FUNDRAISING FOR NONPROFIT GROUPS

FUNDRAISING FOR NONPROFIT GROUPS

Joyce Young, Ken Wyman, and John Swaigen

361.7 pb

Self-Counsel Press
(a division of)
International Self-Counsel Press
USA   Canada

$16.95

7-04

Self-Counsel Press acknowledges the financial support of the Government of Canada through the Book Publishing Industry Development Program (BPIDP) for our publishing activities.

Printed in Canada.

First edition: 1978
Second edition: 1981
Third edition: 1989; Reprinted 1991, 1992
Fourth edition: 1995; Reprinted 1996
Fifth edition: 2002; Reprinted 2004

Cataloguing in Publication Data

Young, Joyce.
    Fundraising for non-profit groups

    (Self-counsel business series)
    ISBN 1-55180-261-9

    1. Fundraising—Canada. 2.Fundraising—United States. 3. Nonprofit organizations—Canada—Finance. 4. Nonprofit organizations—United States—Finance. I. Swaigen, John, 1944. II. Wyman, Ken. III. Title. IV. Series.
    HV41.2.Y68 2002   361.7'068'1   C2002-910976-0

Self-Counsel Press
(a division of)
International Self-Counsel Press Ltd.

1704 N. State Street	1481 Charlotte Road
Bellingham, WA 98225	North Vancouver, BC V7J 1H1
USA	Canada

CONTENTS

INTRODUCTION

1. The Mission

This book is about financing social change. It is about finding the dollars to help you make this world a better place — however you define that.

The fifth edition of *Fundraising for Nonprofit Groups* is a timely renewal. The seven years that have passed since the fourth edition have brought mind-boggling social, political, technological, and economic changes. These changes in turn have profoundly affected the kinds of nonprofit organizations that need to raise money, the available sources of funds, the patterns of giving, and the ways groups raise money.

This edition will reflect changes that have occurred since our last edition in methods available to you to communicate your group's message and raise money. However, in this new millennium, the pace of change seems to be accelerating rather than slowing. Therefore, what groups need is not just an understanding of the current fundraising climate and techniques, but also an ability to adapt to continuing change. Your group's ability to manage change has become just as important as the knowledge and professional skills of your staff members and board members.

We continue to emphasize organizational structure and management skills because success in fundraising and good management are inseparable. As fundraising consultants and as members of social-change groups, we've found that fundraising difficulty was often a symptom of management problems. This book describes ways to integrate fundraising and management functions.

Fundraising is about building understanding, discovering common ground, and ensuring a "win-win" outcome. It's about finding the fit between volunteers and groups, between needs and donors. Fundraising is also about taking responsibility for something out there that's not right, and acting on it. It's about empowering others, be they volunteer fundraisers, clients, or advocates.

People want to give, they want to belong to something bigger than themselves, and they want to spend their money on things with purpose and meaning. The challenge of fundraising is to connect person with person first. Then ask, and the money will come. But you do have to ask.

It is essential that fundraisers and board members put pride and power into fundraising. In the past, there has been a tendency to view it as the dirty work of nonprofit organizations, somewhat sleazy and manipulative, or to view it as begging. Any seasoned fundraiser will tell you that guilt works only once, and begging doesn't work at all! We need to put pride and power into fundraising because that's where the money comes from, and without money, an organization can't achieve its mission.

Fundraising demands discipline from an organization, and that is needed in public interest groups. Undisciplined passion may be part of the birth of new groups, it may be great at demonstrations, but it doesn't build an organization with the staying power to achieve social change. The need to raise money is often the driving force for strategic planning, financial planning, and program design and evaluation.

We have a favorite saying about fundraising: The biggest problem with fundraising is that people don't do it. They worry about it. They talk about it. They read books and hold committee meetings about it. But they don't *do it*. Our goal with this book is to help you, encourage you, and, most of all, make you *do it!* Fundraising works. It will work for you, but only if you *do it!*

2. Who This Book Is For

Fundraising is for people who want to know how to go about raising between $100,000 and $5 million annually for a charitable, nonprofit group. This is the kind of price range with which we are familiar. If you want to raise more money than you do now, raise money from different sources, or try a new fundraising technique, this book will get you started.

If you sit on the board of directors of a nonprofit group, the information in this book will help you better understand your role in creating and maintaining a group that can attract and keep funding. It will help you assess the fundraising efforts and strategies of your group.

If you are a senior staff person responsible for administration or program delivery, this book will help you to carry out your duties in a way that bolsters the efforts of your fundraising staff and volunteers.

For groups that are just starting or want to hire fundraising staff, this book paints a detailed picture of the task ahead. Fundraising strategies for public interest groups that are perceived to be controversial, innovative, or non-traditional are emphasized throughout.

If you are a fundraiser, this book will give you practical advice on every aspect of fundraising, such as —

- finding out whether or not a project is fundable;
- discovering who is likely to give money for this kind of project;
- explaining the project clearly and persuasively;
- budgeting;
- thanking donors and acknowledging their contributions; and
- building a continuing relationship with them after the money has been spent, so that you can count on their continuing support.

3. What This Book Can (and Can't) Do for You

Fundraising is easy to understand, simple, and direct. This book demystifies fundraising and gets you going. This book is lean and mean, just like your organization.

The demand for the charitable dollar far exceeds the supply of money and the number of nonprofit groups continues to grow. Since the last edition of *Fundraising for Nonprofit Groups,* over 17,000 new charities have been registered in Canada and approximately 5,000 more organizations apply for charitable status every year. There are more than 170,000 voluntary organizations in Canada, 45,000 more than when the last edition of this book was published. In the United States, the number of nonprofit groups also increases every year. In 2000, there were more than 724,000 501(c)(3) charitable organizations, plus nearly another 500,000 other nonprofit organizations classified under other subsections of the federal tax code, according to the National Center for Charitable Statistics <nccs.urban.org>.

You are competing for the charitable dollar, and the competition is keen. Well-organized, well-established, and well-known large charities probably already have their chunk of any corporation's or foundation's donations budget secured, so your group is competing for the 5 percent to 30 percent of the budget that is left over. That's not very encouraging, but it's best to know what you are up against. With the help of this book, you will have a head start in the race for dollars.

This book takes you through the strategic and practical steps of fundraising, from preparing a proposal to recruiting a fundraising work-team. It tells you what kind of information a potential donor wants to see and how to present it.

Three essential fundraising tools — the objectives sheet, the annual report, and the funding proposal — are covered in detail, with examples.

After you have put together your fundraising tools, who should you ask for money? To answer that, you need to develop a funding strategy. Figuring out a logical and solid funding strategy is the most challenging, the most difficult, and the most important part of fundraising. Chapter 5 provides a step-by-step explanation with examples of the process.

We deal with raising money from individuals, corporations, foundations, and government sources. Corporate fundraising is covered in depth, because that's where many groups lack knowledge and experience. In chapter 6, the subtleties and the methods of getting in the door to see a funder are discussed. However, many controversial groups have to rely heavily on individuals for support. Therefore, direct mail campaigns, door-to-door canvassing, telephone fundraising, fundraising on the Internet, and organizing special events are explained in chapters 7 to 10, and an example of a direct mail package is included.

How to keep the money coming is an important part of any fundraising program, so examples of reporting and record-keeping systems are provided. Chapter 13 covers these topics.

As volunteers are the lifeblood of many groups, chapter 15 is devoted to developing a solid volunteer network.

This book won't make you rich in five easy steps; if you expect to get rich, you're in the wrong business. But it will tell you all the things we wish we had known when we began fundraising, and what we have learned in 25 very busy years of fundraising, fundraising consulting, and volunteering. This book tells you what you need to know about fundraising so that your group can thrive and accomplish change.

CHAPTER 1
THE FUNDRAISER

Good fundraisers are hard to find and harder to keep. Often they are given too many conflicting responsibilities. A relationship between the fundraiser and group that works well is outlined in this chapter.

1. The Fundraiser's Role

The fundraiser should have an integral part in management and decision making and should not be just a "money magnet" stuck in a corner and told to bring in the bucks. His or her advice on the "fund-ability" of a proposed project or the feasibility of a fundraising technique should carry substantial weight in decision making. A fundraiser should rarely, if ever, be told to raise money for something he or she considers "un-fundable."

Management theory clearly supports the fundraiser's involvement in decision making. Your fundraiser has to sell to the prospective donor your organization's vision, mandate, program, budget, and ability to carry out the program or project efficiently and effectively.

That's not possible if he or she isn't included in thinking these things through. We can take a lesson from the private sector here. "Inadequate product knowledge" is cited as one of the most frequent reasons for failure in sales. To sell the organization, your fundraiser has to believe in it and understand its capabilities.

He or she has to be a part of the team, has to be brought in on the mission, the direction, the program design. Does business exclude its marketing people from the design of new products? Hardly! Important management decisions have fundraising implications, and vice versa. Don't make them in isolation!

While it is important that your fundraiser be determined to bring in the money, he or she must also have integrity, an appreciation of your group's values, a commitment to your cause, and an understanding of the limits of what is acceptable. Raising money is necessary, but not at any cost. If the fundraiser has to compromise your group's principles or misrepresent your group to funders in order to get money, it's money you don't want. There are degrees of compromise, of course, but you can't let obtaining funding compromise your ability to carry out your mandate. Raising money is the means that makes possible the end; it is not an end in itself.

How much money a full-time fundraiser can be expected to raise depends on many factors, including the following:

- Whether your group or its cause is controversial
- Whether you have a track record in fundraising and in successfully completing projects or carrying out programs
- How much money your organization can spend to raise money and what other resources you can invest
- Whether you can demonstrate the effectiveness of your activities
- Whether the money is for short-term financial relief or you are aiming for long-term financial security
- Whether the money is needed for ongoing program support or to fund individual projects
- Whether you have volunteers who are willing to participate in fundraising activities who have the necessary skills, availability, credibility, and connections to donors
- What kinds of fundraising activities are suitable for your kind of program and what funding sources are available

How much your fundraiser can achieve depends not only on his or her skills, but also on the market and the product. The market is your potential donors (how many are they, and how much money do they have to give?), and the product is your organization, its program, and its projects. Too many fundraisers take the blame for a limited market or a poor product.

The reality is that there is a better market for some kinds of products than others. For example, in 1997, in Canada, 51 percent of money donated to nonprofit organizations (excluding government funds) went to religion, 17 percent to health, 11 percent to social services, 4 percent to education and research, 6 percent to philanthropy and volunteerism, 3 percent to culture and arts, 3 percent to international, 2 percent to environment, and 3 percent to various other causes.

In the United States, household giving also favored religious groups, with 60 percent of the donations (excluding government funds) going to places of worship; 9 percent toward human services; 6.5 percent to health; 6.4 percent to education; 4.9 percent to youth development; 3.3 percent to arts, culture, and humanities; 3.2 percent to environment; 2 percent to public or societal benefit; 1.7 percent to private or community foundations; 1.7 percent to international causes; 0.9 percent to adult recreation; and the rest to a variety of causes. (These figures are for 1998 from Independent Sector <www.independentsector .org /GandV/s_hous2.htm>.)

This kind of information can help you to make a realistic assessment of what is feasible for your group. It also helps to know the types of people and organizations that donate to your kind of cause, as well as whether you are in a part of the country where donations are typically larger or smaller.

With this kind of information, you can understand that raising $2 million for a hospital may take the same amount of work as raising $100,000 to operate a food bank or $10,000 for an anti-racism lobby. There are simply too many variables to give a general guideline as to how much money you may expect to raise for your program, but one of the simplest ways to get a realistic picture is to contact another group similar to yours and find out what its experience has been.

In order for your fundraiser to understand the market for your "product" and how your organization can adapt its product to the market, he or she must stay up-to-date on new developments in your issue area and be knowledgable regarding matters in the business, government, and philanthropic communities that may affect the availability of funds. If the corporate sector provides a substantial part of your income, financial publications such as the *Globe and Mail* or the *Wall Street Journal* and the business section of a local daily newspaper are required reading.

If government is an important source of income, you must keep abreast of issues of public concern, what laws and policies the government is considering to address these concerns, and what funding the government may be willing to give to programs designed to address these concerns.

If your organization can afford both a fundraiser and an administrator, your fundraiser should not be distracted by administrative responsibilities, other than those relating to fundraising. But there is one exception. Even if you have an executive director or office manager who is involved in financial administration, your fundraiser should have some responsibility for planning your budget and supervising cash flow and expenditures. In particular, the fundraiser should be involved in planning cash flow. Maintaining cash flow is one of the best incentives to get the fundraiser working hard. It can also help your organization avoid crises caused by unexpected short-term cash shortages. In a small organization, it is a good practice to require the fundraiser's signature and one other signature on all checks. That way, the fundraiser can keep track of how money is being spent and how much needs to be raised. As the group grows, the fundraiser may not have quite such a hands-on role, but must still be kept fully informed.

2. Hiring a Fundraiser

When you look for a fundraiser, you are looking for a personality — a personality that can cope with pressure, demands, occasional ingratitude, and many disappointments. You need a self-motivated person who can work closely with your group.

Some universities and colleges now offer courses in fundraising that are very useful, but the most meaningful credential for many self-trained fundraisers is previous experience. Make sure that the candidate's experience is relevant to your needs and your sources of income. A person who can organize successful benefit concerts may not do well at government fundraising, and vice versa.

Fundraisers should be effective, agile communicators. In fundraising meetings, they need to impress and influence a wide range of people. The fundraiser must be able to conduct a discussion smoothly and lead it to a positive conclusion — money! But beware of people who only talk a good line. Too often they can't produce results. You want an honest and hard worker in this position particularly.

Good, straightforward writing skills are essential. Fundraisers write letters and proposals all the time. The writing must be interesting, clear, and concise, because boring proposals won't get read. Ask to see samples of the candidate's writing or make a writing assignment part of your hiring process.

Your fundraiser must look presentable in a business setting and should be as comfortable in a suit as in blue jeans.

The fundraiser's most important duty is to mobilize volunteers who will do the actual fundraising work. Fundraisers who do the work themselves are quickly overwhelmed and burned out. Even when they are successful, they are not strengthening the diversity of people and skills that are essential to a nonprofit's stability. No organization can survive if it depends on just one person's skills, knowledge, or contacts. One day the fundraiser will leave. The organization should be self-reliant and independent long before that day comes.

These days there are more jobs for fundraisers than there are experienced candidates. Publicize the opening well. Ads and free listings can be placed with local chapters of the Association of Fundraising Professionals (formerly called the National Society of Fund Raising Executives) or other professional groups. New Internet sites for fundraising jobs are also being created, such as <www.charityvillage.com> in Canada and <charitychannel.com/careersearch> in the United States.

When you are interviewing people for the fundraising job, get a successful fundraiser from another group to sit in with you. The outside fundraiser can ask the tough questions and objectively assess candidates. If you are desperate to find a fundraiser, this outside perspective could spare you the cost of a poor decision made in haste.

3. Firing a Fundraising Staffer

This is an unpleasant topic, but a crucial one. In a small organization, the fundraiser's success is often critical to the group's survival. Therefore, a fundraiser must either raise a reasonable amount of money or leave — voluntarily or involuntarily. To maximize the likelihood of success of a new fundraiser, the organization must set clear and realistic goals and expectations, communicate them clearly to the fundraiser, provide him or her with as much orientation, training, and support as its (often extremely limited) resources allow, and give the fundraiser regular and positive — but honest — feedback on how he or she is doing.

However, at the end of a probation period, the group must be prepared to fire a fundraiser who is not up to the job.

When interviewing fundraising applicants, describe the probation period clearly. (All staff in nonprofit groups should have probation periods. You can't afford dreamers and shirkers; you need people who can produce. There should be no such thing as tenure in nonprofit groups.) For the fundraising position, a period of 6 to 12 months is reasonable. It takes up to six months to get decisions on funding requests. It's only fair to give fundraisers that much time to prove themselves.

If your group is new, or is new to fundraising, a six-month probation period for a fundraiser is too short. It will take time for your group to establish a reputation in the funding community. A fundraiser for a new group should be given at least a year and initially should be judged by the amount of work he or she is putting out, not results.

But if you aren't getting the dollar results within 6 to 12 months, you must act. Few concerns raise the collective blood pressure of a board of directors as high as the issue of firing someone. Firing, dismissal, termination, downsizing, right sizing — call it what you will — is fraught with a level of emotional upheaval comparable only to the stir that a lawsuit or near bankruptcy evokes.

Because it's such a difficult thing to handle well, firing is usually mismanaged in one of two ways:

a) The board puts its head in the sand, holds its breath, and prays that the whole nasty business will go away.

b) The board gathers the courage to fire the person and handles the firing badly.

Let's look at each scenario in turn.

3.1 The head in the sand

If the problem is serious enough to warrant high-level attention in the first place, odds are that it will escalate if left unattended. When you start getting complaints from staff or board members who do not normally call you directly, you know the problem has grown. If staff start to resign, you likely have a situation that needs fast, decisive action.

3.2 How not to fire someone

How the firing is handled has a tremendous impact on many facets of the organization. Whether the employee you fire bad-mouths the organization or brings a legal suit is not all there is to it. It affects morale and is the sort of thing over which board members resign. It affects your organization's reputation with clients, with funders, and with regulatory agencies. It will also affect your ability to attract good candidates to fill the job.

Here are some examples of handling termination badly:

a) The whole board is involved in the decision to fire the employee. Can you imagine what that does for the employee's reputation? How would you like to be fired by 10 or 20 people?

b) The employee first learns about it from a subordinate, or a well-intentioned board member who leaks the information, or the morning paper.

c) From the employee's perspective, it happens out of the blue: no feedback, no warning, and no opportunity to improve performance.

d) The employee is not given the option of resigning and leaving with confidentiality and dignity.

3.3 Pointers for terminating employment

Following are some suggestions on how to tackle this unpleasant task so that everyone emerges with dignity:

a) Prevention: Boards and executive directors are often guilty of doing too little too late. Take action and give attention to the small problems as they arise, before they escalate. This involves the executive director bringing problems to the fundraiser's attention and providing support and assistance. The Executive Director (or ED) must also keep the board informed of the fundraiser's progress and let it know about any serious warning signs.

b) See that the procedure for dealing with termination is spelled out, either in your contract with your employee or your personnel policy. This includes establishing who has authority to fire — the ED or an officer or committee of the board — and setting out grounds for termination.

c) Keep the number of people who know about the situation and who are involved in making the firing decision as small as possible.

d) For the few people who are involved in the decision, allow the time that is needed to work through each person's thoughts and feelings on the matter. Give your group all the information it needs to make an informed decision. Fear and ignorance in this area are the main reasons for a head-in-the-sand response. It will go more smoothly if you can come to consensus and if each person truly believes it is the only solution, or the best solution.

e) Get legal advice from a lawyer who knows employment law. Termination is a complex matter and the legalities depend on the specifics of each case. Find out where you stand.

f) An employment reference for someone who has been fired can be difficult to handle. Try to be fair both to the employee and to the prospective employer, but also take care to avoid liability for comments you might make.

If possible, work out in advance an agreement with the employee specifying what you will and won't say. If this is impossible, give only an employment-related reference (i.e., confirm details such as the length of time the employee worked for you, the job title and responsibilities, and salary, if that is relevant). Decline to give any subjective evaluation. Particularly in the litigious climate of the US, many employers refuse to say anything.

Recommend to the employee that he or she get his or her own personal references. For example the employer or the immediate supervisor may be unwilling to provide an evaluation, but the employee might have had better relations with other supervisors or coworkers and is free to ask one of them to provide a reference.

The best approach is to help the person you fire to find more suitable employment elsewhere, rather than to have him or her unemployed, if it is possible to assist without misleading the prospective employer. Just because the person did not work out in your organization's context does not mean they are not competent fundraisers. They may do brilliantly in a different type of group.

Few people will pat you on the back for doing a good job of firing somebody, but you aren't an ogre with an axe. You are a leader who isn't afraid to put the well-being of your organization ahead of your own popularity. You won't win an award for this one, but you will deserve one if you handle it well.

CHAPTER 2
ORGANIZING FOR EFFECTIVE FUNDRAISING

1. Are Volunteer Organizations Different?

Some people think the voluntary sector is a nice, sheltered place to work. After all, we are going to make a better world, and besides, the nonprofit sector is not "the real world." Right?

Wrong! Nonprofits are not nice, sheltered places to work. They are the toughest organizations in which to participate. There is more uncertainty, complexity, difference, and conflict than in profit-based organizations, and far fewer resources to deal with it all, so be proud and stand tall for doing this kind of work. The nonprofit sector does not have a monopoly on making the world a better place, and the attitude that it does alienates a great many potential partners in government, foundations, and industry.

There *are* differences between volunteer organizations and profit-based companies, however, and these differences have nothing to do

with one sector being "better" or "easier" than the other. The following examples illustrate this point.

After one turbulent board meeting, a client said to Joyce, "If any of my staff ever pulled a stunt like that, I'd fire them. They would be out of here! But you can't fire a volunteer. You can't tell them what to do either. It has to be *consensus!*" He was a vice president of Xerox who was 18 months into his first experience on the board of a volunteer organization.

Joyce's neighbor, who makes her living as a management consultant and who was recruited to the board of a community organization, called, obviously upset. "Joyce, I can't believe it," she said. "The meeting starts 15 minutes late, and for the next half hour, people continue to arrive. The chairperson interrupts the meeting to welcome them, asks how their kids are doing, and then brings them up to speed on what we were discussing. I don't know how a place can function with a board like that!"

Ken, too, had a similar experience when he consulted with a particular nonprofit. The new chair of the board was a senior vice president of a major bank. The chair asked for a progress report on a significant project, and was dismayed to learn that the overworked staff and cautious volunteers had been studying the situation for three years, with no conclusion in sight. After all, with donors' money at stake, they wanted to be sure they made the right decision. The chair, on the other hand, insisted on action within the next three months. He was used to the fast-paced business climate that demanded quarterly results, and was willing to take multimillion-dollar risks to stay ahead of the competition. Who was right? Both, and neither. But the culture clash would take effort to resolve.

You may recognize the culture shock of these new initiates. You may remember learning the ropes in your organization: it wasn't what you'd expected. Ask anybody who has been a board, committee, or staff member, and they will agree that volunteer organizations are different from profit-making companies.

Does it matter? Yes, because if you can grasp why and how volunteer organizations are fundamentally different from profit-making ones, important possibilities emerge. The possibility of doing more with less, of being more effective with the same level of resources. The possibility of structuring the organization in ways that will provide timely decisions and better coordination. The possibility of ensuring longer-term, productive volunteers. The possibility of predicting conflict and crisis so you can better manage them. The possibility of moving beyond a hand-to-mouth financial existence.

By looking at four important aspects of nonprofit groups, you will begin to understand why they are different from businesses and government agencies and how you must take these differences into account to effectively structure and operate your organization.

1.1 Volunteer labor

A new manufacturing company will start out by *borrowing money,* which it uses to hire the staff and buy the raw materials and the technology it needs to manufacture a product. It then sells the product to the consumer. The money from sales is fed back into the organization to maintain production and to pay for the cost of the borrowed money. In time, the start-up debt is repaid. In a very simple and general way, that's how a private company gets started.

Now, look at the volunteer group. The founders begin the organization by *donating labor,* which is used to provide a product or service to a consumer, often for free. No money may change hands in these early stages, or if it does, it is usually money that is "given" by the same people who give the labor.

Those are very different scenarios. The fact that the volunteer organization began with the free labor of its founders might explain a few things. Consider this example. The hypothetical ZIP Organization began with John, Mary, Elsie, and a few others meeting in each other's living rooms on Monday nights. Then more people got interested, ZIP grew, and the members started meeting down in the church basement. Well, it was such a helpful thing and word spread and pretty soon there were Monday night meetings in church basements all over the city.

If you project this flourishing organization seven years into the future, you might witness the following. It is the meeting of the provincial board of ZIP, which now has 12 chapters. The executive director is presenting her proposed budget for the next fiscal year. It includes a 7 percent salary increase, the addition of health and dental benefits, the purchase of liability insurance, and the purchase of computers and a photocopy machine. Then there's the $1,000 for rental of a hotel conference room in which to hold the annual general meeting.

John, Mary, and Elsie are exchanging glances across the 20-person oak boardroom table on the thirty-fourth floor of a downtown office building. They aren't too enthusiastic about this budget and they are wondering how it came to this. It's still Monday night, but this is no church basement!

When an organization changes from being led and run by volunteers to having a financial life of its own, the founders are displaced. They no longer "own" the organization and often, they don't even understand or recognize it anymore.

The start-up debt, which is still owed to founders like John, Mary, and Elsie, is an emotional debt. It can be repaid only by giving recognition and respect to the founders and to their vision and values for the organization. The importance of this goes beyond keeping your founders happy and preventing them from reacting and trying to maintain control. The vision and values that gave a few people the energy to give birth to a new organization will help to sustain that organization. The vision will evolve, but the original vision should serve as an anchor, keeping the organization directed and purposeful.

The fact that most volunteer organizations begin with volunteer labor rather than venture capital and are financed indirectly by a third party (the funders) may be the beginning of the following chronic problems:

a) *The start-up debt is hidden and not repaid.* The start-up debt is what is owed to the founding members who got it all rolling in the first place.

b) *Staff are underpaid.* The only variable is how badly underpaid they are. The staff or board may even believe it is virtuous to be underpaid. The board members are often those who used to do the staff's work without pay, so they view staff work as replacing their free labor. The problem of uncompetitive salaries manifests itself in problems ranging from incompetence to high turnover.

c) *Volunteer organizations are undercapitalized.* They do not have the equipment they need to do the job, and thus much valuable volunteer time is wasted running errands. Productivity is low, which makes it harder to raise funds, which means no equipment can be bought, and the vicious cycle continues.

1.2 Funding

A second point of comparison is the difference in the sources of money for the two types of organizations. In profit-making companies, the consumer has the choice whether or not to purchase a product in the first place, and whether to purchase your brand or a competitor's. The first choice depends on the need for the product or service; the second on aspects of quality, availability, and price. Consumers' dollars are the major source of funds for the company, and the consumers' buying behavior gives the company feedback about how well it's doing, imposing a standard on the quality of the product or service. If a product does not meet the consumers' standards, the company knows immediately by a drop in sales. If it does not adjust to the needs of its customers, it will go out of business.

If you look at these same variables in volunteer organizations, you will see that they operate very differently. First, there is often the absence of a direct and visible consumer. In the case of an advocacy organization, if we say that their "product" is information, it would be clear that the users of that information are politicians, government organizations, and private corporations. However, the people who benefit from their efforts are an entirely different group.

Even when there is something approaching a consumer, the service is often free. Rarely does another group offer the same service to the same consumer group, so there is no competition for consumers. Finally, a third-party funder, such as a foundation or government agency, provides the money for all this.

For instance, a social welfare agency may provide service for "consumers" — people who have a problem and may be too poor to donate — while donors who do not share the same problems may give to provide services they value but do not use.

Even a performing arts organization, with an the audience that pays for tickets to watch the performance, must satisfy the wishes and whims of third-party funders. It is extremely rare for all the costs of a production to be covered by the ticket buyers.

What does all this add up to? It means that the funders' and the volunteer organizations' criteria — and not that of the consumers — become the measure of "need" and "quality of service" and "efficiency." In some cases, what the consumers want and what the funders will fund are in absolute conflict. The volunteer organization is in the middle of that conflict. In addition, the organization and the funders don't get the kind of direct feedback from the consumers that a drop in revenue provides to a profit-based company. These facts can become the source of many problems, and the only solution we know is to try to get funders and clients together. This is happening with some US foundations that are getting trustees out into the field and getting clients into their boardrooms.

1.3 Values

Volunteer organizations are *value driven*. The logic of what your organization does is often based on an unarticulated, emotional, personal, nebulous thing called values. Members of the group are driven by their commitment to those values. The power of shared values to motivate and coordinate people is so great that many corporations are trying to emulate it.

Ultimately, however, moneymaking companies are profit driven. They may be ethical corporations with high moral standards, but their primary goal is still to make money. Therefore, if a question of values arises, the company will not

necessarily be torn apart by this conflict. A value-driven, volunteer organization, on the other hand, could very well be destroyed by such a conflict. Though they may share a general goal, all members of a group do not have exactly the same values, and when the differences between their values become greater than the similarities, the organization is in trouble.

For the power of values to work for your group, the board and the staff need to be able to talk about values and work them through. You need to recognize value conflicts when they arise, and confront them fast. This calls for a lot of interpersonal strength and maturity.

1.4 Volunteer leadership

Nonprofits are volunteer-led organizations. While in the past decade staff have become more sophisticated and professional, boards continue to be made up of people from many levels of society. This difference leads to increased board-staff conflict and conflict within the board itself. Conflict in an organization can be healthy, provided you learn to express it and deal with it. Conflict can also take over your whole agenda, and then you need outside help.

2. Incorporation and Charitable Registration

This section is not a definitive work on the topic; it will not tell you whether you should incorporate or how to do it. You should seek a lawyer's advice on that. This section simply gives a basic overview and points out the fundraising implications of incorporation and charitable registration.

If you expect to be around for a few years and your annual budget will exceed $25,000, you will probably want to incorporate. Incorporation means constituting your group as a legal entity separate and distinct from your membership or board of directors. It establishes your group as a more permanent structure, reduces the taxes the group must pay, and limits the personal liability of the staff and the board members.

Corporations and foundations prefer to fund incorporated groups; many require incorporation. Nonprofit corporations are perceived to be more permanent, accountable, and credible. Funders feel that a donation to an incorporated group is safer and that there will be a long-term benefit from their charitable investment.

In Canada and the United States you can incorporate either at the federal level or at the state or provincial level. Provincial or state incorporation is more flexible, has fewer regulations and reporting requirements, and can be accomplished more quickly and inexpensively. You will probably need a lawyer's help, but you may be able to find a lawyer who is sympathetic to your cause and will do the job as a public service.

If you are in Canada and the activities of your group are of a "charitable" nature (i.e., religious, educational, scientific, artistic, or social), you can apply to Canada Customs and Revenue Agency (formerly Revenue Canada) for tax exemption registration. (This is called charitable registration throughout this book.) If your application is accepted, you will be issued a charitable registration number. This number entitles you to issue receipts to donors that permit them to receive tax credits for the money donated. It also exempts you from paying income tax and some sales taxes on your group's purchases of goods and services. It is not unusual for groups to wait up to a year or more for approval.

In the United States, nonprofit corporations can apply for federal tax exemption under section 501(c)(3) of the Internal Revenue Code.

You do not have to incorporate to obtain charitable registration status in either Canada or the United States.

In the United States, both incorporated and unincorporated nonprofit organizations can apply for an exemption from paying income tax. In addition, both registered charities and other nonprofit organizations can register for income tax exemption. There are different requirements for different kinds of organizations.

To obtain tax-exempt status, contact the Internal Revenue Service and ask about filing for federal tax exemption. The government has free publications dealing with how to obtain tax-exempt status that you can order through your local IRS tax forms office. You should request Publication 557, *Tax Exempt Status for your Organization,* which explains how to apply for tax-exempt status.

Depending on the purpose of your group, you should also request either Package 1023 or Package 1024. Package 1023, called *Application for Recognition of Exemption under Section 501(c)(3) of the Internal Revenue Code,* is for use by charitable, religious, educational, scientific, and literary organizations, as well as certain other groups. Package 1024, *Application for Recognition of Exemption under Section 501(a)* is for civic leagues, social welfare organizations, labor, agricultural and horticultural groups, social and recreational clubs, and business leagues, among others. Also request Form SS-4, *Application for Employer Identification Number.* You are required to submit this with your application to obtain tax-exempt status even if your group has no employees.

You should also ask for Form 8718. If your group's income is less than an amount specified by the Internal Revenue Service, you may be considered tax-exempt even without filing for tax-exempt status. However, obtaining formal tax-exempt status has an advantage in that the government will issue you a "determination letter" if you also fill out Form 8718. This determination letter is public recognition of your tax-exempt status and may prove useful when dealing with donors or the public. It gives advance assurance to donors that their contributions will be deductible, grants exemption from certain state taxes and certain federal excise taxes, and gives your group access to some discount mailing privileges available to nonprofits.

Some of these application forms are lengthy and require you to provide detailed financial information as well as information about your objects, activities, and board members. You probably need the help of a lawyer to submit these applications.

Most groups will not need to know the details of obscure and technical tax laws that apply to nonprofits. However, if you do, you can order the IRS agents' own manual on exempt organizations. Contact the government printing office in Washington DC and ask for IRS Manual Section 7751.

Charities and fundraising activities are closely regulated in the United States. To understand your rights and obligations you need to examine not just the federal laws, but also the legislation affecting your group at the state level. Many states now have laws affecting matters such as —

a) the composition of your funding base,

b) the requirements for reporting contributions received,

c) the percentage of your total budget required for fundraising costs, and

d) the licensing of fundraisers or fundraising consultants.

Charity Web sites have created new legal technicalities over jurisdictions. A donor can access a Web site and may be able to donate online from anywhere in the world. Government regulations may apply not only in the area where the charity is based, but also in the area where the donor resides. If your charity actively solicits or regularly receives donations beyond the boundary of your home state or province, check with a lawyer specializing in charity law.

Charitable registration status is an absolute prerequisite for raising money from corporations and foundations.

Foundations and corporations will seldom give donations to groups that are not registered charities. While this is not legally prohibited,

their preference for government approval is strong.

Corporations do not require a charitable tax receipt, since they can usually write off donations as a business expense, with the same tax savings. CCRA has reported that half the tax receipts issued to corporations by Canadian charities are never used. Ask corporate donors if they want an "official tax receipt" or merely a letter of confirmation that the money was received.

The Canadian government requires charities to spend 80 percent of the donations *for which they issue tax receipts* on their charitable purposes within one year. This restriction does not apply to donations for which the charity does not issue a tax receipt. Since charities often need more than 20 percent of their funds to pay for administration and fundraising costs, it is in the interest of any Canadian charity to issue tax receipts only when the donor wants them.

Most government funding sources do not require charitable registration. In fact, if you get a grant from a government source, do not issue them a receipt for a tax credit for the donation; it will only confuse them.

Annual membership fees are not tax deductible in Canada. You can issue receipts for donations over and above the membership fee. Similarly, if you are holding a special charity event, such as a fundraising dinner, you can issue a receipt only for the portion of the fee that exceeds the cost of putting on the event. (For example, the dinner may cost $40 but you charge $100 to attend. You can issue a receipt for $60.) When doing membership or direct mail campaigns, you should distinguish between membership fees and donations. Include a check-off box for the donor to show if he or she wants a tax-credit receipt issued.

In the US, the ticket price for attending a special charity event can be claimed as a donation, but only for the amount that exceeds the fair market value of putting on the event. The rules are complex, and you should consult an accountant who has special knowledge of the peculiarities of charity regulations.

The canceled check is a sufficient receipt in the United States for donations under $250 in a single gift. Tax credit for one-time donations over $250 requires the donor to submit a canceled check for $250 and a donation receipt from the organization stating the balance of the donation.

The IRS allows annual membership fees to be fully or partly tax deductible, depending on the benefits a member receives.

The tax laws change regularly in every country, however, so check with your local tax office about the best way to proceed.

For a more detailed discussion of incorporation and charitable registration, consult one of the reference works listed in the Appendix.

3. Establishing an Effective Board of Directors

Once an organization has more than 30 or 40 members, it becomes impossible for everyone to meet regularly and participate in making decisions. At this point, organizations will often elect or appoint a smaller group that has authority to make decisions that will bind the members. This group is usually called a board of directors or a board of governors or trustees. Also, once a group of volunteers hires staff, it is, for practical purposes, impossible to operate without a board of directors that has authority to direct the work of the staff, or at least direct the executive director who directs the staff.

In addition, having a board of directors is a legal necessity if you want to incorporate. Corporations must have members, and these members are required to elect a board of directors.

To be effective, a board should be neither too big to be cohesive nor too small to get the work done. Twelve to 18 is often an optimal number of directors. However, the size of the board should depend on the kinds of skills needed to operate effectively and the availability of good people.

In the case of corporations, federal, state, or provincial laws may dictate the minimum or maximum number of directors permitted. Within these legislated limits, you can specify in your bylaws how many directors your organization can have. These bylaws can be amended, if desired, by the members of the corporation.

If you want to get a lot of help from your board, you should give a lot of thought to whom you choose and how you recruit. Remember that the board member is a volunteer. Chapter 15, which discusses working with volunteers, also applies to working with board members.

3.1 Who should be on the board?

The board is an important part of your group's identity. Prominent, respected people in your field of endeavor should be on the board. If your group is controversial, these people are doubly important because they lend credibility to your existence and activities.

However, it is often difficult to find prominent people who are not only willing to lend their names but also willing to spend a lot of time on the day-to-day routine work of a board, such as monitoring the activities of staff and ensuring the organization stays within its budget.

Your board may be a "figurehead" board or a "working" board, or a combination of both. Figurehead board members satisfy legal necessity and business credibility, but do not have much involvement in the day-to-day running of the group. Working board members work closely with the staff. Figurehead board members lend you their good names, and working board members give you their time.

In practice, to be successful it helps to have a combination of both, but not necessarily on the same board. One approach that some groups use is to have a working board and a separate "honorary board." The honorary board members are not expected to participate in the day-to-day governance of the organization, but they are expected to make themselves available from time to time, especially in support of fundraising efforts.

Another approach that some groups find useful is to create a separate group of volunteer fundraisers or fundraising consultants called "The Friends of. . . . " (If your group were called the Society for the Preservation of Martian Mice, this group would be The Friends of Martian Mice.) Such a group can be populated by people prepared to devote their energy to fundraising. They don't take the power away from the working board, or, as it is sometimes called, the managing board. This arrangement also means the nonprofit doesn't have to undertake the often-impossible task of transforming existing board members (who may have many wonderful skills) into fundraisers. Nor do they have to fear that fundraising leaders, who may not understand the issues as well, will wreak havoc on the board. Larger organizations often institutionalize the "Friends of" by turning it into a legal foundation. Hospitals and universities do this a lot.

It is a good idea to have a lawyer and an accountant on your board. They may do your legal work and your books at cost or for free, but their importance goes beyond that. Every business has a lawyer and an accountant because these people are necessary. They help to round out your business identity, and they can warn you of the legal or financial implications of projects you are planning. They also add credibility, reassuring donors that the organization is well managed. When you list their names in your annual report or grant applications or even on letterhead, show their credentials.

Recruit at least two board members who are outside "the cause" of your organization. Outsiders will give time to your organization for many different reasons. A volunteer accountant once said, "I wanted to do something with more meaning and purpose than helping the rich get richer." At the board meeting of a bereaved parents' group, a newly recruited outsider said simply, "There, but for the grace of God, go I." Insiders sometimes fear that outsiders — who are not bereaved parents, retired ballet dancers, recovering alcoholics, survivors of breast cancer, or

what have you — will not fully understand the issues and can't be trusted. However, every cause has blind spots that only outsiders can see. Blind spots are values, beliefs, attitudes, and assumptions that don't work in the outside world. By recognizing and challenging the blind spots, the outsiders can help your group to see them and correct them. Funders don't like blind spots. You may not expect it, but you can recruit outsiders and they are invaluable.

You need at least two strong board members who will champion fundraising, make it fun and exciting, and give it prestige and resources. Fundraising must be a strategic, mainstream function at the board and staff level. Give the fundraising function a power base within the board of directors. We've seen too many boards give low or no priority to fundraising, and then cry "help" when they "suddenly discover" the group is in the red. Find the board leadership that fundraising needs and deserves. Draw on sales and marketing people from the private sector, for example.

Last, but by no means least, you should have a few business people on your board. The lack of business people on boards of lobby groups and arts groups is a common shortcoming. Business people can help you with fundraising, but if you want them to help raise funds, you should let them know this when you invite them to be on your board. Find out what kind of commitment they are willing to make. If they are willing to help with fundraising, they can do the following:

a) Directly solicit prospective donors on your behalf.

b) Go with you to fundraising meetings with important potential funders. The fact that the board members are willing to invest that kind of time shows the potential donor that they are very committed to your group. It also puts more peer pressure on the potential donor.

c) Write to those people on your behalf, indicating their involvement with your group and requesting that they take the time to meet with you. (This doesn't guarantee any money, but it usually means that you will get a meeting and a chance to make a pitch for money.)

d) Suggest senior people in the business community who they think would be sympathetic or interested in your cause.

You should select all board members because of their commitment to your cause. You don't want a token lawyer; you want a lawyer who is interested in your field of endeavor. You don't want a businessperson who is only there to "be seen" as a good corporate citizen; you want someone who cares about your cause and will invest time and energy to see it succeed. It's a real balancing act to assemble a board that has diversity and cohesion.

Board members cannot be paid for serving on your board but, generally, paid staff members can be members of the board, provided that they do not vote on matters in which they have a conflict of interest between their roles as staff members and their duties as board members (for example, on salaries and benefits). Having staff members on the board can help make up for poor working conditions and low salaries and bolster staff morale. But don't put too many staffers on the board; a staff-dominated board makes funders nervous. From their point of view, there's not enough control or accountability in staff-dominated boards.

3.2 Recruiting board members

Common errors in board recruitment include leaving it to the last minute and asking someone to join the board without giving thought to what kinds of skills are needed on the board. To avoid both pitfalls, it is useful for the board to appoint a recruitment team shortly after a new board is elected. This recruitment team can ask the board to consider what "holes" exist in the skills of board members and report back on this at least three months before the next board election, so

that the recruitment team can start seeking appropriate candidates. That way, instead of trying to find a board job that the new member can do well, the team can pick a candidate who is willing and able to do a job that it knows needs to be done. It is also useful to include staff members in identifying what kinds of people are needed for the board and to ask them to suggest names.

With a list of "job vacancies" in hand, the team should search for the best possible candidates by asking for referrals from friends, donors, clients, foundations, government departments, corporations, and other nonprofit groups.

Once the team finds people who they feel can make a useful contribution as a board member, the chair of the board should approach the candidates by spending time with them, explaining the history and goals of the organization, and discussing the kinds of contributions they might make to the work of the board.

The chair should ask if the candidates are willing to make a commitment to attend board meetings regularly, to take on their share of the legal responsibility, and to spend time working on special projects or committees of the board, such as the fundraising taskforce.

Successful organizations interview at least two people for every position and choose the best. Yes, it is permissible to interview potential volunteers, even at the board level, and select the person who best fulfills your criteria. While some nonprofit people feel this will insult powerful people, the opposite is true. Interest in serving on such a board grows with the respect for its high standards.

Ideally, no one should join the board of a nonprofit group until he or she has served several months or a year on a committee or working team. This stipulation provides the opportunity for mutual assessment, and avoids the potential for unfortunate matches. It is a lot like dating before marriage. Skipping this step is risky. As a consultant, Ken often hears from groups trying to find a nice way to cut the dead wood from their boards. It's much better to prevent the problem in the first place by —

a) interviewing and carefully selecting candidates,

b) providing a clear job description to avoid surprises,

c) having a "trial marriage" at the committee level before appointing anyone to the board, and

d) setting a policy limiting the number of years board members can remain in office before mandatory retirement.

All board members should contribute financially to the organization, in addition to their time. The amount should reflect their ability, and a board member with limited resources might give only a token amount while others who are better able give much more. A simple standard is that board members put your cause near the top of their charitable giving list. They may give more to two or three other charities, but many more than that and they are not sufficiently excited about your work. Discuss this expectation with your candidates during the recruitment process. Don't surprise the board members later. Since it may be hard to convince board members to give, a simple solution is to reverse the process and look among your donors for board members.

Now you are ready to present good candidates for election to the board.

If the candidate responds positively, he or she should be introduced to staff and key volunteers, tour the office, be brought up to date on recent plans and activities, and be introduced to the other board members. It is also helpful to give new directors a manual that sets out the mandate of the organization, its policies, past and present activities, the mandate of each board committee, the names of all directors, the names and positions of the staff members, the dates of all board meetings for the coming year (if this has been determined), and other useful information. This way, the newcomer will be well oriented in the organization.

It is better to have a steady flow of retirements from the board and new people coming in than to have to replace the whole board at once. Some groups set a "term" for board members and have to replace them all when the term is up. This is most common when the board members are elected by the general membership.

It's best to have board members and staff work on recruiting new board members before others retire, as doing so provides continuity. Do not try to get the retiring members to find their own replacements. They are not necessarily equipped to be good recruiters, and their choices may prove to be weak. (This assumes that the board is not democratically elected but largely self-appointed, which is often the case.)

When people decide to leave the board, it is important to let them retire gracefully. If people are made to feel guilty when they want to leave, they will come away with a sour taste from their volunteer experience, and they will be more reluctant to volunteer for something else. You can't expect the same people to do all the work, all the time, forever. It is usually true that 20 percent of the people do 80 percent of the work, but you have to keep the membership of that 20 percent dynamic by allowing those who feel they have done their part to step down and by bringing in new energy.

3.3 Responsibilities of the board

The responsibilities of the board can be divided into three main categories: policy, monitoring, and management. If the organization has paid staff, many of the management functions will usually be delegated to the staff and the board will focus more on the first two responsibilities.

a) Policy

The board should develop both short- and long-range goals to help your group fulfill its mission and it should decide priorities for spending funds. It should regularly evaluate programs, staff and volunteer performance, and its own performance. It should also represent and promote the organization within the community.

The extent to which the board of directors sets or controls policy and positions on issues will vary from group to group. Whether or not they exercise it, the directors do have the ultimate decision-making power and responsibility for the group and its actions. If they are experienced and committed directors, their advice on the management and direction of the group can be very valuable; they have both background and perspective, which the staff often lacks.

b) Monitoring

Once the board has established policies and set the direction for the group, it falls to staff to implement the policy. In theory, the board steers, the staff rows; although in practice the relationship between board and staff is more complex than this. The role of the board does not end with setting direction. The board also has a duty to monitor how well staff are carrying out its policies and directions. The board should expect regular reports on the financial status of the organization, staff relations, the progress of projects and programs, compliance with laws, and any unforeseen or unusual situations that can affect the welfare of the organization (such as unfavorable news coverage or significant complaints).

c) Management

Planning the budget, planning and supervising the fundraising (if not actually doing a lot of it), ensuring that expenditures are kept within the budget and that projects are carried out on schedule, and seeing that financial records are kept are all functions of the board. It may delegate some of this work to staff, but the board is ultimately accountable for legal obligations.

The board will hire and fire the most senior staff person (often called the executive director) and may also recruit important volunteers. It is the board's job to resolve any internal conflicts among board members or between board and staff. If there is a serious dispute and the people can't work it out, a member of the board should deal with it quickly. The longer you wait, the harder it gets.

Many groups list the board of directors on their letterhead. When you are starting out, the only credibility you may be able to demonstrate is your board of directors.

List more than the names of your board members. The more potential donors know about your board, the more credible your organization becomes.

A board member named "Jane Doe" might be anybody. Add any degrees so potential donors can be reassured that you have a lawyer and an accountant on the team. Note other "respectable" titles, such as doctors, clergy, other health professionals, and so on. "The Rev. Dr. Jane Doe, BSW, MDiv, PhD" is much more impressive.

Show where the people work to further identify them. It can provide the added credibility by association with another organization. "The Rev. Dr. Jane Doe, BSW, MDiv, PhD, President, Utopia University" or "Vice President, Human Resources, Widgets Inc." adds credibility.

Some people worry that this practice discriminates against valuable people who have fewer of these socially acceptable credentials. A mini-biography of those people may solve this problem. For example a group like Artists for Fair Wages might list "John Row, full-time artist for ten years."

3.4 Board development

Although the board has all these duties, some board members aren't very good at carrying out these functions. This is where the chairperson and the executive director should work very closely.

If board members aren't coming to meetings or aren't working, the chair of the board should try to encourage them to contribute more. Often a review and renegotiations of mutual expectations will get everyone back on track. If that doesn't work, find a tactful way to get them to resign and replace them with people who are willing to work.

Sometimes board members lack skills in matters such as running a meeting, making decisions, setting policy, or dealing with finances. They may have expertise in understanding and relating to the community, but lack these management skills. The executive director and the chairperson can get together and work out a plan for board development, which is a nice way of saying training. The training needs to be approached in a way that won't offend the respected board members, so it helps to have the chairperson involved with it.

Board development might consist of a simple presentation on how to make decisions in a group, how to chair a meeting, how to do a budget, or different methods of fundraising. Staff can do informal board training by making presentations on topics they have studied in courses. However you go about it, board training is a necessary investment. The Canadian Centre for Philanthropy or the Foundation Center can help you to find competent trainers. So can the United Way. In many communities there are now college courses on fundraising or volunteer management.

Successful organizations have funds available for both staff and board training, and have educational activities year-round. A skill-development session or a presentation on your cause can enhance interest in board meetings, improving attendance and performance at the same time.

The book *Working with Volunteer Boards* is a great help on this topic. It is available from Volunteer Canada (see the address in the Appendix).

3.5 Committees and work teams

One way to reduce the board's workload is by creating working committees, such as a fundraising committee or a management committee, made up of a few working members of your board. Committee membership, however, does not have to be limited to board members. Board members heading up a committee can recruit new members from outside the board; this is a good way of bringing in new people. For example, a fundraising committee could be composed of one or two board members and a number of prominent members of the business community recruited by your board members. Later, committee members might be invited to join the board when there is a vacancy.

A fundraising committee can be of great help to you, but before you rush off to arrange it, ask yourself whether a committee structure is going to be any more effective than volunteers working individually for the organization. For certain types of fundraising to be effective, you need businesspeople with clout, and people with clout are busy. It's more important that these people go out and raise money for you than spend time in committee meetings. Arranging committee meetings and reporting on them also takes your time, and your time is valuable. Don't assume the structure; design the structure to suit your group's needs and the needs of your volunteers.

The word "committee" might be best avoided. Too often this word implies endless meetings discussing what other people should do, rather than action. Instead, call them "task-forces" or "working teams" or "action groups" to make it clear they have a goal to achieve within a limited schedule.

4. Managing Growth

The rapid growth and expansion of organizations is more of a problem in the voluntary sector than you might think. It seems nonprofit groups are so accustomed to a "struggle and survive" mentality that when growth knocks on the door, we are immediately seduced. Growth can derail a group just as quickly as bankruptcy, so you should know what it looks like and how to manage it.

First, get a perspective on the growth of your organization. Comparing your group to another in the same field or same community won't help. Where you are now, compared to a year ago or a year hence, is what matters. Indicators of growth in your organization include increases in —

a) your annual operating budget,

b) the number of people served (clients, students, audience, participants, members, or whatever you call them),

c) the number of volunteers and paid staff,

d) the number of new programs or services, or art shows,

e) your fundraising projections,

f) your sphere of influence, and

g) the number of chapters, branches, or divisions.

These are just a few general "growth and change" parameters for your organization that will help you identify and quantify growth in an objective and rational way.

Organizations can experience two kinds of growth: organic and artificial. Organic growth is an orderly and incremental development that arises naturally from within the organization. It will cause some growing pains but it's manageable. Artificial growth is created by a major change outside the organization. New legislation, new technology, new major funding sources, or a suddenly elevated social or political profile are only a few of the external changes that can spark artificial growth.

Artificial growth is explosive, fast changing, and, often, out of control. It is compelling and seductive; it begs you to accommodate it. It requires astute management to keep it harnessed and directed. If you are looking at doubling your annual budget in one year, hiring five or more paid staff for the first time, adding three new target groups or services, or merging with another organization, you are dealing with artificial growth.

On one occasion, Joyce consulted with several groups who were facing at least three of these items in their next fiscal year. Only one of them managed to say no to artificial growth. This group could see that they would burn out their volunteer base, program quality would suffer, and the reputation they had worked so hard to build would be at risk. Instead, they chose to work at expanding their volunteer base first. They plan to be able to properly accommodate half of the originally projected growth a year from now.

Artificial growth is not always bad, and you should not always decline it, but you must recognize it as a major change and understand it is not necessarily desirable. Carefully assess both the opportunities and the risks it poses for your organization. Then make a deliberate decision about whether to take it on and how you will manage it.

5. Networking

Networking has become an essential activity for job seekers, fundraisers, managers — in short, for everybody. It is a powerful tool for getting access to important people or information and for building coalitions. It is a way of doing more with less. Unfortunately, some networkers have forgotten, or never knew, the rules of the game.

A network is an informal system of one-to-one, usually face-to-face relationships. Information and access are the business of the network. There is a set of shared values and goals, a sense of kindred spirit and colleagueship that holds a network together. Without that, you don't have a real network.

There are three roles that members of the network can fulfill: "Asker," "Giver," or "Link," and there are rules for each role.

If you are the Asker, your first task is to be specific and realistic about what you want from the Giver. You should do everything possible to make it easy for the Giver to help you, and knowing precisely what you want is the first step. Another way to make it easy for the Giver is to ask for time on the phone, rather than a meeting. Respect the Giver's time, and intrude as little as possible. Finally, if the Giver helps you, a brief note explaining what happened is a must. That's how you say "thank you."

There are rules for Givers, too. Sometimes Givers just give out a lot of advice without taking the time to listen carefully to the Asker and determine the Asker's needs. Too often, Givers promise something and then don't deliver. It's better to simply say no.

Finally, there are the Links, the people who connect the Askers to the Givers. The Links need to exercise judgment to find a good fit between an Asker's needs and a Giver's resources. When you make a linkage, that reflects on you and affects your relationships with the Giver and Asker. You want to protect both relationships and be careful not to overuse any one Giver.

Most people play all three roles at different times. Being a good Giver and a Link is what allows you to network successfully when it is your turn to be an Asker. The creation and maintenance of an effective network enables individuals and groups to accomplish more in less time, with fewer resources. It is an essential activity for fundraisers.

CHAPTER 3
FUNDRAISING TOOLS

Before you bought this book, you probably read the front and back cover to help you decide whether or not to buy it.

Right now, a corporate executive may be reading printed material from your group and deciding whether or not to donate a few thousand dollars, or a government official may be reading a proposal and deciding whether or not to give you a grant. A concerned citizen may be looking at your Web site or a fundraising letter and deciding whether or not to send you a donation.

Printed matter and electronic communications are to a nonprofit group what appearance is to the individual. They create a first impression, they build an image, they show a style, they create expectations, and they can build interest and curiosity. Whether the presentation will achieve its purpose depends greatly on the quality of the printed material or electronic message.

Some of your most important tools as a fundraiser are the printed and electronic materials your organization produces, and the annual report, objectives sheet, and funding proposal are

particularly vital to your efforts. They must be concise, good-looking, and contain essential information. Donations administrators have to deal with many requests from all kinds of groups, and you want to make it easy and pleasant for them to take a look at your group on paper. It is very important that there be no spelling mistakes, typos, or arithmetic errors in these materials. If there are, the potential donor can easily say, "If these people can't put out a pamphlet without mistakes, how can we trust them to carry out a $40,000 project successfully?"

In this chapter, you will learn about writing, design, and print production generally and about specific fundraising materials. The emphasis will be on good communication and cost-effectiveness.

1. Presenting Your Organization in Words and Images

As a fundraiser, you need a wide range of skills. One of those skills is presenting your group on paper and via the Internet, in a variety of formats, to a number of different audiences. Nor should your interest in presentations be restricted to fundraising materials, because every piece of paper, every e-mail, every phone call that goes out of your office represents your group. Try to set an organization-wide standard of quality for printed materials. If possible, all your important print documents should be professionally printed. Publications don't need to be flashy or expensive. After all, you don't want donors to get the impression you are spending their money to impress them! But they should be clean, neat, attractive, and have a style consistent with your organization.

1.1 Content and audience

Before beginning any writing project, answer the following important questions:

a) What do you want to say?

b) Why do you want to say it?

c) Whom do you want to reach?

d) What image do you want the reader to have of your group?

If you don't work out the answers to those questions very carefully, you are already wasting money by pursuing a vague goal. However, if you can give precise answers to those questions, you will save yourself time, money, and a lot of headaches along the way.

While the first question is pretty easy to answer, the second question, "Why?", often gets an indefinite answer like "to increase public awareness." That's not good enough. Usually you want to provide certain information to motivate people to take a certain action. The question may be easier to answer if it is restated as "What do you want readers to do after reading your material?" Do you want them to attend an event? Do you want them to give you money? Do you want them to be kinder or more understanding toward a person with a disability? Do you want them to participate in a lobbying effort? Try to be as specific as possible.

Your answer to the third question, "Whom do you want to reach?" may be, "The general public, of course." Wrong. Unless you have the advertising budget of American Express, you had better forget about reaching the general public *on paper*. (Electronic communication, discussed below, is a different matter.) The only way a nonprofit group can afford to reach the general public on paper is if it deals with an issue newsworthy enough to get free radio, television, and newspaper coverage. In that situation, reporters will likely interview you, or you can bring your views to their attention through news releases and news conferences.

What image do you want? Earthy or elegant? Local or global? Low budget to the point of tackiness or chic to the point of extravagance? Should people who have only basic language skills be able to read your material, or is it aimed exclusively at highly educated professionals? Do you want to warm the heart with human-interest stories and/or focus on statistics and facts? Will your print brochure have to catch the readers' eyes from crowded literature racks, where only the top third of the cover page is visible? Many donors are old enough to need bifocals: will the print be too tiny for them? Many are color-blind: will your graphics or colored print and backgrounds make sense? Do you need to use more than one language? People viewing your Web site may have older equipment, slower modems, outdated software, no speakers, or other barriers to enjoying complex designs. Do you need to make it easy for them to see a version of your site?

In this era of brand identity, all your materials should consistently convey the same message, with the same logos, colors, designs, and even typefaces.

Identifying the audience is the toughest part of planning your publication. It requires intuition, experience, and hard-headed thinking. When you are trying to define your audience, consider the following factors:

a) Age group

b) Income bracket

c) Occupation

d) Cultural background

e) Lifestyle

f) Values

g) Casual interests and hobbies

People who work for nonprofit groups tend to be highly motivated, often politically aware people with a cause. We are all, in some way, trying to make the world a better place. That's tremendous, so long as you don't forget that your burning cause doesn't even enter into the reality of some others. To reach people, you must try to get inside their minds and understand their experience, their goals, and their concerns. Try to put yourself in your audience's shoes. You have to find a way to touch their reality, and their reality is different than yours.

Joyce illustrates this briefly with a story from the time she worked at Pollution Probe:

Walking home from work each day, I would see garbage cans overflowing with take-out food containers and think, "What a waste of money and resources!" I would see cars lined up along the road and think of all the chemicals from those automobile exhausts that were going to be washed into my drinking water. I would see stores filled with consumer goods and wonder how we were going to slow down all this frantic consumption in time to leave some resources for our children. Then I would look at someone near me in the street and know that he or she wasn't seeing any of the things I was seeing. That person was thinking about what to cook for dinner, getting the car fixed, the kids' measles, and just getting by. In order to communicate effectively in person or in a publication, you must remember that your cause is only one among all the causes and concerns that make up our busy, complex society.

Athletes may wonder why others are sedentary when they could run, jump or at least walk. Artists may see the world as a poem or a potential symphony. All of us see things differently from the way our neighbors do. How can you get them to see things your way for a moment?

Once those first questions are answered, you should be able to outline the contents of your publication and decide on a style of writing and a graphic design.

1.2 Writing

If your publication is not well written, it's not worth the paper it's printed on or the bits and bytes it takes up in a computer. A badly written brochure, fundraising letter, or grant application won't be read or understood. The Canadian Pacific Charitable Foundation (CPCF) receives "more than 2,000 formal proposals each year; however, this does not include the informal requests and questions, fielded by phone, e-mail, mail, or fax." Former CPCF donations officer Hollie L. Zuorro a few years ago said, "Many proposals are of very poor quality. They don't state their name, address, charitable number, purpose, goals and objectives, accomplishments, or reason for fundraising. They do not define their clients or service area. And they do not explain their local, regional, or national affiliations."

Happily, the quality of proposals has improved since the last edition of this book, reports the new CPCF donations officer Sheila Carruthers: "This [concern] is no longer as accurate as it may once have been. We have made a concerted effort to better communicate the strategies and focus of the Foundation's grants program, and as a result, receive many proposals of a high quality and sufficient detail to efficiently consider support." Ms. Carruthers' comments only emphasize how important it is for you to research a donor's requirements before you write, and tell them, clearly, what they need and want to know.

The writing should be clear, concise, and direct. Use proper grammar. Avoid jargon; it alienates people who don't understand it. If you must use jargon, define it when it first appears in your text, and spell out acronyms at least once. Sometimes you don't even recognize your own jargon as jargon, so have at least one other person look over what you've written. Get somebody completely outside your organization to look over your writing and give you a reaction. A member of your board of directors should examine any publication that will have broad distribution before it goes to print.

When you've written something, set it aside for at least a day before you go over it again. You will be better able to critique your own writing if you have had a rest from it. If you don't use a computer for writing your first draft, get your work on the word processor before you look at it again. You can be much more objective if you are looking at clean, typed copy.

If you can't write well, hire a freelance writer or editor. If you've answered those first four questions in section **1.1**, it shouldn't be difficult or expensive to have a freelance writer pick up your basic idea and do your writing for you.

1.3 Design

The components of designing a publication are —

  a) choosing a format,

  b) designing a layout,

  c) preparing artwork, and

  e) final computer production.

Once those steps are completed, you have material that is ready for printing and binding.

a) Format

Format is the shape and size of the publication. It influences communication effectiveness, cost, distribution, and the amount of information the publication can convey.

There are standard formats for brochures, newsletters, annual reports, and books. Size affects the cost of a publication. To keep costs down, select a standard size. Printers buy paper in large sheets, and if your publication is in a standard format (such as 8" x 11" or European A5) your printer will be able to cut your paper with very little wastage. If you choose an unusual format, there will be paper wastage in the cut, and you pay for that wastage. It will also affect the size of envelope required, and you may have to pay for a larger envelope than would otherwise be necessary.

When choosing format, don't forget to consider the way your publication will be distributed. Will it be posted, handed out, mailed, or displayed? If it is to be mailed, you can save some money with a design and format that can be mailed without an envelope. This is often done with direct mail pieces or newsletters for a large-volume mailing. However, postal regulations change often. Before you print, make sure that your design meets the specifications. If you are using an envelope, postal rates may be lower if you use standard-size envelopes or smaller envelopes or lightweight paper.

Make sure the design fits comfortably in a regular envelope. For example, an 8" x 5" booklet will require an odd and unsightly fold to fit into a standard #10 envelope, which is 9" x 4". If it is to be displayed, you want to make sure it will fit in the display rack.

You have already defined your audience. Put yourself in their shoes now and ask, "What print formats are they familiar with?" Everybody is familiar with newspaper formats. But if you are appealing to potential funders, you may want something more sophisticated, such as an 8" x 22", two-page spread. The format should always be appropriate for the audience.

b) Layout

The next step is layout, or your plan of where to put everything in your publication. Layout influences readability, attractiveness, type size, and the amount of information you can fit into your document. In your layout, be sure to break up blocks of type with white space, lines, symbols, graphics, and photographs, if you can use them. The captions under photographs are the first part of the page most people read. Make them interesting. Use them to add to the information conveyed by the photo; don't just repeat the obvious or add names. Avoid italics; type designers find that italics are hard to read if they are more than a few words.

Wall-to-wall type is unattractive and hard to read. If you leave enough white space (areas without type or pictures) in your layout, it will also help break up and balance the inked areas.

c) Choosing type fonts and sizes and column widths

We won't go into detail about type sizes and column widths, but we will point out some basics. For readability, 55 to 65 characters per line is optimal. To count characters, count the letters, the spaces between words, and all punctuation marks.

Type size, the size of the letters in your publication, is measured in points. This book is set in 10-point type. There are 72 points to an inch, measured vertically. Column width is measured in picas. Column length is measured in agates. For continuity in your publication and to save money, keep the number of different typefaces to a minimum. If you have never worked with typeset copy, get a graphic artist to help you with these decisions. Buying a little expert help is a lot cheaper than changing all the codes. Computer graphic design is harder than it looks. Despite the power of the layout options in modern software, people often turn out pages that are hard to read. Avoid justifying the margins (so that the right margin is an even line) if it leaves rivers of white spaces through your text.

d) Artwork

Artwork and graphic design are very much a matter of personal preference, but no matter what your taste, it pays to use an experienced professional, either paid or volunteer. You may pay a fixed amount for the job or an hourly rate. Rates for freelancers vary depending on experience and the complexity of the job. Be sure to establish your contractual terms with the artist at the outset:

- How much are you going to pay per illustration?

- How many illustrations will there be?

- Will you be able to see a rough sketch or concept before the final (costly) work is completed?

- If you are going to see finished artwork only, what happens if you don't like it?

Since artwork is a matter of personal taste, it is important to decide who in your group has the ultimate say on production matters. In this situation, decision making by committee can be a very expensive form of democracy.

In the past, once you had all the copy typeset and had collected your photographs, drawings, and other graphics, you had to manually paste them where you wanted them onto paper. (This was called paste-up.) Today, photos and drawings can be scanned into a computer and inserted electronically, and computer software permits you to insert symbols and graphics electronically, eliminating crooked manual paste-up.

Layout and paste-up are now part of the same electronic process. If you have a good design sense and good technical computer skills, you can do your own layout and paste-up using desktop publishing software and graphic arts software. However, amateurish design or computer work can ruin an otherwise good-looking publication, so hire a professional if no one in your group has these skills.

e) Proofreading

In the past, once you had a typed manuscript on paper, you decided the layout you wanted, including typefaces, type sizes, and column widths, either on your own or by hiring a designer. Then you gave the typed copy with instructions on layout to a typesetter before it went to a printer. The typesetter retyped everything on a machine in different sizes and types of fonts and column widths according to your instructions. After the manuscript was typeset, you had to proofread every word carefully to make sure that in retyping your manuscript, the typesetter didn't drop lines, repeat lines or introduce spelling mistakes.

Then it went to the printer.

Today, almost every document is typed on a computer and the designer or printer is given a computer disk to work from or the copy is sent electronically as an e-mail attachment and is downloaded from a modem. Even if you still provide typed words on paper, this information can often be "scanned" onto a computer disk using a machine called, not surprisingly, a scanner. As a result, in most cases, the typesetting step has been eliminated.

Regardless of whether you still give typed or hand-written copy on paper to a typesetter or provide a computer disk to a printer, be sure that you provide the printer with perfect copy. Your copy should be typed rather than hand-written and perfectly readable; if there are corrections, cross-outs, and scribbled-in additions, the chances are high that the typesetter or printer will make a mistake. Be sure he or she doesn't have to guess at anything.

If there are mistakes in the copy you provide, the printer will simply print those mistakes. Printers are not editors or proofreaders. Proofread the copy carefully before giving it to the printer. Important documents like funding proposals, annual reports, newsletters, and other publications should be proofread by at least two people.

Remember to keep a copy of whatever you give the printer, because you should not be charged for corrections made necessary by the printer's mistakes. If you have a copy of the material you sent, you can easily determine whether a mistake was yours or the printer's. Don't expect your printing to be done in one day. Depending on the size of the job and how busy the printer is, it could take three days to two weeks to get the material printed.

If you type on a computer, as most people now do, be sure to use the spell check feature. But don't count on computer software alone to check your spelling adequately. It may miss simple errors that substitute the wrong word, spelled correctly, but out of context. Ken has a list of awful errors that can easily slip through, such as 'asses' for 'assess,' or 'pubic' when you meant 'public.' By the same token, don't trust spreadsheets to do the math correctly. Late changes may mean the formula does not add up all the numbers in a column, for example.

f) Printing and binding

If you are providing text on a computer disk, or transmitting it through a computer modem to be downloaded by the printer, first discuss fonts, formatting symbols, hidden text, and other potential problems with your typesetter or layout artist.

Get written quotations from at least three different printers before giving the job to anyone. To estimate the cost, the printer will need the following specifications:

a) Size

b) Number of pages

c) Number of sides to be printed

d) Quantity

e) Paper type, weight, recycled content, and colors

f) Ink types, environmental friendliness and, if you are using colors, how many, and what is required for *registration* (do they touch or are they close together?)

g) Bleeds (where the printing goes right to the edge of the page with no margin)

h) Number of half tones or screens (photographs specially rendered into dots so they can be printed clearly). The printer will need to know the gradation on the screens, usually a percentage.

i) Folding

j) Collating

k) Binding or stapling

To print your publication, the printer will use different techniques depending on the type of job, for example, the size of the press run, and the number of ink colors. Generally, the more ink colors, the higher the cost of printing.

Printing jobs have an economy of scale. The more items you print, the cheaper the unit cost because many of the costs in printing are fixed. Whether you are printing 200 newsletters or 2,000, the printer still has to set up the press.

Black ink is the cheapest. Using a colored ink instead will be a little more expensive.

A bleed means that the ink appears to run right over the edge of the page because the margins of the paper are cut off. Bleeds are an additional cost.

There is an infinite range of papers, varying depending on weights, textures, and colors. A higher quality paper will hold the ink better and give you a nicer-looking job. Brochures are often printed on 50-pound paper, but if you are printing on both sides, you might want to use a heavier stock such as 70-pound paper to reduce see-through. Your printer will show you sample books so that you can select a paper type and weight. You can also select your ink from sample cards. If you select a paper or ink that the printer does not have in stock, it will delay your job.

Folding and collating are pretty straightforward.

The cheapest way to bind a 50- to 200-page report is either by stapling it (sometimes a special

tape is put over the bound edge to look more finished), or coil binding (plastic or metal). A booklet would be either saddle-stitched or perfect bound. Saddle stitch means it is stapled at the fold. This book is perfect bound. Perfect binding is the more expensive of the two, but once you get over 100 pages, saddle stitch becomes unattractive.

If you don't understand the printing process, you can make some very expensive mistakes, such as publishing a book that loses its pages after the first reading because you skimped on the cost of binding. Funders would not be impressed!

Print production is an art and a science. There is an incredible amount of detail involved and you have to make a lot of decisions along the way. But when you get the package of printed material back from the printer, it's like getting your first donation from a new funder. It's all worth it!

2. Key Documents

2.1 The objectives sheet

Your objectives sheet organizes all essential information about your group on one piece of paper. It is a very important document. If you can't afford to print anything else professionally, at least have your objectives sheet printed. Give a good deal of thought to the design and layout. You want a potential funder to be able to look at the objectives sheet for a couple of minutes and get a good overview of your group. (See Sample 1.)

The core of the objectives sheet is the statement of objectives. We can't overemphasize the importance of getting this statement right. It tells why you are doing what you're doing, not how, or what, or when. That comes later. State your objectives positively and avoid jargon.

You can have more than one objective, but the first one should be all encompassing. The objective statement should be no longer than a sentence you can read aloud in one breath. Think through every single word and phrase in that statement. Every one counts.

SAMPLE 1
OBJECTIVES SHEET

THE SOCIETY TO SAVE DEAD ELM TREES
Five Year Objectives 2003–08

To promote and demonstrate the importance of full forest ecology, both urban and rural

To be the catalyst for involving business, government and the public in environmental improvement

To advocate wise management of forest resources

To continue to promote environmental education in public schools

To encourage the adoption of national and local forestry policies with an emphasis on forest renewal

To demonstrate the environmental and economic soundness of green forest management

Within this framework, the Society to Save Dead Elm Trees is undertaking the following major projects

PROGRAMS 2003–08

Forest Management:

Form a coalition for preservation of trees, wood lots and forests in our region. Specifically, join with local environmental groups to protect the 700 acres of Sleepy Hollow's woods threatened by the Greater Metropolitan Sleepy Hollow Regional Council's plan to expand urban boundaries.

Conserver Education:

- Alert the public to environmentally damaging consumer products and wasteful packaging
- Design a "Tree-mendous" poster to help individuals maintain and improve their personal environments
- Continue to respond to over 500 information requests per week from the public
- Provide teachers with current information on our special area of concentration, including The Elm Elves Club, Backyard Forests, Art and the Environment, Literature and the Environment, and guides to 20 environmental tours in Sleepy Hollow

Health Research:

We will develop a campaign explaining the links between trees and clean air, protection from skin cancer, soil conservation, cooler climates and water purification.

We will study the effects on pubic health of logging and tree planting, including paper production and the release of toxins into the environment.

Note: We will maintain organizational flexibility so that we can respond to urgent environmental problems as they arise.

Funding:

Donation and grants from individuals, foundations, ethically screened corporations and governments meet the Society's yearly budget.

The Society is a registered charity in Canada (# 123-4567890) and a 501(c)3 nonprofit in the United States.

The Society's accounts are prepared under the supervision of the Global Caring Accounting firm.

Funding objectives for 2003–08:

Forest Management	$55,800
Conserver Education	$80,000
Health Research	$13,000
Total	**$148,800**

Note: Included in the above is —

Program Administration	$15,000
Fundraising	$35,000

Fundraising objectives also include —

Existing donor renewal	85%
New individual donors	1,750

Volunteer objectives for the 2003–08:

Program	Retiring	Retain	New	Total
Forest Management	2	12	7	21
Conserver Education	10	20	12	42
Health Research	5	10	5	20
Total	**17**	**42**	**24**	**83**

Contact information:

The Society to Save Dead Elm Trees
1 Elmsvale Crescent
Elmada, MI 04309
Phone (555) 362-DEAD
Fax   (555) 362-1234
Email: fundraising@deadelm.com
Web: www.DeadElm.com

You are writing this for potential donors. If your group is controversial, you have to search for a diplomatic way to state your purpose. Usually, there is some common ground, some area of agreement between what you are working for and what your funders find acceptable:

- A gay and lesbian group might state its objective like this: "To foster understanding and tolerance of nontraditional human and sexual relationships."

- A daycare center might say, "To provide a supervised learning and development situation for children two to five years of age."

- A local environmental group might say, "To educate the Jamesborough community about the wise use of our natural resources."

- A community legal clinic might say, "To provide a full range of legal advice and services for low-income people in Marysville."

2.2 The annual report

If your group has been going for less than a year, you won't have published an annual report, but at the end of your first fiscal year you should prepare one (see Sample 2).

Next to your objectives sheet, the annual report is your most important fundraising tool. It identifies your group as a business, albeit a nonprofit business. All publicly traded corporations and government agencies and some foundations publish annual reports. If you are seeking funds from any financial institution, such as a bank, insurance, or trust company, the first thing it wants to see is your annual report.

When businesses want to check out their competitors or are considering investing in another company, the first thing they look at is that company's annual report. Your group's annual report shows your businesslike approach. With it, you can present your group in a language and format

that corporations and foundations understand and respect.

a) General considerations

If possible, have your annual report professionally designed and printed. It must be neat, well written, and contain the essential information outlined below. If you've never done one before, take a look at the annual reports put out by similar nonprofit groups. (They are also a good place to find names of potential funders!) To a large extent, corporations and foundations are going to judge your group on the basis of this one document. So put due time, thought, and, if you have it, money, into the annual report.

Try to get the annual report out as soon as possible after your year-end. If you organization's financial records are subject to an independent audit, you can't print it until you have the auditor's report, but you can get it ready for printing while you wait for the accountant to finish.

The length of your annual report will depend on the size of your group and how many activities you have to describe. For small groups, a one-page, two-fold pamphlet will do the job. Large groups will need a small booklet to convey the information. Keep it concise and stick to basic, essential information.

b) Essential elements of an annual report
Financial statements

The financial statements are the real reason behind an annual report. Hand your annual report to a corporate president and he or she will turn straight to the financial statements. The financial statements — set out by categories — your income, expenditures, and balance at the year-end. As a guideline, if your group's annual income is $50,000 or more, you should probably have an annual audit of your financial records by an outside accounting firm. In some cases, an independent audit is a legal requirement. However, even

www.sierralegal.org

2000 | Annual Report

Sierra Legal Defence Fund

Year in review | Too busy to celebrate

Dear friends,

Around the time of Sierra Legal's tenth anniversary, we weren't able to celebrate properly; we were hard at work. Two of our lawyers were in Ottawa's Supreme Court of Canada, trying to protect the right of local governments to enact regulations to restrict the use of harmful pesticides. Two others were in Vancouver's Federal Court of Appeal trying to protect Banff National Park from inappropriate development.

Another was attending a Montreal meeting of the NAFTA Commission on Environmental Co-operation, while another was meeting with representatives of other North, Central and South American environmental law organizations in Costa Rica. With our investigators in the field, only a handful of staff were around to enjoy the "endangered species" chocolates that Raffi brought us to commemorate the day.

After ten years we have a lot to celebrate. In the margin of this annual report, we're showcasing ten of our most potent cases and the lasting changes they have made to Canada's environmental protection.

Looking ahead, we're positioning ourselves to meet a growing demand for services throughout the country. Our Challenge Project, launched this past year, seeks to bolster our financial reserves so that we can, with confidence, increase the depth and strength of our legal and scientific teams and offer more service in more regions of Canada; see page 14 for more details. Watch our website (www.sierralegal.org) for updates on the Challenge Project, as well as improved coverage of our cases and reports.

With growth, inevitably, comes change and this year, we will see some significant change. We say farewell to a number of people whose passion and commitment created and positioned Sierra Legal to become the mainstay of Canadian environmental litigation.

The managing lawyer of our Toronto office, Stewart Elgie, is leaving Sierra Legal to work on boreal forest issues. As a young law-school graduate, Stewart articled in the Alaska office of the U. S. organization the Sierra Club Legal Defense Fund (now known as Earthjustice Legal Defense Fund). What Stewart learned there about the effectiveness of environmental law convinced him that Canada needed a similar organization, and Stewart played a central role in starting Sierra Legal. He later joined Sierra Legal as a senior litigator, and his legal acumen and personal commitment are

10 HITS, 10 YEARS

After 10 years we have a lot to celebrate. In the margin of this annual report, we're showcasing ten of our most potent cases, and the lasting changes they have made to Canada's environmental protection.

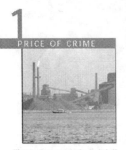

PRICE OF CRIME

Waged private prosecution on behalf of concerned citizen that led to the City of Hamilton being fined a total of $450,000 – the largest environmental fine in Canadian legal history – for allowing polychlorinated biphenyls (PCBs), pesticides and ammonia to leach into a fish-bearing creek and Lake Ontario.
Client: Lynda Lukasik; 2000

legendary in the organization. Stewart was the legal mastermind behind pivotal Sierra Legal victories, including a large proportion of the "greatest hits" featured in this year's annual report; he also worked tirelessly for the introduction of strong endangered species legislation in Canada. While his skills will certainly be missed at Sierra Legal, Stewart is sure to be a powerful advocate for the environment in his new position.

Professor Chris Tollefson retires from being chair of our board this year after serving as a director since June 1992. Chris rolled up his sleeves at the beginning, advising our first executive director on our early cases and strategies, as well as fundraising. His sage advice, hard work and humour were essential to me as I took on the role of Executive Director, and I know we'll all miss his contributions greatly.

Long-time director Don Lidstone is also leaving the board. Don has served on every one of Sierra Legal's board committees, and has devoted countless hours to ensuring Sierra Legal's smooth operation; his calm assessments and dry sense of humour leavened long meetings and injected clarity when issues appeared complex.

At the same time, new recruits to both Sierra Legal's board and staff continue to amaze me with their talent and dedication. The decade to come can't help but be full of more brilliant recruits and days worth celebrating.

 Karen Wristen, Executive Director, is one of Canada's leading experts in defending against SLAPP suits (Strategic Lawsuits Against Public Participation), having successfully defended the Friends of the Lubicon against a SLAPP brought by the transnational logging company Daishowa – a case that confirmed the right of citizens to mount consumer boycotts. A graduate of Toronto's Osgoode Hall Law School, Wristen ran her own law firm in Toronto for ten years before moving to the West Coast. She joined Sierra Legal in 1994 and, since being appointed Executive Director in 1998, has presided over a period of rapid growth and strategic planning.

FREEDOM TO PROTEST 2

Won final round at appeal of our precedent-setting victory at the Ontario Court of Justice, established the right of Friends of the Lubicon to promote a consumer boycott of Daishowa, a multinational company that planned to log the Lubicon Cree's traditional territory in northern Alberta.

Client: Friends of the Lubicon; 2000

Docket | 00

Walkerton, oil sands, beehive burners, raw sewage, watersheds, the Taku River, forest practices, Candu nuclear reactors, whistleblowers, Canada's most contaminated sites, radiation, the Oak Ridges Moraine, urban sprawl, electricity deregulation, endangered species, fish habitat, trichlorethylene, advocates' rights, national parks... Over the past year, Sierra Legal has tackled these and many more of Canada's most pressing environmental issues both in and out of court. The docket that follows is a representative, not exhaustive list our efforts toward achieving natural justice.

AIR

ISSUE	ACTION
oil sands	Argued in Federal Court to challenge the federal government failure to conduct adequate environmental assessment of Suncor's major oil sands development in northern Alberta; awaiting decision. *Client – Toxics Watch, Environmental Resource Centre, Prairie Acid Rain Coalition*
woodwaste burners	Challenged the issuance of permits to three severely polluting beehive woodwaste burners in the Bulkley Valley, B.C.; awaiting provincial Environmental Appeal Board decision. *Client – local residents Laurie Mutschße, Dave Stevens, Dr. Biz Bastien*
power generation	Used freedom of information legislation to obtain massive disclosure of Ontario Power Generation's air emissions and resulting health impacts. *Client – various*
	Filed application under Ontario Environmental Bill of Rights petitioning the Ontario government to impose strict emission caps on power stations as part of a planned electricity sector deregulation; more stringent regulations were then imposed. *Client – Ontario Clean Air Alliance*
natural gas power generation	Filed petition to federal minister of environment calling on Canada to oppose proposed natural gas fired power plant at Sumas, Washington; minister subsequently spoke out against proposal. *Client – Municipal and regional governments, British Columbia Lung Association, conservation groups*
coal-fired power generation	Assisting residents near East Selkirk, Manitoba, in fighting pollutant emissions from nearby coal-fired power plant. *Client – local residents*
	Provided scientific data and legal expertise in publication of *Countdown Coal: How Ontario Can Improve Air Quality by Phasing Out Coal-fired Electricity Generation.* *Client – Ontario Clean Air Alliance*
air pollution activism	Provided legal and scientific assistance in publication of *cleanair.ca citizen's action guide.* *Client – Environmental Law Centre, University of Victoria*
chemical fumigations	Provided legal and scientific support to citizens group in Elmira, Ont., investigating chemical fumigations by Uniroyal; assisted in convincing provincial Ministry of Environment to lay charges. *Client – APT Environment*

WATER

ISSUE	ACTION
Walkerton	Won the right for a coalition of three national and international organizations to participate at Ontario's Walkerton inquiry to address systemic problems facing municipal water supplies. *Client – Great Lakes United, Council of Canadians and Canadian Association of Physicians for the Environment*
rivers/fish habitat	Filed submission resulting in the North American Commission for Environmental Cooperation issuing factual record that harshly criticized Canada for failing to enforce its own Fisheries Act and allowing B.C. Hydro to destroy fish and fish habitat. *Client – B.C. Aboriginal Fisheries Coalition, B.C. Wildlife Federation, Steelhead Society of B.C., Trout Unlimited (Spokane Falls Chapter), Trail Wildlife Association*
	Set to challenge in Federal Court the issuance of permits without an environmental assessment by National Energy Board to an arm of B.C. Hydro for power exports. *Client – Steelhead Society of B.C., B.C. Wildlife Federation*
	Successfully intervened on behalf of residents of Sunshine Coast to help them gain water licence for Fisheries and Oceans fish conservation purposes. *Client – SPAWN to be Wild*
aquifers/urban sprawl	Won right to appeal a municipal plan that lays the groundwork for a development explosion that would drain aquifers in ecologically sensitive moraine and erode a rare green corridor north of Toronto. Also filed request with Ontario government to review the environmental assessment of a major sewage pipe extension based on new information about the potential effects on the headwaters of the Humber River, a National Heritage River. *Client – King City Preserve the Village Inc., Concerned Citizens of King Township Inc., Nobleton Alert Residents Association, Save the Oak Ridges Moraine Coalition*
	Filed request under the Environmental Bill of Rights that Ontario government review urban planning laws and policies to ensure protection of ecologically sensitive Oak Ridges Moraine pursuant to Ontario Environmental Bill of Rights. *Client – Federation of Ontario Naturalists, Save the Oak Ridges Moraine Coalition*
mining pollution	Filed formal complaint with the North American Commission for Environmental Cooperation alleging that three abandoned B.C. mines are violating the Fisheries Act by leaching effluent into fish-bearing waters; awaiting response. *Client – Environmental Mining Council of B.C., Sierra Club of B.C., Taku Wilderness Association*
water use	Assisted on Cheakamus consultation committee and multi-stakeholder Fisheries Technical Committee in effort to improve water flow from B.C. Hydro's installations. *Client – British Columbia Environmental Network*
watersheds	Provided scientific and legal advice to groups opposed to the development of a gravel mine in upper Pitt River, important fish habitat; proposal later rejected. *Client – Pitt River Area Watershed Network*
	Brought an application for judicial review of governmental refusal to grant designated watershed protection to local water users. *Client – Red Mountain Residents Association*

WATER CONTINUED

ISSUE	ACTION
Taku/transboundary watershed	With U.S. group EarthJustice, filed transboundary complaint demanding that U.S. government exercise powers under Pelly Amendment to ensure that Canada protects Taku Watershed of northern B.C./Alaska, one of the last roadless wilderness watersheds in North America. Formed Transboundary Watershed Alliance, a coalition of Canadian and U.S. conservation groups, to protect watersheds on Alaska/B.C. border. *Client – Taku Wilderness Association*
natural gas pipeline	Advised coalition concerned about plans to build a second large natural gas ocean pipeline from B.C.'s Lower Mainland to Vancouver Island. *Client – local residents, SPEC, David Suzuki Foundation*
ocean dumping	Appealed to Federal Court of Appeal against decision that allows dumping of metal debris from naval weapons in Nanoose Bay testing range, in Georgia Strait. The court held that naval ships were not subject to anti-dumping laws. *Client – Nanoose Conversion Coalition*
raw sewage	Laid charges against the Capital Regional District for discharge of raw sewage into the Strait of Juan de Fuca. B.C.'s Attorney General intervened, then stayed charges. *Client – United Fish and Allied Workers Union Local 24*

FORESTS

wildlife/First Nations	Launched challenge to Ontario's authority to issue forestry permits to Abitibi Consolidated in Northwestern Ontario on the basis that the permits allow forestry practices to interfere with wildlife populations, thereby infringing on the local First Nations members' right to trap. *Client – Joe Fobister, Andrew Keewatin Jr, Willie Keewatin*
watersheds	Produced *Muddied Waters: The Case for Protecting Water Sources in B.C.*, a 58-page report highlighting the destruction wrought by watershed logging on salmon habitat and sources of clean drinking water. *Client – B.C. Tap-water Alliance, B.C. Watershed Stewardship Alliance, Sierra Club of B.C., Red Mountain Residents Association, Tuwanek Ratepayers Association*
	Reviewed impact of past and proposed logging in Chapman and Gray Creek watersheds, near Sechelt, B.C. *Client – Tuwanek Ratepayers Association, John Marian*
fish habitat	Filed a submission resulting in the North American Commission for Environmental Cooperation requiring the federal government to answer our allegations that Canada is systematically failing to enforce Fisheries Act against logging companies that damage streams. *Client – Greenpeace, Sierra Club of B.C., David Suzuki Foundation, Northwest Eco-systems Alliance and Natural Resources Defense Council*
forestry practices	Drafted report identifying the environmental shortcomings of the B.C. Innovative Forest Practices Agreement. *Client – Natural Resources Defense Council*
	Submitted separate complaints to Forest Practices Board addressing the protection of endangered marbled murrelets, stream damage and preservation of recreation trails in Robson Valley. *Client – Vancouver Island Forest Watch, Fraser Headwaters Alliance, Sierra Club of B.C., respectively*
	Published *Grounds for Concern: An Audit of Compliance with Ontario Forest Protection Rules*, which documents widespread non-compliance with wildlife and waterway protection standards. Also conducted field investigations of access roads in Northern Ontario and forestry operations in Carolinian forest. *Client – Wildlands League*
	Prepared comprehensive review of need to reform forestry standards to better protect environmental values. *Client – Sudbury Naturalists, World Wildlife Fund Canada, Federation of Ontario Naturalists, Earthroots, Environment North, Wildlands League*
wildlife	Conducted field investigation that led to government enforcement action against forestry company for breaking wildlife habitat protection rules. *Client – Environment North*

PAGE 8 | SIERRA LEGAL DEFENCE FUND

drinking water	Brought application for judicial review of order to chlorinate local drinking water; chlorination is routinely required in B.C. now because industrial logging leads to increased pathogens in surface water. *Client – Erickson Water Users Society*
raw log exports/jobs	Examined the legality of exporting unprocessed wood from B.C. – thereby reducing forestry employment – on behalf of a group of forest industry workers. *Client – Woodworkers for Fair Forest Policy*
forest tenure/jobs	Mounted B.C. Supreme Court challenge of a tree-farm licence on grounds that the licensee, Canfor, had failed to comply with the Forest Act by failing to maintain or create wood processing jobs, then appealed decision dismissing our petition. *Client – Woodworkers for Fair Forest Policy*
wood waste	Began Federal Court challenge of constitutionality of provincial log salvage regulations; current regulations encourage waste of logs, which clog marshes and degrade vital salmon rearing habitat of Fraser River estuary. *Client – Beachcomber Shirley Weisuhn, Early Recovered Resources*

FOREST WATCH PROJECT

Forest Watch of B.C. is a province-wide network of more than 200 citizens trained to monitor forest practices and take legal action against logging companies that violate public-forest regulations. Currently a project of the Sierra Legal Defence Fund, the B.C. network will eventually become an independent non-profit organization.

forestry practices	Conducted training workshops in Terrace, Nelson and Squamish on methods of monitoring forestry practices, bringing together people from First Nations with loggers, silviculture contractors, environmentalists, fisheries officials and others. Investigated existing and proposed forestry cut-blocks in B.C.'s Chilcotin region. *Client – First Nations, Silva Forest Foundation and others*
	Forced Ministry of Forests compliance officers to reassess causes of a three kilometre landslide in the West Kootenay region after identifying poor forestry practices that had damaged an endangered bull-trout stream. *Client – West Kootenay Forest Watch*
	Developed comprehensive checklist for concerned citizens to assess Forest Development Plans, B.C.'s principal land-use planning document. *Client – First Nation and Silva Forest Foundation*
	Submitted four complaints to the provincial Forest Practices Board covering "significant non-compliance", threats to endangered marbled murrelets, the destruction of a wetland and other breaches of forestry legislation. *Client – various*
professional accountability	Filed complaint with the Association of B.C. Registered Professional Foresters which led to the disciplining of a member for inadequate investigation of illegal logging near Prince George. *Client – Prince George Forest Watch*
eco-certification	Produced reports on forestry practices on Vancouver Island and near Prince George to assess efforts by Western Forest Products and Lignum Forest Products to gain the seal of approval of the Forest Stewardship Council, the leading ecological forestry certification. *Client – Greenpeace, others*
forestry	Assisted in writing *Canada's Forests At a Crossroads: An Assessment in the Year 2000*, first publication of the new organization, Global Forest Watch Canada. *Client – Global Forest Watch Canada*

ISSUE	ACTION
forest practices	Conducted an assessment of all approved logging in the Great Bear Rainforest of B.C.'s mid-coast to support a conservation mapping initiative and ongoing conservation negotiations. *Client – Sierra Club of B.C., others*
development in parks	Launched Alberta Federal Court appeal of judge's ruling that refused to review federal environmental assessment of proposed development at Lake Louise in Banff National Park. *Client – Bow Valley Naturalists, BEAR Society*
	Filed submissions on proposed process of environmental assessment of new developments in Ontario's provincial parks and conservation reserves system. *Client – Federation of Ontario Naturalists, Wildlands League*
	Won injunction and order requiring provincial environmental assessment of a proposed logging road which would run through Bruce Peninsula National Park; road construction has since been postponed indefinitely. *Client – Canadian Nature Federation, Canadian Parks and Wilderness Society, Federation of Ontario Naturalists, Chippewas of Nawash First Nation, Chippewas of Saugeen First Nation, Wildlands League*
	Filed an application for review to stop a mine slated for the newly established Mellon Lake Conservation Reserve; a claim was staked there just before the area was declared protected. *Client – Federation of Ontario Naturalists, Wildlands League, World Wildlife Fund, No Quarry at Mellon Lake*
	Challenged Vancouver Park Board decision to allow expansion of causeway through Stanley Park. B.C. Supreme Court ruled that the causeway had "valid park purpose" and dismissed the petition. *Client – Society Promoting Environmental Conservation, Friends of Stanley Park*
	Through Freedom of Information Act appeals, obtained crucial information regarding proposed golf development in Bronte Provincial Park; proposal subsequently scrapped. *Client – Bronte Creek East Preservation Association, Wildlands League*
development near parks	Filed petition seeking federal environmental assessment of proposed logging operations adjacent to Bruce Peninsula National Park. *Client – Chippewas of Nawash First Nation, Chippewas of Saugeen First Nation, Wildlands League*
	Successfully defended our 1999 Federal Court victory in the Cheviot Mine case on appeal, which forced a new environmental assessment of a proposed massive open-pit coal mine located in critical wildlife habitat close to Jasper National Park. The proposal has since been abandoned. *Client – Alberta Wilderness Association, Canadian Parks and Wilderness Society, Canadian Nature Federation, Pembina Institute and Jasper Environmental Association*
development in protected areas	Obtained Court of Appeal ruling enabling Sierra Legal to continue prosecuting a quarry operating without a permit. The quarry is on the Niagara Escarpment, a UNESCO World Biosphere Reserve. *Client – Rita Landry*
hunting in parks	Filed complaint under Ontario's Environmental Bill of Rights and launched two Freedom of Information Appeals to stop sport hunting in wilderness parks. *Client – Wildlands League, Thunder Bay Field Naturalists, Canadian Environmental Law Association, Earthroots, Canoe Ontario, Federation of Ontario Naturalists, Animal Alliance and Environment North*
parks protection	Acted as legal advisors to commission revising the federal National Parks Act to protect the ecological integrity of parks. Many of our recommendations were incorporated into the strengthened Act. *Client – Parks Canada Panel on Ecological Integrity*
	Advised conservation groups on proposed revisions to B.C. Parks Act. *Client – B.C. Environmental Network Parks Caucus*
environmentally sensitive lands	Filed complaint over peat operation non-compliance with environmental laws at Wilfrid Bog, Ontario; enforcement action was subsequently taken. *Client – South Lake Simcoe Naturalists*

TOXICS

ISSUE	ACTION
toxic waste-water discharges	Published *Who's Watching Our Waters?*, which used official data gained under the Freedom of Information Act to expose industries and municipalities that have violated water pollution regulations, and dramatic increases in violations in recent years. *Client – various*
heavy metal pollution	Continued providing legal and scientific advice to groups opposing development of toxic waste dump at Brittania, the worst point source of heavy metal pollution in North America. *Client – Environmental Mining Council of British Columbia*
groundwater contamination	Provided expert legal and scientific advice to Beckwith, Ontario residents about contamination of wells with trichlorethylene (TCE). Submitted a petition to the federal Auditor General requesting a decrease in the allowable limits of TCE in water; awaiting federal response. *Client – Beckwith Water Contamination Committee*
pulp mill pollution	Developed complaint to North American Commission for Environmental Cooperation and public report on federal law violations by pulp and paper mills in central and eastern Canada and government enforcement negligence. *Client – Great Lakes United, Quebec Environmental Law Centre*
pollution from nuclear facilities	Advised clients and Ontario Environmental Commissioner on the Ministry of Natural Resources' response to our request for an investigation into heavy metal discharges from nuclear generating facilities. *Client – Great Lakes United, Energy Probe and Sierra Club of Canada, Eastern Chapter*
toxic discharges	Brought private prosecution challenging the discharge of polychlorinated biphenyls and other toxic substances into fish-bearing creek flowing into Hamilton Harbour, resulting in a conviction and a $450,000 fine against the City of Hamilton, the largest ever levied against a Canadian municipality for an environmental crime. *Client – Lynda Lukasik*
pesticides	In four separate cases around B.C., conducted field assessments and/or appeared as an expert witness to appeal issuance of pesticide-use permits; won modifications to two permits, forced one to be withdrawn and awaiting decision on fourth appeal. *Client – Raincoast Conservation Society, Tsawataineuk Band Council, Skeena Environmental Coalition*
arsenic/heavy metals	Argued case against the Province of Ontario for discharges of arsenic and other heavy metals from the Deloro mine site, known as Ontario's "most contaminated site"; awaiting decision. *Client – Janet Fletcher*
polycyclic aromatic hydrocarbons	Investigated the discharge of toxic polycyclic aromatic hydrocarbons into the Thames River in London, Ontario; formally requested that Environment Canada investigate; remedial measures now being implemented and/or planned. *Client – Dr. Joe Cummins*
radioactive water pollution	Trained people to sample wastewater discharges, sediments and groundwater seepage from low-level radioactive waste sites near Port Hope and Port Granby. *Client – Port Hope Environmental Advisory Committee*
radiation	Brought private prosecution against the Ontario Ministry of Environment for permitting dangerous radiation discharge from the abandoned Deloro mine site. *Client – Tom Adams*
	Investigated tritium contamination of Inverhuron Provincial Park caused by nearby Bruce Nuclear Generating Station. Publication of our investigative results forced Ontario Power Generation to commission studies of the impact of the tritium plume on local fisheries. *Client – Bob MacKenzie*

SAMPLE 2—CONTINUED

ISSUE	ACTION
dioxin/heavy metals	Successfully challenged an Ontario Ministry of the Environment order that permitted under-regulated use of liquid waste containing dioxin and heavy-metals, as a dust suppressant on Ontario roads; obtained strict conditions for use during period when alternatives are developed and implemented. *Client – Federation of Ontario Naturalists, Federation of Ontario Cottagers' Associations, Quinte Watershed Cleanup, seven individuals*
raw sewage	Convinced the Ontario Ministry of the Environment not to issue a permit to a company intending to dump raw human sewage, containing known carcinogens, from portable toilets onto agricultural lands. *Client – Citizens in Hillsburgh, Ontario*
Canadian mining companies overseas	Investigated the environmental effects of the Bellavista mine in Costa Rica, proposed by a Canadian mining company. *Client – Inter-American Association for Environmental Defence, other groups*

ADVOCATES RIGHTS

ISSUE	ACTION
rights of whistleblowers	Intervened successfully in defence of Health Canada scientist Margaret Haydon (who had alleged she was pressured to approve bovine growth hormone) to win Federal Court ruling defending right of public servants to speak out in public interest. *Client – National Farmers' Union, Canadian Health Coalition, Council of Canadians, Sierra Club of Canada*
public access to public forests	Set legal precedent by convincing B.C. Supreme Court to strike down an injunction barring public access to old-growth forests being logged in the Elaho Valley, part of the Stoltmann Wilderness of southwestern B.C. *Client – Western Canada Wilderness Committee*
	Convinced B.C. Supreme Court to balance public and private rights in granting an injunction to International Forest Products in Elaho Valley. The injunction, which replaced an earlier injunction struck down by the Court, barred Interfor employees from having physical contact with protesters and prohibited logging of a cutblock in which a Goshawk was nesting. *Client – Western Canada Wilderness Committee*
right to public protest	Defending local opponents of a residential/commercial development at East Sooke, Vancouver Island, against intimidating SLAPP-type (strategic legal action against public participation) suit brought by developer. *Client – Residents of East Sooke, B.C.*
government liability	Conducted research with Environmental Law Centre at University of Victoria on renewing the law of government liability in environmental decision making. *Client – with the Environmental Law Centre, University of Victoria*
local control	Obtained right to intervene in Supreme Court of Canada case to defend the right of local governments to restrict use of harmful pesticides. At issue is the ability of citizens to protect their immediate environment through locally elected representatives. *Client – World Wildlife Fund Canada, Nature-Action Quebec, Federation of Canadian Municipalities*
	Awaiting decision after petitioning B.C. Supreme Court to set aside building permit that contravenes local bylaws and statutory duties. *Client – Galiano Conservancy Association*
freedom of information	Succeeded in convincing B.C. Ministry of Forests to hire more staff to expedite processing of Freedom of Information requests, after filing complaint about ministry's lengthy delays in responding to such requests. *Client – various*
	Filed a petition with the federal Environment Commissioner seeking a more stringent screening, regulation and labelling regime for genetically modified organisms. *Client – Canadian Institute for Environmental Law and Policy, Council of Canadians and two university professors*
	Successfully defended the public right to information about sulphur content in gasoline against court actions by Canada's six largest oil refiners to stop Environment Canada from releasing the information. *Client – Friends of the Earth*

PAGE 10 | SIERRA LEGAL DEFENCE FUND

| freedom of speech | Won final round in Ontario Court of Appeal, bringing successful end to a SLAPP suit mounted by forestry company, Daishowa, in attempt to stop consumer boycott organized by Friends of the Lubicon. Daishowa agreed to not log traditional Lubicon Cree lands in Northern Alberta. *Client – Friends of the Lubicon* |

| environmental assessments | Awaiting application by Atomic Energy of Canada Ltd. for leave to appeal to Supreme Court of Canada, after twice defeating AECL's attempts to deny public access to documents. Case challenges Canada's export of CANDU reactors to China without environmental assessment. *Client – Sierra Club of Canada* |

WILDLIFE

endangered species	Participated in national coalition working to pass a strong federal Species at Risk Act, which died on the Order Paper with the federal election call. *Client – Coalition of over 120 groups*
	Filed a complaint about the Ontario government's failure to protect many of its species at risk under the Ontario Endangered Species Act. Two endangered birds subsequently listed for protection and others expected to follow. *Client – Federation of Ontario Naturalists*
wildlife habitat	Challenged adequacy of environmental assessment of proposed large-scale diamond mine in the Northwest Territory in critical wildlife habitat. The mine proponent then agreed to fund a study to assess limits to development in the central Arctic. *Client – Canadian Arctic Resources Committee*
migratory birds protection	Brought a petition before the federal Auditor General requesting a review of federal government's improper issuance of permits authorizing harm to migratory bird nesting grounds. *Client – Ontario Field Ornithologists, Friends of the Spit, Animal Alliance*

EAGLE PROJECT

Environmental-Aboriginal Guardianship through Law and Education has a mandate to empower First Nations to protect the environment in their territories. Currently a project of the Sierra Legal Defence Fund, EAGLE is in the process of becoming an independent non-profit organization.

forests	Represented the Haida Nation in a case challenging the replacement of a Tree Farm Licence in the face of a reasonable assertion of aboriginal title. *Client – Council of the Haida Nation*
	Provided legal advice and assisted with retaining an expert to assess the impact of logging on old growth forests in a culturally and ecologically unique and sensitive boreal forest ecosystem. *Client – Fort Nelson First Nation*
development	Assisted lawyers for Skeetchestn with an appeal of a B.C. Supreme Court decision that upheld the Registrar of Land Title's refusal to register notice of aboriginal title litigation over lands proposed for a major golf course and related residential and hotel development. *Client – Skeetchestn Indian Band*
education	Developed materials for mining workshop with the Environmental Mining Council of B.C. Developed curricula for workshops in Water, Fisheries, Oil and Gas and Forestry. *Client – First Nations*
threatened species	Continued to provide support for the negotiation of a co-management agreement for Thompson River coho. *Client – Adams Lake Indian Band, Neskonlith Indian Band*

SIERRA LEGAL DEFENCE FUND | PAGE 11

Board chair | Litigating with attitude

2000 was yet another period of growth and change for Sierra Legal. And amid the sprint towards year-end (things around here seldom seem to slow down), it's worth pausing to reflect on why it is that thousands of Canadians like you have come to support us so loyally.

I recall vividly my first Sierra Legal board/staff meeting, held in the backyard of our first executive director, Greg McDade. It was a small but highly animated group. There was a sense we were charting new waters. We wanted to be a different kind of environmental law firm: one with attitude. After much debate, we generated a wish-list of strategic cases that we thought could leverage real benefits for the environment. Our main worry was that the money would run out before these cases could be litigated.

Nearly nine years later, we have worked our way through much of that original list and added to it. And though our meetings are now bigger, the Sierra Legal attitude (summed up by some as the unwillingness to think "inside-the-box", or to take "No" for an answer) has endured. It is an attitude that our current executive director, Karen Wristen, has in abundance. And, I think, it is this attitude – and its results – that count most with our supporters and friends across the country.

I am retiring from the board in January, and on the eve of my retirement I feel enormously fortunate to have worked with so many talented and committed people. I have relied heavily on the board for advice and support, and especially on members of the management committee, current and past. I have also thoroughly enjoyed my dealings with the folks who are the heart of Sierra Legal: our amazing legal, scientific, fundraising and administrative staff. To the board, to the staff and to you, our loyal supporters, thank you for a great decade.

3

LAST RESORT

Our lawyers went all the way to the Supreme Court of Canada to secure a ruling that an environmental assessment be done for a planned major expansion of a ski resort in Banff National Park. This action helped trigger concerns about the over-development of Canada's entire national park system.
Client: Canadian Parks and Wilderness Society; 1997

[signature]

Current Sierra Legal Board Chair Chris Tollefson is a professor of law at the University of Victoria, and the Executive Director of the University's Environmental Law Centre, Canada's only curricular public interest environmental law clinic. Chris has published on a wide variety of environmental law and policy topics, including authoring the book *The Wealth of Forests* (1998), and, most recently, *cleanair.ca: a citizen's action guide*, published in August 2000. Chris has served as a Sierra Legal Director since 1992, and has been Board Chair since 1998, shepherding the organization from its small-scale beginnings to the influential force for change it is today.

PAGE 12 | SIERRA LEGAL DEFENCE FUND

4

BOARD OF DIRECTORS: Dr. John Brennan (appointed January 2000), Jutta Brunnee (appointed January 2000), Liz Crocker (appointed January 2000), Meinhard Doelle (appointed October 2000), Tom Heintzman, Lynn Hunter, Don Lidstone, David Love, Leslie J. Muir, Judge William A. Newsom, Buck Parker, John Rich, Clayton Ruby, John Swaigen, Chris Tollefson, Tom Wickett (appointed January 2000), Lori Williams, Dr. Jeremy Wilson (appointed January 2000).

HONORARY DIRECTORS: Robert Bateman (appointed January 2000), Gregory J. McDade, Q.C. (appointed January 2000), Dr. David Suzuki (appointed January 2000).

COMMERCIAL RIGHTS

Intervened in a Supreme Court of Canada case to overturn an interpretation of the Charter of Rights and Freedoms that would have allowed corporations to challenge environmental laws that interfere with their commercial interests.
Client: Council of Canadians; 1998

VANCOUVER, HEAD OFFICE STAFF

Melissa Abram, Mitchell Anderson, Dorothy Bartoszewski, Stella Bastidas, James Boothroyd, Elizabeth Jane Brandon, Laurel Brewster, Wilma Brown, Jerome Cheung, Randy Christensen, Fereshteh Daelhagh, Mark Dunphy, Lisa Fleming, Heather Hall, Lisa Holden, Lucille Hough, Timothy J. Howard, Bridget Jenson, Angela McCue, Lisa Mckenzie, Aran O'Carroll, Ben Parfitt, Jessica Plescia, Tina Reale, John Richardson, William Roberts, Clarice Save, Cheryl Sharvit, Kate Smallwood, John Soanes, David Thompson, Ruth Tovim, Margot Venton, Vicki Vishniakoff, Heidi Ward, John Werring, Sharon Wilkie and Karen Wristen.

TORONTO STAFF (photo left)

Claudia Alvarado, Marlene Cashin, Doug Chapman, Elizabeth Christie, Lynda Collins, Jerry DeMarco, Stewart Elgie, Elaine MacDonald, Carol McDonald, Suzana Stos.

EAGLE STAFF

Wilma Brown, Mai Rempel, Cheryl Sharvit, Ruth Tovim, Terri-Lynn Williams Davidson.

Natural justice | The next challenge

Secured legal acknowledgement of First Nation's "interest in the forest," in a landmark ruling that threatens the stranglehold of multi-national corporate control of public forests.

Client: Council of the Haida Nation; 1997

I joined Sierra Legal on July 1, 2000 with a novel challenge: to raise $1.5 million in new gifts from individuals by October 31, 2001. Working with my Toronto colleague, Carol McDonald, executive director Karen Wristen, and board members from across the country, I have every confidence that we will be successful in exceeding our goal.

This "Challenge Campaign" has grown out of a generous "Challenge Grant" given to Sierra Legal by the Brainerd Foundation in 1999. Sierra Legal was one of only six groups in the Pacific Northwest to receive one of these special grants, the goal of which is to take the selected groups to "the next level of effectiveness."

In Sierra Legal's case, we determined that, in order to reach the "next level of effectiveness", Sierra Legal would need to diversify our sources of support. A more diverse funding base will decrease our reliance on any one source of funding, and thereby improve our organizational stability and our ability to plan for the future. New sources of funding will also allow us to take on crucial cases currently beyond our capacity.

Andrea Seale, my predecessor, and Mike Magee, our former Director of Communications and Development, laid the groundwork for the Challenge Campaign. Thanks to them and a definitive fundraising feasibility study, we know that Sierra Legal is well-situated to meet this new challenge.

The Brainerd Foundation's faith in our work and in our capacity to become even more effective is matched by the enthusiasm of the staff at Sierra Legal, and the incredible donors who are committed to helping us reach our goals.

Thank you, in advance, for helping Sierra Legal meet the challenge of providing strategic legal services that do justice to Canada's extraordinary environment.

William Roberts

William Roberts comes to Sierra Legal with seven years' experience working with non-profit organizations throughout Canada consulting on strategic planning and revenue development. He has worked closely with board members on major gift programs as well as working with management and staff to develop successful annual, capital and planned giving programs. Prior to this consultancy work, William served as the Member of the Alberta Legislature for Edmonton Centre for seven years. As an MLA he was actively involved in many health and environmental issues, and worked with a variety of non-profit groups in his diverse downtown constituency.

PAGE 14 | SIERRA LEGAL DEFENCE FUND

For the defence

Sierra Legal's supporters are united in their commitment to justice and to the environment. Whatever the size of the contributions, their support reflects a belief that the environment deserves the full protection of the law, and that giving to Sierra Legal is an effective means of achieving that protection. While we only have room to acknowledge donors who gave $500 or more in the past year, we sincerely thank all those who gave.

6

BUFFER ZONE

Convinced Federal Court to quash approval for a massive open-pit mine slated for the outskirts of Jasper National Park. This victory established the importance of buffer zones around national parks and will strengthen key environmental laws.

Client: Alberta Wilderness Association, Jasper Environmental Association, Canadian Parks and Wilderness Society, Canadian Nature Federation, Pembina Institute; 1999

SENIOR PARTNERS
1155599 Ontario Ltd.
Barbara Blouin
Charles R. Chamberlin
Dr. Bernard J. Benson
Earthjustice Legal
    Defense Fund, Inc.
Edith R. & Theodore H.
    Fitz-Selmen
Elinor Kelly
Gordon N. Tyndall
Hilda F. Pangman
Husky Injection
    Molding Systems
Key Trust Company of Ohio
Louise Brittain
Marna Disbrow
McCuaig Desrochers
Patagonia Fund
Rockefeller Brothers Fund
The Estate of
    John A. MacDonald
Top Shelf Feeds Inc.
VanCity Enviro Fund
W. Laurence & Mary T. Jones
World Resources Institute
World Wildlife Fund Canada

PARTNERS
Adanac Corporate Services Ltd.
Madeline M. Carter
Terry Good
Cortlandt & Jean Mackenzie
Robert & Betty McInnes
United Way of
    Peterborough & District
Jan Zwicky

ADVOCATES
Ascot Computing Inc.
Flora & Arne Baartz
Robert & Birgit Bateman
Phyllis M. Bowell
    & Ethel M. Parsons
Mona Campbell
Clarica
Comox Indian Band
Harold S. Cusden
Harry Dahme
Joan and Rolph Davis
Minnie De Jong
J. H. Eldridge
Environmental Fund of B.C.
Dr. M. Virginia Evans
Ms. Irene Fedun
Mr. David Feeny
Fledermaus Investments Ltd.
James H. Firstbrook
Geoff Fridd

Friends of the Lubicon
Galiano Conservancy
    Association
D. Moira Glerum
Jacqueline Greene
Mary & C.G. Hampson
Anne Harfenist
William J. & Ria Hart
Irene Harvey
Marjorie & Robert Henry
Mike & Barbara Keilhauer
Dr. William Knight
Heidi Krogstad
Erik Lockeberg
Malcolm R. Macfarlane
    & Lela Korenberg
Charles Douglas McCallum
Victoria Olchowecki
Diether & Heidi Peschken
Louis W. Ray
Ruth Reid
Pamela Bessey
    & Hugh Reynolds
Dr. John T. Roberts
James E. Seidel
Audrey I. Sillick
Jean Smith
Ruby Emily Stauffer
Dorothy J. Stewart
United Way of Peel Region
Ted Williams

SIERRA LEGAL DEFENCE FUND | PAGE 15

7

POLICING POISONS

Convinced the Supreme Court of Canada to uphold a critical anti-pollution law by ruling that the federal government has both the right and responsibility to police the handling of dangerous chemicals across the country.

Client: Pollution Probe, Great Lakes United; 1997

ASSOCIATES

E.P. & T.M. Aboussafy
Bacon Basketware Ltd.
Rick Baker
Michael Barden
Dr. Suzanne E. Bayley & Dr.
  David Schindler
William & Pierrette Beaton
Judith & B. Paul Bock
Elizabeth Borek
Emma Bradley
John Brennan
Mary Anne Brinckman
Brian A. Bronfman
Armelda A. Buchanan
Canadian Friends
  Service Committee
Phillip Carter
Constant Temperature
  Control Limited
Cynthea Cooch
M. W. Cooke & Elizabeth Cooke
Gregory A. Corbett
Dorothy Cutting
Harwood Davies
Albert & Reva Dexter
The Diocese of Ontario
Ruth Donnelly
Jacqueline J. Eccles
R.P. & H.E. Edwards
Dr. Martin H. Edwards
Epstein Equestrian
  Enterprises Inc.
Lieselotte A. Eschenauer
John H. Esling
David Estrin
Joan M. Forman
Bryen F. Fowlie
Friends of Strathcona Park
  Society
The Friends of Wells Gray Park
Genevieve M. Gamache
Jane L. Glassco
Richard & Nicolina Gleasure
Paul Godkin
Dr. Thomas F. Godwin

David A. Goodings
  & Judith M. Goodings
Margery M. Gregg
Martin & Florence W. Haase
Priscilla F. Hafner
Elwood E. & Joanne K. Henning
Rosemarie Herrell
Douglas H. Hitchins
Trevor C. Holding
Nancy & Alan Hopkinson
Jessco Structural Formwork
Shin Imai
Richard Ivey
John Iwanic
H. Dale Jones
Lloyd Karges
John & Ingeborg Kassner
Miriam Kesselring
Colleen E. Keys
Verna M. Kingsley
H. & E. Kirkpatrick
Martin Krippl
Quentin Lake & Galina Laks
Patricia Law
Ruth Leavens
John W. Lee
Franca Leeson & Tim Hurson
Judith Leykauf
John Liver & Winnifred Liver
Nora L. Long
Joseph Lotzkar
David & Kathleen Ann Love
Jocelyn Lovell
Margaret Lunam
Iver Lund
Mary W. Macaree
Ian B. MacKenzie
Louise M. MacMaster
Mendi Malkin
Barry & Judith May
Michael McDerment
Dr. and Mrs. James A. McGregor
Leonard G. and Joanna E. Miller
Robert J. Minden
K. Montgomery
Robert D. Moore

David Morgan
Mrs. V. Morgan
Agnes Morrison
A. David Morrow
James Murphy
Dugald H. Nasmith
Barbara R. Nicholls
Valerie & Bryce Nolan
Oakdale Estates Ltd.
Dr. John O'Driscoll
Dr. Lynne M. Paton
Shirley E. Pearce
M. Aileen Pelzer
Brian Pinch
Scott Poole
Dr. Margaret E. Prang
Edna M. Ralston
Red Deer River Naturalists
John & Kim Rich
Martha Richardson
  & Keith Beckley
R. W. Rinn
Jennifer L. Rosebrugh
Lothar & Liane Rosenberg
Tom A. Roycraft
William Russell
  & L. Patricia Townson-Russell
Murad Saadi
Yuji Sakuma
William & Dorothy Salter
Richard G. Sayers
Barbara J. Scott
Peter Seixas & Susan Inman
The Sisterhood
  of Saint John the Divine
Margaret E. Stedman
Stefan Roland & Co. Ltd.
Amy Stewart
Isaac & Judy Thau
Ann L. Thompson
  & Stephen A. Gurman
Michael Traynor
Jane Underhill
United Way of the
  Lower Mainland
Willem & Susan Van Iterson

Jeff Weddell
Judith & Gordon White
Audrey Wild
Russell Williams
Catherine E. Wilson
Michael Wilton
Marion Woodman

DEFENDERS CLUB

(monthly donors who provide steady
and reliable income for our work)

Deborah Anderson
Robert L. Ayers
Diana Bainbridge
Lorraine Bell
F. Roy Blair
Mrs. Jocelyn N. Braithwaite
Cindy Breitkreutz
Edward J. & Curlena M. Brooker
Michael Brown
Jane & Craig Campbell
Catherine C. Campbell
    & Andrew Tardif
James A. Carscallen
Carol Cochrane & James Hasler
Susan Dahlgren
A.J. Dawson
Dawne Deeley
Terry DeMarco
Dana V. Devine
Erica K. Dhillon
Erwin & Eva Diener
Ann Louise Emanuel
Dianne Fahselt
Charlotte Ferree
Dean W. Flemming
Bristol Foster
Kenneth A. Gamey
Carol Givton
Sharon E. Godkin
Herman & Enid Gorn
Jean F. Hampson
Mark Harris
Don Hedges
Andrew Heintzman
Eleanor F. Hoeg

Ted A. Holekamp
Paula & Emam Khan
Dr. Charles King
Eric Kraushaar & Erin McGoey
Godwin Lai
Vanita Lokanathan
    & Ellen Windatt
James Macdonald
Patricia Jean Macquarrie
Alan Major
Mary B. Martin
Ruth J. Masters
Greg & Lynne McDade
Seaton Stuart McLean
Mieneke Mees
Heather More
Nathan and Gwyndolyn Nicholas
Ms. H.M. Victoria Page
William & Joan Paterson
Carol-Anne & Don Pease
Mike J. Peel
Colin Rankin
Dr. Mary France Richardson
Bart Robinson
Duncan P. Rueger
Sandra Sakofsky
Basil & Gillian J. Seaton
John Seckar
Ilse Stein
Catherine & John Syrett
John & Barbara Taylor
Gordon Thompson
Norman Todd
Rudy L. Van Der Vegt
    & Dorothy Field
Liis Veelma
Fred Voglmaier
Douglas H. Waterman
    & Kathy Waterman
Karolyn Waterson
Nina Wilkoyc
Lori Williams
Manfred & Isolde Winter
Alan J. Witherspoon
Ronald Wright
T.D. Pearse Resource Consulting

FOUNDATIONS AND TRUSTS

Acorn Foundation
Arcangelo Rea Family
    Foundation
Beatrice & Arther
    Minden Foundation
Brainerd Foundation
Bullitt Foundation
Bulrush Foundation
C.S. Mott Foundation
Eden Conservation Trust
EJLB Foundation
Endswell Foundation
Flavelle Foundation
Frank Weeden Foundation
George Cedric Metcalf
    Charitable Foundation
Helen McCrea Peacock
    Foundation
Henry P. Kendall Foundation
Kongsgaard-Goldman
    Foundation
Krauss Family Charitable Trust
Lannan Foundation
Laura L. Tiberti Foundation
Law Foundation of B.C.
Lazar Foundation
McBride Foundation
McLean Foundation
Muttart Foundation
Percy R. Gardiner Foundation
Richard Ivey Foundation
Robert Schad Foundation
Shooting Star Foundation
Summerlee Foundation
Turner Foundation
Vancouver Foundation
Victoria Foundation
W. Alton Jones Foundation
Walter & Duncan Gordon
    Charitable Foundation
Wilburforce Foundation
One anonymous donor

8 PARK PROTECTION

Convinced court to stop clearcut
logging in Wood Buffalo National
Park on the edge of the Prairies.
The park is a United Nations World
Heritage Site and home to free-
roaming buffalo, endangered
whooping cranes.

Client: Canadian Parks and Wilderness
Society, 1992

Fiscal 2000 | Financial statement

Sierra Legal Defence Fund Society statement of operations and changes in fund balances for the year ended October 31, 2000[1]

9

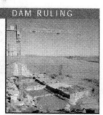

DAM RULING

Won Supreme Court of Canada ruling that forced the federal government to carry out an environmental assessment of the Oldman Dam. The ruling provoked the passage of the Canadian Environmental Assessment Act.

Client: Friends of the Earth, Cultural Survival, Sierra Club of Western Canada and other groups; 1992

	2000	1999
REVENUE		
Foundation grants	1,908,273	1,571,660
Contributions from other community groups	106,763	137,241
Cost awards and recoveries	114,608	206,835
Donations[2]	1,561,407	1,014,170
Other income	104,279	41,055
Total	3,795,330	2,970,961
EXPENDITURES		
Amortization	71,312	56,938
Audit and consulting	14,781	9,063
Capital assets acquired	142,536	84,216
Equipment rental and maintenance	10,368	25,079
Facilities	188,038	123,901
Fundraising	34,767	83,418
Litigation – direct costs	354,327	309,234
– projects	197,158	111,586
Loss on disposal of capital assets	2,334	-
Newsletter	83,287	92,768
Office administration	156,367	146,408
Organizational development	25,617	35,760
Professional licences and fees	17,868	25,103
Staff benefits	167,180	148,624
Staff remuneration	2,081,620	1,674,139
Telephone / telecommunication	85,113	59,386
Travel	20,578	14,722
Volunteer programs	20,930	11,394
Write-down of marketable securities	9,050	-
Total	3,683,231	3,011,739
Excess (Deficiency) of Revenue over Expenditures	112,099	(40,778)

[1] This statement was previously called the Statement of Revenues and Expenditures, and is condensed from Sierra Legal's independently audited financial statements. Full audited statements are available upon request.
[2] Donations net printing costs, mailing costs and consultant fees.

SAMPLE 2—CONTINUED

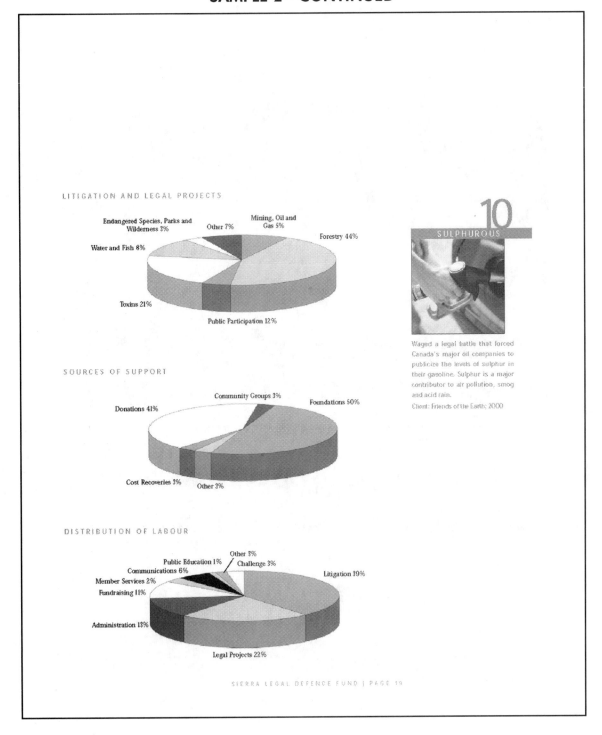

LITIGATION AND LEGAL PROJECTS

Endangered Species, Parks and Wilderness 3%
Other 7%
Mining, Oil and Gas 5%
Forestry 44%
Water and Fish 8%
Toxins 21%
Public Participation 12%

SOURCES OF SUPPORT

Community Groups 3%
Foundations 50%
Donations 41%
Cost Recoveries 3%
Other 3%

DISTRIBUTION OF LABOUR

Other 3%
Public Education 1%
Challenge 3%
Communications 6%
Member Services 2%
Litigation 39%
Fundraising 11%
Administration 13%
Legal Projects 22%

SULPHUROUS 10

Waged a legal battle that forced Canada's major oil companies to publicize the levels of sulphur in their gasoline. Sulphur is a major contributor to air pollution, smog and acid rain.

Client: Friends of the Earth; 2000

SIERRA LEGAL DEFENCE FUND | PAGE 19

Sierra Legal Defence Fund empowered BEAR (Banff Environmental Action and Research (BEAR) Society) and Bow Valley Naturalists to legally stand up for the health and future of Canada's first National Park, Banff. We send our sincerest thanks to you ... for your help, courage and generosity.

– Ed Whittingham, BEAR Society, Banff, Alberta, commenting on our Federal Court challenge of proposal to expand a convention centre at Lake Louise.

SIERRA LEGAL DEFENCE FUND is a Canadian charity (BN 13474 8474 RR0001) that provides free legal and scientific services to environmentalists in Canada. Our sister organization in the United States is Earthjustice Legal Defense Fund. We are completely separate from the Sierra Club.

B.C. HEAD OFFICE
Suite 214
131 Water Street
Vancouver, B.C. V6B 4M3
Tel (604) 685-5618 • 1-800-926-7744
Fax (604) 685-7813
E-mail: sldf@sierralegal.org

ONTARIO OFFICE
Suite 900
30 St. Patrick Street
Toronto, ON M5T 3A3
Tel (416) 368-7533
Fax (416) 363-2746
E-mail: sldfon@sierralegal.org

EAGLE OFFICE
Semiahmoo Reserve
16541 Beach Road
Surrey, B.C. V4P 3C6
Tel (604) 536-6261
Fax (604) 536-6282
E-mail: eagle@eaglelaw.org

www.sierralegal.org

where an external audit of financial records is not required, an audit gives comfort to potential funders that their money will be spent properly. The auditor's opinion letter states (we hope) that your financial records have been prepared following proper accounting procedures and that they appear to be accurate. This will be printed in your annual report next to your financial statement.

The potential donor wants to get an idea of your financial size and management. Before giving you money, he or she wants some proof that you know how to manage money wisely. Good balance sheets don't tell lies.

If you have a deficit, be prepared to explain to a potential donor why you have it and how you intend to get out of it. Look at your deficit and calculate it as a percentage of your annual income. A deficit greater than 5 percent of your annual income will look particularly bad. It might be useful to have your bookkeeper do a rough balance sheet a few months before your year-end, so that you can get an idea of the size of the deficit and decide if there are any emergency measures that can be taken.

If you have a running deficit, the balance sheet will show what it was at your present year-end and what it was the year before that. It's very bad to have a deficit in the first place, and if that deficit is growing every year, it's worse! That tells a potential donor that you aren't a good money manager. If your deficit keeps growing, your donors are going to decide that they are throwing money away by funding you, and they are going to say NO.

One group that was facing a deficit at year-end asked staff to forego salary for one month in order to clear the deficit on the books. So, in effect, the staff actually paid the debt. It was a drastic measure that hurt in the short term, but it managed to put the group in a much better position to raise funds in the coming year. Groups that are in the red make donors nervous. A surplus may also make donors nervous, oddly enough. If you are carrying funds on your books that are earmarked for specific projects and can't be used for other work, make that clear.

Activities and achievements

Point out the impact you had on your community in the past year. You want to impress your readers by presenting a positive past and a rosy future. Specifically, you should answer the following questions:

a) What did you do last year? You could cite conferences, policy papers, research, campaigns, publications, or services, for example.

b) How many people did you serve? Mention telephone and written inquiries, and speaking engagements, if applicable.

c) What did you achieve? Be as specific as possible, but don't be afraid to brag a little. If you are lobbying for certain changes in legislation or social attitudes, show what progress you have made. Philosophize a little.

If you are a service group, running a daycare or a halfway house or assisting disabled children, for example, you will want to put more emphasis on activities and on the number of people your group served in its different capacities. Paint a picture of what your service meant to these people. Include photographs or quotations that support your points. Point out that you provided this service economically.

If you are an issue group, you may be able to point out that you played a role in achieving some concrete changes. But don't make claims to fame that you can't back up.

History

Write a few paragraphs about when your group was formed, what its purpose is, where you've come from, where you're at, and where you're heading.

Donors and Sponsors

List all corporations, foundations, and government agencies that funded your group or sponsored events during the fiscal year unless they say that their contributions are to be anonymous. Be sure to spell their names correctly and exactly the way they have it on their letterhead. (The same practice should be applied in your correspondence with them.) Don't forget anybody! Don't show how much they gave, just who gave. List them alphabetically. Donors often appreciate extra recognition when they have given a bit more, so many groups list donors in categories by the amount they give, such as —

- Donors (under $1,000)
- Benefactors ($1,000 to $2,499)
- Sustainers ($2,500 to $4,999)
- President's Circle ($5,000 to $9,999)
- Angels ($10,000 to $14,999)
- Platinum Society ($15,000 or more)

Companies who gave you their services for free or at cost, such as the accounting or legal firm you use, and companies who gave free envelopes, paper, or whatever should also be listed as donors. The more contributors you can justifiably list, the better your group will look, and this is one of the best ways to acknowledge donors' contributions.

Board of directors

List the full names of the people on your board, and, if the members will let you, where they work, or other relevant positions they hold. A miniature biography, showing their degrees, credentials, or relevant experience may impress funders.

Staff

Be sure to include the executive director's and fundraiser's names and phone numbers. You can list names, phone numbers, and titles of all permanent staff if you like. Again, degrees, credentials, and a mini-bio may add to the organization's credibility.

Volunteers

If you have volunteers other than your directors, be sure to thank them collectively, and where appropriate, individually. Stating the total number of hours donated by all your volunteers can also impress potential donors and encourage others to donate their time.

Contact Information

Provide the organization's full address in the annual report. These days, the address is likely to include not only a telephone number, but also a fax number, e-mail address, and in many cases a Web site address.

c) Distribution of the annual report

Send your annual report to all corporations, foundations, and government sources you approached for funding in the past year, not just those who gave you money. Send it to the corporations and foundations you plan to approach next year. Any individuals who gave you a large sum of money ($100 or more) should also receive a copy of your annual report. Send it to key volunteers, elected officials (if you want government funding), the people you serve (if you want them to feel like equal partners), and staff (if you want them well-informed).

Some organizations also post their annual report on their Web site.

You should send it to your local media as well: it may help you to get valuable news coverage. Media attention contributes to a high profile, which translates into successful fundraising.

In the United States, send your annual report to the Foundation Center's cooperating collection in the city or state where your group operates.

In Canada, send it to the Canadian Centre for Business in the Community. The Centre is a nonprofit organization sponsored by the Conference Board of Canada. The Centre is set up to provide more than 100 large corporations, which are its members and affiliates, with information and advice about how to conduct their business in a socially responsible manner. This includes encouraging "corporate community investment" and ethical business practices, promoting hiring of members of aboriginal communities, and encouraging corporations to protect the environment. In their own words, "the Canadian Centre for Business in the Community at The Conference Board of Canada helps (a company) become a leader in Corporate Social Responsibility (CSR) through breakthrough strategies and practices that: ensure long-term business success, make a difference in the community, encourage ethical business practices, and enhance corporate reputation and stakeholder relationships."

The Centre promotes corporate giving, but it doesn't help nonprofits find funding. It does not match nonprofit groups with corporate donors. However, the Centre wants to have information about all the nonprofits who are seeking financial support from corporations to share with its members and affiliates. If a company wants more information about a nonprofit group than is provided in the funding proposal or wants to verify information in the funding proposal the CCBC will provide it from the annual reports sent to it.

The Centre recommends that any group making donations requests to corporations send information about itself to the Centre's office. You will find the address in this book's appendix.

2.3 The funding proposal

Many projects are born on impulse, raised on love and overtime, and then join the ranks of other unpublished masterpieces. Why? Because they weren't well planned and they weren't properly funded. Writing a funding proposal will help you overcome both hurdles: to write a successful project-funding proposal, you will have to plan the project first, and once your proposal is completed, it will aid in raising the dollars to make your project a success.

To begin planning, determine the following:

a) Why should the project be done? (Prove it hasn't already been done.) Help the donor understand what societal problem you are trying to fix.

b) How will it be done?

c) How long will it take?

d) How much will it cost?

e) Who will do the work and why are they the right people?

f) What end product or impact will result and how will it be measured and evaluated?

In the actual proposal, these components are given more sophisticated names. A description of what is required in each of these sections follows. If you have not done many proposals, try to look at a few done by other groups in your locality before you start.

When your proposal is complete and ready to present, don't forget to include a covering letter.

a) Key components of the proposal
Introduction and rationale (Why?)

State the project's objective and define the need for this project in concrete and meaningful terms. You may know the project is needed but you have to define and describe that need well enough to convince someone else it's needed. The staff of issue-oriented groups tend to be so committed to their cause that they don't have a realistic perspective on it. What you do may well seem obscure and irrelevant to most people. The key to writing a convincing rationale is to put your issue in perspective with other social issues, and to show why and how it affects many people.

Explain why your group is best suited to do the project. Outline your previous interest and accomplishments in this field.

This section of your proposal is vital because if your introduction and rationale are not convincing, a funder won't read any further. Try to excite an interest; write an upbeat, appealing rationale. Avoid jargon if possible; if you must use it, define it. Watch your assumptions.

Project description (How?)

How will you accomplish your objective? How will you fill the need you have defined? How are you going to provide the needed information or service?

Be specific. For example, if you proposed to write and produce a booklet, this section would include a table of contents. If it is being printed, will you use photocopies, laser printer quality, or offset printing? How many illustrations and how many pages will there be? What is the size of the pages? You need to make these kinds of decisions in order to budget accurately, so show them in this section. It will prove that you know what you're doing.

Schedule (How long?)

Break the project down into phases and show how long each will take. For the booklet example above, you might present a time schedule for: research, writing and editing, printing, promotion, and distribution. Show the schedule in numbers of weeks or months. Don't say, "Research: January to March." Say, "Research: three months." You never know how long it will take to fund the project, so you don't know exactly when you will be able to put your schedule into effect.

Budget (How much?)

Budgeting is a science — a science that intimidates many people. The biggest challenge is to budget accurately, and that requires research, unless you are familiar with current prices.

Some fundraisers play a silly game of "Ask for twice as much as you need because they will only give you half of what you ask for." If that is your attitude, you underestimate the intelligence of the person who will evaluate your proposal. Funding administrators can spot a padded budget at a glance. You will lose credibility and respect if you pad budgets. Joyce once saw a project budget that required an aerial survey. It happened that the plane was owned and operated by the project coordinator. Plane rental was budgeted at $200 an hour. Commercial rental of a private plane with pilot then cost about $80 an hour. The funder requested an adjustment for this item.

Since you will be providing a staff profile in the proposal, make sure that the staff salaries you list are consistent with staff qualifications. Assign a figure that is near market value for that person's skills.

It's important that the cost of a project be reasonable and realistic. Step back and take a long, hard look at the cost in relation to the project and the issue. That's exactly what a potential funder is going to do and, unless it looks sensible, he or she is not going to fund you. For some types of projects you can gauge this by calculating a unit cost. For example, if a writing, research, and publishing project has a total budget of $20,000 and you print 500 books, the cost per book is $40. If you print 2,000 books, the cost per book is $10. Similarly, a service group could calculate the cost per client served. Is it a reasonable cost compared to other groups?

Be sure to include all project costs in your budget. Postage, fax transmissions, courier service, computer time, and long distance telephone calls are often forgotten. It is usually acceptable to include an item called "contingency," which can be no greater than 10 percent of your total budget. The contingency money will take care of unforeseen and unavoidable cost overruns. Calculate a budget that includes salary time for project supervision and management. This takes a good deal of time, and it's a necessary part of the project, so budget for it.

Printing costs are difficult to budget. Once you make the decisions on size, format, and number of copies, phone a few printers and get estimates. If the project is over $5,000, include a written estimate from a printer in the proposal appendix. (When you do the job you should get bids from three different printers.)

A proposal with a budget of $30,000 or more should also include a bookkeeping or auditing fee. Government agencies and many foundations require detailed accounting for grants.

Sample 3 is an example of a budget for the writing, production, and distribution of a short book. The book will be 7" x 9" (18 cm x 23 cm), 60 pages long, typeset, and printed on an offset press. Five hundred copies will be printed. This sample is presented to illustrate budget format and detail. The prices are meaningful but not intended to be 100 percent accurate.

Personnel (Who?)

The proposal will show your group's previous experience and interest in this field and your charitable registration number. Letters of support are helpful, but make sure that they are directly relevant to the specific project. If you are approaching a government source, a letter from your mayor, governor, or member of parliament/senate/congress is valuable. If your group or project is controversial, a letter of endorsement from a respected authority in the field will lend credibility.

Include a staff profile of the person(s) who will carry out the project, giving the name, education, and relevant experience. You need to convince prospective donors that you have the personnel to successfully complete the job. Only list those staff and volunteers who will be directly involved in the project. Also list all board members and what credentials, skills, or experience they bring to this project.

Anticipated results (What?)

Describe the project's end product. How many people will benefit and how? What will you have to show for the time and money invested? What changes in public awareness, database, legislation, or services can be expected? Be as specific as possible. Quantify your results. You are explaining how you are going to evaluate the project once it is completed. Funders have no way to evaluate their contribution or your success unless you evaluate the project. By doing this, you are setting a goal and making a commitment to donors. It should be realistic and achievable, but should be significant enough to justify the financial investment. This section should answer the toughest question a funder can ask: "So what?"

Funders increasingly demand a rigorous evaluation process. If, for example, the project involves printing a booklet, they want to know not only that you printed it, but also how you plan to find out if people actually read it. If people do read it, the funders want to know how you plan to find out if it had any impact on them. They want to know what lessons your group expects to learn from this project, and how you will share them with other groups.

Sample 4 is an actual project funding proposal prepared by the Canadian Environmental Law Research Foundation. The proposal contains the essential parts of a proposal described above. It is a good illustration of how to phrase a project dealing with a controversial issue — public interest litigation — in terms that are understandable and acceptable to funders.

3. The Thank-You Letter and Phone Call

Thanking donors is essential both to raise funds initially and to keep the money coming.

There are at least three occasions when you must thank donors: after you have met with potential donors; after you have received a rejection letter; and after you receive a donation. You may also thank people who have pledged money during a telephone campaign.

SAMPLE 3
BUDGET FOR A SHORT BOOK

Item	Budget	
1. Salaries (part time)		
Research: 4 months @ $2,200/month	$8,800.00	
Writing, editing: 3 months @$2,600/month	$7,800.00	
Secretary to take book orders/ship books: 3 months @$1,900/month	$5,700.00	
Print production and supervision:1 month @$2,000/month	$2,000.00	
Graphic design and art work:	$2,000.00	
Promotion	$2,500.00	
Sub total	$28,800.00	
Staff benefits @ 28% of above	$8,064.00	
Total		**$36,864.00**
2. Office		
Rent, heat, light, water: 8 months @ $500/month	$4,000.00	
Office supplies	$559.00	
Computer rental: 3 months @ $280/month	$840.00	
Photocopy and scanning (supplies and equipment)	$360.00	
Telephone (long distance and local)	$200.00	
Total		**$5,959.00**
3. Production		
Printing: 60 pages @ $30/page	$1,800.00	
Covers:	$400.00	
Binding (perfect): 500 copies @$1.50	$750.00	
Shipping envelopes	$200.00	
Total		**$3,150.00**
4. Other		
Travel to Hamilton and Ottawa	$560.00	
Shipping costs (courier)	$1,000.00	
Contingency (10%)	$4,570.00	
Total		**$ 6,130.00**
Grand total		**$52,103.00**

SAMPLE 4
PROJECT FUNDING PROPOSAL

PUBLIC INTEREST ADVOCACY HANDBOOK

A PROPOSAL FROM THE
CANADIAN ENVIRONMENTAL LAW
RESEARCH FOUNDATION

I. Introduction and Rationale

A real estate developer sued a citizens' group for $500,000 for conspiracy to interfere with its business. The group had asked its municipal council to prevent the development of ravine lots along the Credit River. When the case came to trial four years later, the developer's lawyers abandoned the suit against the group. Had the case against the citizens' group been successful, their homes and life savings might have been at stake. Also, such a precedent would threaten freedom of speech of residents before their elected representatives.

Even though the case was dropped and costs were awarded to the citizens, for four years they lived under a cloud of uncertainty. The lawsuit effectively stifled their work as a group over that period. Rather than submitting briefs to various public agencies on matters of environmental concern, the group was forced to spend most of its time trying to raise funds for the legal costs of its defence.

A community legal clinic provided legal services to members of the public who would not likely have been covered by the Ontario Legal Aid Plan. The clinic suggested that the tenants pay their rent into a trust fund rather than pay their landlord, because he failed to keep the premises in good repair.

In court, the landlord was successful on an application to evict the tenants. The court also ruled that the trust fund for rent was not authorized by the Ontario Landlord and Tenant Act. The landlord's lawyer asked the judge to award costs against the tenants' lawyer who was one of the staff of the legal clinic. Only after considerable discussion did the judge refuse to order the lawyer to personally pay the court costs. He admitted that the clinic was trying to fill a social need, but felt that it was irresponsible for an organization to undertake and sponsor litigation without having due regard to legal costs.

Environmental groups, civil rights organizations, consumer groups — all public interest groups and their lawyers — face unique legal problems seldom encountered by the average litigant (party to a lawsuit) or his or her lawyer. Many of the lawyers practising in community legal clinics or specializing in public interest law are young and inexperienced. It is often difficult for these lawyers to advise their clients about the unique problems that might arise, or to protect their clients and themselves from sophisticated forms of harassment designed to intimidate them. Very little has been written on the subject of some of these forms of harassment. They have not presented a serious problem until recently, when the frequency and consequences of public interest litigation have become more serious.

The staff of the Canadian Environmental Law Association and the Canadian Environmental Law Research Foundation have had nine years of experience in the practice of public interest law and have been called upon frequently to deal with questions such as, What can we say to the press while our case is in progress? What is my liability if I lose my case? Can I legally join a demonstration or picket line? Is it ethical to deliberately set up a test case situation?

II. Project description

We propose to write and publish a booklet explaining to both potential public interest litigants and their lawyers some of the issues that might arise during the course of public interest litigation, and what they can do to protect themselves.

The booklet will include chapters on the following subjects:

1. The Test Case: Is it legal? When the law is ambiguous or unclear, some segments of society take advantage of this to engage in practices which are oppressive. In such circumstances, the test case, taken not only to protect the rights of the individual acting as plaintiff, but to clarify the law for others in the same position, may be a useful step toward ending the oppressive practice.

   Perhaps the best-known example in Canada was a case taken by the Canadian Civil Liberties Association on behalf of a black person who was refused service in an Ontario restaurant in the 1950s. However, engaging in this form of litigation may impose practical problems on the litigant and ethical problems for his or her legal advisors, particularly if they deliberately set up the factual situation to be used in court.

2. Picket Line Etiquette: What can (or can't) I do during a demonstration? Rights to freedom of speech and freedom of assembly guarantee the right to peaceful and legal demonstrations. Public interest groups sometimes feel that such a peaceful demonstration is the best way, and in some cases the only way, to "get their message across." However, if such groups trespass or impede the flow of traffic they may be breaking the law.

   Protestors and demonstrators have been arrested, sometimes properly and sometimes improperly. They should be aware of their rights and duties before undertaking this activity. Two lawyers have been charged with criminal and quasi-criminal offences in recent years as a result of their attendance at demonstrations to advise their clients. Both were acquitted, but only after costly legal proceedings.

3. Contempt: What can (or can't) I say to the press about my case? Contempt is any act that is calculated to embarrass, hinder, or obstruct the court in the administration of justice, or which is calculated to lessen its authority or dignity. In public interest cases, clients are often approached by the press for comment while the case is in progress. They ask their lawyer for advice. Some guidelines as to the line between freedom of speech and contempt are given.

4. Defamation: Defamation is the offence of injuring a person's character or reputation by false and malicious statements. This includes libel, which is a written defamatory statement, and slander, which is a spoken statement. Public interest groups and their lawyers find more and more reasons to believe they may be sued for libel for anything they say, in an attempt to muzzle them on important issues.

5. Costs: What is the liability of the public interest litigant and his or her counsel for costs in a public interest lawsuit.

    The general rule in Canada is that costs follow the event: that is, the loser in a civil action case pays approximately two-thirds of the legal expenses of the winner. The court in its discretion may make an exception in a public interest case.

    On the other hand, some parties who have succeeded against public interest litigants have argued that the lawyer for the public interest group should personally bear the costs. Both the lawyer and client should know in advance the general rules regarding costs and special considerations that have been applied to public interest cases.

6. Charitable Status and Public Interest Activity: There are approximately 80,000 registered charitable non-profit organizations in Canada. In recent years, many of them have been tempted to engage in litigation or political activity as methods of furthering their goals. In some cases, involvement in public interest litigation or political activity could lead to revocation of a group's charitable status.

    Community legal clinics and public interest lawyers are being asked for legal opinions on what effect certain activities might have on the group's charitable status. Moreover, many public interest lawyers in Canada practise as employees of charitable organizations and must advise their board of directors of the implications of certain activities.

III. Project budget*

Lawyer: 250 hours at $80 per hour	$20,000
Paralegal researcher: 130 hours at $40 per hour	$ 5,200
Secretary: 8 weeks at $460 per week	$ 3,680
Expenses:	
(i) photocopying; 750 pp at $0.20 per page	$ 150
(ii) travel; 2 trips to Ottawa	$ 1,000
(iii) mileage; 300 miles at $0.40 per mile	$ 120
(iv) supplies and miscellaneous	$ 225
(v) long distance phone calls	$ 275
Publication: 50-page handbook, paperback size, 2-color cover, saddle-stitched (includes artwork, typesetting, page assembly, paper, printing, binding and cover), 2,000 copies	$ 3,685
Administration and Project Supervision: quotations, editing and proofreading, indexing, and all production duties	$ 2,100
Promotion: design and printing of flyer, media coverage	$ 1,500
TOTAL	**$37,935**

*Note: The budget format shown in Sample 3 should be used. A breakdown of the publication costs and written estimates from printers would also be included.

IV. Project schedule

1. Legal and paralegal research	6 weeks
2. First draft of manuscript	12 weeks
3. Editing of manuscript	4 weeks
4. Book design	2 weeks
5. Typesetting	6 weeks
6. Layout and art work	3 weeks
7. Printing	4 weeks
Total from starting date to completion:	9 months

V. The audience

With the assistance of colleagues at other public interest groups, we will establish a target list of individuals and public interest groups.

This would include Community Legal Clinics, the Consumers' Association of Canada, the Canadian Civil Liberties Association, the Ontario Federation of Labour, ratepayers, landlord and tenant groups, public interest lawyers, lawyers in private practice, law schools, and libraries. They will then be notified of the publication by mail, with telephone follow-up.

VI. Project staff

John Swaigen was one of the first lawyers in Canada to specialize in environmental law. He has practised for the past 15 years as general counsel to the Canadian Environmental Law Association and as a prosecutor and policy advisor for the Ontario Ministry of the Environment. In these roles, he has had first-hand experience conducting legal proceedings involving citizens' groups and lawful advocacy.

John Swaigen has been a consultant on environmental issues to the Economic Council of Canada, the Law Reform Commission of Canada, the Public Interest Advocacy Centre, and environmental groups in Indonesia.

He is the author of several books and hundreds of papers, studies, and scholarly and popular articles on environmental, energy, and resource issues. While in university, he obtained training and experience in journalism as a reporter for the University of Toronto student newspaper. He has written a column for Alternatives magazine, and has contributed feature articles to the Globe and Mail, the Toronto Star, and the Hamilton Spectator.

VII. Anticipated results

With the help of this handbook, public interest groups and their lawyers will be better able to use public interest litigation to further their goals. Groups will also be less likely to succumb to those who would use the law for intimidation or harassment. Finally, this book will provide a small but significant contribution to the effectiveness of public interest groups in shaping public policy and making democracy work

Recent research has proven how important a good — and timely — thank-you can be. Fundraiser Penny Burk conducted a "Thanks Test" with the Canadian Paraplegic Association (CPA) and their Ontario chapter. CPA sent out a direct mail acquisition piece that attracted 1,965 new donors, about one per cent, which is normal. They gave an average of $26.28. CPA chose 10 percent of these new donors, and within 24 hours of receiving their gift, a CPA board member called to thank them for their gift.

Three months later, the CPA asked all the new donors to give again. Those who had been thanked promptly gave average donations 39 percent higher than those who had not been called. The people who had been thanked donated $34.24 on average, compared to $24.59 from the others.

More than a year later, all the donors had received six more requests to give. Those who had been thanked promptly with a phone call after their first donation were now giving 42 percent more ($35.00 on average compared to $24.57). Evidence also suggests that many of the donors who had been thanked quickly were focusing more of their giving on the CPA and had stopped giving to other charities after the one-on-one contact.

Burk has repeated the test, and says it's safe to call to say thanks within 48 hours of receiving a gift. However, if you leave the thank-you call longer than that, donors think that you're calling to ask for another donation.

Burk's findings are available in her book *Thanks! A Guide to Donor-Centred Fundraising.* <www.donorcentred.ca>.

The kinds of letters that should be sent under various circumstances are described in chapters 6 and 9.

Sample 5 is a thank-you letter to an individual donor.

4. Presenting Your Organization on the Internet

For many organizations, including fairly small ones, it is no longer sufficient to provide information about their mission, programs, projects, and publications on paper. It is often less expensive and faster to send the information by e-mail or post it on a Web site than to print it and send it through the mail. When designing a publication to be sent out as an e-mail attachment or posted on a Web site, the same kinds of design considerations apply. Although the technology is different, layout, typefaces and sizes, and graphics still must be visually appealing and writing must be of the same quality as print materials.

4.1 Using a Web site to communicate

It may save you time and money to post information and key documents such as your mission statement, objectives, annual report, newsletter, and other publications on your Web site rather than sending them out to people. Even if you do print these documents, some people will find it more convenient to read them and download them from the Internet than to call or write to request them.

In other words, communicating through your Web site can be cheaper and faster both for you and for people who want to know more about you.

In addition, Web sites can be designed to be interactive, so that there is two-way communication. Not only can you tell people about your organization, but they can give you feedback, ask you questions, order publications, buy products, and make donations. (More about using Web sites to raise money in chapter 10.)

In addition to designing individual documents, a group that plans to have a Web site should design the overall Web site so that it is attractive, appears quickly on the visitor's computer

ST. ALBAN'S BOYS' AND GIRLS' CLUB

843 PALMERSTON AVENUE TORONTO CANADA M6G 2R8 FAX : (416) 534-8860 TEL : (416) 534-8461

Celebrating Our 50th Year of Service to Our Community

Founded 1949

August 9, 2000

Dear: John Swaigan
83 Olive Ave
Toronto, Ontario M6G 1V2

In receipt of your generous donation to St. Alban's Boys' and Girls' Club, we would like to extend our thanks. Your donation will go a long way towards providing children, youth & their families with the necessary programs aimed at supporting and encouraging happy, healthy lifestyles.

St. Alban's Boys' and Girls' Club runs programs year round – providing children & youth with the opportunity to participate in activities in a safe, welcoming and positive environment. With priorities such as ensuring children a healthy head start in life, providing mentors and role models for youth, providing otherwise impossible opportunites for young people, we are continually seeking financial support to ensure high quality programs.

Your dollars translate into swim lessons, available summer day camp spaces, basketball tournaments for youth, youth employment training and so much more. We hope that with your continued support our community will continue to receive the much needed educational, recreational & social programs we aim to provide.

Enclosed is a tax receipt for the amount of your donation. Thank you again for your continuing support.

Sincerely,

Chris Foster
Executive Director

Member Agency of the Boys and Girls Clubs of Canada and Regional Ontario
"Every Kid has Potential"

screen, contains useful information presented in an interesting manner, and is easy to navigate. In addition, a Web site requires maintenance. That is, information must be updated regularly.

a) Is establishing a Web site a worthwhile investment?

Assuming that you do not intend to do any serious fundraising through your Web site, you should carefully consider the costs and benefits before deciding whether to establish a Web site. Building a Web site that is attractive, easy to navigate, interesting and informative, and keeping that Web site up to date, is not inexpensive. Setting up the Web site will probably cost several thousand dollars. Web sites that are effective are often designed by professionals, either paid or volunteers. However, some groups have the good fortune to have a staff member, board member, or other volunteer who is willing to design a Web site for free. Other groups have been able to find a talented high school student to design their Web site for a relatively small fee.

If you do decide to set up a Web site, consider seeking an "in kind" donation of professional design services to set it up. If a professional will donate his or her services, this will save thousands of dollars. Another form of contribution is sponsorship. Donors may be willing to "sponsor" your Web site in return for prominent mention on the Web site. Or you may even "sell space" on the Web site. If your group does not object in principle to carrying commercial messages on the Web site, it may display a banner ad for the products of a Web site sponsor.

To decide whether to set up a Web site, and if so, what information to put on it, your group should ask itself what information it wants to disseminate and why. If your mission is to operate a food bank, there may be little or no need to tell the whole world about what you are doing. On the other hand, if your mission is to educate the public about the problem of hunger, the need for food banks, and how to set up and run a food bank, you may want to take advantage of this opportunity to reach out to a wider audience. The nature of your mission will determine not only how much you want to tell the public, but also how much the public wants to know. If your phone is ringing off the hook and your staff cannot keep up with the requests for information about your organization and the issues it deals with, being able to send people to your Web site for this information instead of spending time on the telephone or mailing out information can save a great deal of time and money.

The second question to ask is, "If we build it, will they come?" Just because you set up a Web site doesn't mean anyone will look for it or choose it from among the hundreds of Web sites if they search for terms like "poverty" or "hunger" or even "food bank." If your need to communicate is greater than the public's need to receive information, your site may not be in great demand. But if the public's thirst for information is greater than your organization's ability to impart information, you may not need to do anything more to draw people to your Web site than to put the needed information on the Web site and put your Web site address on your letterhead and in your brochures, newsletters, news releases, annual reports, and other materials.

On the other hand, if your supply of information exceeds the demand for it, you may have to do more than provide electronic access to the information; you may also have to devote time and energy to stimulating the demand for the information.

This is what Internet fundraising consultant Adam Corson-Finnerty refers to as "push" and "pull." People are drawn or "pulled" to a Web site because it offers them something they want. This may be information, entertainment, or an opportunity to obtain a service or product. A "pull" strategy focuses on putting information on the site that is so valuable that people will seek it out on their own. You may have to keep changing or adding information, products, or services if you want to keep "pulling" people.

If there aren't a lot of people who feel a great enough need for the information or services provided by your Web site to seek it out on their own, what are the alternatives? Either do not create a Web site or be prepared to spend time and money "pushing" people to it. A "push" strategy involves promoting your site. Advertising is the most common form of "push" strategy. People read the newspaper or turn on the radio or television because they want information or entertainment. But they buy the products advertised in these media because the information or entertainment is periodically interrupted by enticements to purchase. A Web site "push" strategy may be as simple as putting your Web site address on all your written material or as complex as sending out e-mails with a link to your site inviting people to enter it, arranging for your site to be advertised on other Web sites, or setting up links between your Web site and other Web sites.

b) What information should you put on your Web site?

Look at other Web sites to get ideas. You will find that most Web sites for nonprofit groups contain some or all of the following:

- "About us": a page with a brief description of the history, mission, and activities of the organization.

- Staff list.

- "What's New": a page describing recent achievements, new projects, awards, etc.

- News releases: a page that may have the text of news releases issued by the organization, news items in which the organization has been featured, or both.

- List of the organization's publications: Sometimes there is a summary of the contents of each publication. Sometimes by clicking a button, this list will take you to the full text of the publication, which can be made available for downloading (printing it out) or for viewing only.

- "How to contact us": a page that may have a mailing address, telephone number, fax number, and e-mail address.

What all of these contents has in common is that they are "one-way" communications — from the organization to the viewer.

However, at a higher cost, Web sites can be made "interactive." They can permit direct communication from the viewer to the organization through the Web site. Several large nonprofit organizations now use their Web site to establish two-way, ongoing communication with their supporters and potential supporters. To see how this works, visit the Web site of the Nature Conservancy <www.nature.org> or the CARE Web site <www.care.org>.

It is these interactive Web sites that have the greatest potential for direct fundraising and money-saving activities. On a fully interactive Web site, a viewer can send messages and even arrange for the electronic transfer of money to the organization by clicking buttons.

The viewer can —

- sign up for membership in the organization or membership renewal;

- show what information the viewer would like to receive and in what form, such as news releases, newsletters, annual reports, information about special events or opportunities to purchase products, or even — here it comes — click "yes" to the question "Please send me information about how I can contribute";

- donate online or click through to a specialized portal where a donation can be processed;

- "sign" a petition by authorizing his or her name to be added to it;

- ask questions about your organization (by searching a page of Frequently Asked Questions or by sending e-mail, or in a live chat, or by clicking through to a live telephone operator;

- make suggestions for improving the services provided by the organization or the information and layout of the Web site;
- join a special interest news group or chat room;
- view photos or even a live Web cam of your work;
- link to other sites;
- send an e-mail to the group though a pop-up window;
- sign up to receive e-mail news bulletins from the group;
- send an electronic postcard or greeting card on the group's topic to a friend or a politician;
- purchase books or other materials either directly from the nonprofit group or from an allied online store which may give part of the purchase price to the nonprofit group;
- take a quiz, participate in a survey, play a game, or join in another interactive process;
- chat with other people who have similar interests.
- chat live with a staff member or volunteer who is in the middle of an exciting assignment, such as reporting live from a disaster zone, or with a celebrity who endorses your work;
- listen to music or watch a video related to your work; and
- sign up to receive a free e-mail address for life. (Many universities, for example, now give these to their alumni, because (a) it increases the sense of identification, which is useful when asking for a donation, and (b) they always know how to find the alumni.)

CHAPTER 4
TYPES OF FUNDING

The type of funding you are looking for affects your funding strategy.

1. Core Funding versus Project Funding

Core funding is the money that you need to operate an office and pay for rent, office supplies, computers, telephones, a secretary, and other day-to-day expenses. Projects, on the other hand, have a definite start and finish and involve a tangible end product. Things like speaking tours, writing and publishing a booklet, making a slide show or film, or undertaking specific research can be considered as projects.

Core funding is more difficult to obtain because the people who fund your daily operations have fewer ways to judge what you accomplished. Project funding is more popular because donors feel that they are playing a measurable role in a tangible activity, without getting locked into funding an ongoing activity that is difficult to evaluate.

Corporations, foundations, and the government all prefer to supply project funding for the following reasons:

a) Projects are finite. They may run for months or years but they don't go on indefinitely.

b) Projects usually involve a tangible result, which can be evaluated.

c) Projects can be assigned a definite, adequate budget figure. Core costs tend to keep growing due to increases in staff, higher rent, and inflation.

However, government sources are generally more willing to fund core costs than either foundations or corporations.

Try to raise core funding from individual supporters or your membership, who might be more willing to provide this type of funding. You might have a moneymaking aspect to your group such as the sale of a publication or a nominal charge for certain services, which can go toward core costs. Any unallocated funds that you raise should be put toward your core costs or other activities that you can't fund directly.

If you are a service group, it is even harder for donors to evaluate whether their contributions were well spent. Provide them with statistics about how many people used your service, and provide client evaluations of your service. The best way for a service group to get around the difficulty of raising core funding is by describing part of the core service as a project. The work of most staff people can be packaged as a project. A portion of your overhead or core costs is required to support the project staff person, and this portion of overhead becomes a legitimate project cost.

Many groups are burdened by a large portion of their budget labeled "administration, overhead, and core costs," which the donors find unappealing. Most of these costs should be, in full honesty, considered part of the project costs. For example, a group raising funds to print a booklet may wrongly assume that the only project cost is the printer's bill. In fact, it should include staff time to plan the project, research the facts, write the material, proofread changes, distribute the booklet, answer the phone and take requests for the booklet, write letters to people who comment on the booklet, and so on. It should also include a fair share of the rent, electrical, heat, and telephone bills, as well as postage and couriers. It should include the cost of an advertising and publicity campaign so that people know the booklets are available. Don't forget the computer, printer, desks, and chairs as well as office insurance and bookkeeping.

Think like a restaurateur. The cost of pizza includes far more than flour, cheese, tomato sauce, pepperoni, and mushrooms. It also includes the cook's labor, the waiter, the dishwasher, and the manager. It includes heat for the ovens and the restaurant. It includes advertising, a van for delivery, a phone, and much more. The pizza itself is only a fraction of the cost — often less than one-third of the total.

If you are a small group, with less than ten staff people, here is a simple way to budget your projects. Calculate your total annual overhead cost for office rent, heat, cleaning, insurance, telephone, postage, photocopying, etc. Add to that the salaries of secretaries, the bookkeeper, and the fundraiser. Divide this total by the number of "project staff" people. That will give you the overhead per project staff and make it easy to check whether you have budgeted project overhead correctly.

If all of that seems a bit elaborate, just remember that a lot of fundraising is really marketing — honest marketing. A well-packaged project will be easier to sell.

2. Seed Funding

"Seed funding" is a special one-time-only kind of core funding. Although most funders are reluctant to provide ongoing core funding, some will give enough money to "kick-start" the operations of an organization.

For example, a donor may give enough funding to a group that has no paid staff to hire one or more full-time staff people and rent an office for one year. Or the donor may give a group enough money to try out a new kind of fundraising technique; for example, a group that has always relied on submitting funding applications to government, corporations, and foundations may receive a grant to conduct a direct-mail campaign. If successful, this campaign will have opened up a new source of ongoing funding for the group.

To obtain such start-up money, you will need a proposal that shows how you will use the funding effectively to establish a base upon which you can continue to build. This requires establishing a board in whom the funder can have confidence, setting out the need for the services your new organization will deliver, developing a realistic budget, establishing short-term and long-term goals and objectives, and identifying potential future sources of funding. In short, you must create a "business plan" or "prospectus." This is like the plan a person seeking a start-up loan from a bank or money from investors would produce to demonstrate the viability of the business and persuade the lender or investor that there is a high probability of repayment of the loan or profit from the investment.

3. Capital Projects

Raising money for a building, filmmaking equipment, a computer system, a library, or some other expensive "thing" requires capital funding. In the fundraising trade, capital projects are referred to as "bricks and mortar" because, traditionally, they have been for buildings.

Large corporations and foundations used to participate heavily in capital campaigns because there was a definable need, a highly visible end product, and usually a brass plaque on the building recognizing the company's contribution. Capital projects are no longer as popular because the donor's participation in them is expensive. Capital campaigns usually start at $500,000, and participation is going to cost a donor at least $5,000. Many donors aren't willing or able to give such a large chunk of money, especially to a smaller, innovative group.

Many groups considering a capital campaign worry that it might bankrupt the organization's core or project funding. That's a legitimate concern because, if it isn't properly managed, it may do just that. However, a well-managed capital campaign can be used to attract new funders and approach sources that specialize in capital funding. If it's done right, it should increase your group's public profile and broaden your funding base.

The next few pages will give you some tips and warnings about capital campaigns, but they are by no means a complete road map. Capital fundraising is specialized and sophisticated; you should look beyond the information presented here before making the decision to take on a capital project.

You are competing with large established institutions such as universities, hospitals, churches, and YM-YWCAS.

The second thing to remember is that you can't build half a building or use half a piece of equipment — a capital campaign is an all-or-nothing proposition. If you buy a building, for example, but can't afford heat, electricity, or staff, the building is useless. Your funding proposal must show your plans for operation and maintenance of the project after it is built or bought.

Show in your proposal if you have set up a trust fund and name the bank and branch. You can invest this money and collect interest until you have reached your objective. Set a target date that gives you enough time to have a good go at it, and if you don't raise all the money by that time, or at least 75 percent of the total, give back the money you have raised, with a note of thanks. That's how it works.

Remember: Donations for a capital campaign cannot be used for any other purpose.

Tell your donors how their contribution will be recognized and try to think up appropriate and inexpensive ways to do this. For instance, if you are building a library, you might hand out bookmarks for the first year listing your donors. Contributors to a capital campaign do deserve a little extra recognition!

Leadership funding plans are often used for capital campaigns. If you need to raise $100,000 for building renovations, consider the following giving chart:

3 donors @ $10,000	=	$ 30,000
6 donors @ $ 5,000	=	$ 30,000
12 donors@ $ 2,500	=	$ 30,000
General contributions	=	$ 10,000
TOTAL	=	$100,000

Then you would carefully select at least five potential donors to approach for $10,000 and so on. One advantage of a leadership plan is peer pressure. Corporations and wealthy individuals have their pride. Before you can put together a leadership-funding plan that will work, you have to know the money-giving scene well. You have to know which donors are leaders in innovative funding and who will follow their example.

You might also break up your funding objective by source, indicating, for example, that you expect to raise 30 percent from corporations, 30 percent from foundations, 30 percent from individuals, and 10 percent from government contributions. (There is no standard proportion)

Matching gifts can challenge more donors to give, and/or give within a deadline. In this method, one donor (or more) might promise to match any other donor's gift, giving a dollar for every dollar others contribute. The match may be $1 to $1, or $2 to $1, or 50¢ to $1. The matching offer may have a ceiling limit, perhaps up to $100,000. It may come with a time limit, perhaps December 31. Matches may even focus on a target population, such as a car dealer challenging other car dealers.

If your group has undertaken any sort of capital campaign previously, give a brief history of this success (or failure) in your funding proposal. That will tell potential donors that you have the experience and the capability to carry out what you are proposing, or what you will do differently this time.

Do a little "market research" first. Select a number of foundations and corporations that you think you might approach. Write to them, or visit if they have time for you, and say your group is considering undertaking a capital campaign to build such and such; ask if they have a capital funding program and if they might consider an appeal from your group. You want to find out what kind of money is available for what you are proposing to do. They will respect your initiative.

If they say that they do contribute to capital programs, try to find out what size of a contribution they have made in the past, and to whom. It is generally easier to get this kind of information from foundations than corporations. Corporations do have policies on this, but they don't make their policies public as often as foundations do.

Phone the person who answered your letter and politely ask a few exploratory questions. Try to get a feeling for whether the foundation is interested in your capital project, and try to find out what they have done in the past. You've got nothing to lose by asking a few polite questions, and before you launch a capital campaign, you've got a lot to learn.

Alternatively, you could hire a fundraising consultant to do a feasibility study on the capital campaign you are considering. The consultant will make sure you have thought through all the important aspects, and then will interview leaders in the philanthropic community to see if they would support the project.

Capital campaigns should not begin on impulse. Once you launch a capital campaign you are putting your group's reputation to a test in the philanthropic community. The repercussions of failure could be serious, but you don't want to fail, so investigate first.

There are fundraising consulting firms that specialize in capital campaigns and this is one area in which experienced fundraising consultants are well worth their fee. If nobody in your organization is experienced in capital fundraising, at least have an exploratory meeting with a consultant. Tips for working with consultants are given in chapter 14.

In a capital campaign, the first donation is the hardest to get. One corporation, foundation, or government agency has to stick its neck out and endorse your project by making that first donation. Nobody wants to make the first move. Try to get the first donations, or at least a commitment on paper, before you launch your campaign fully and publicly. Ideally the leaders should all be asked, and half to two-thirds of the money should be pledged, before you approach mid-level donors or publically announce your campaign.

4. Deficit Funding

Some people can live comfortably with debt, be it personal debt or organizational debt, but it is very bad for a nonprofit group to be in debt. As a registered charitable organization, you don't have the right to make a profit and you don't have the right to live in debt either. However, if you are reading this, you may well have a debt, so what do you do about it?

First of all, don't let it get any bigger. Don't let it grow because it can get out of hand. Second, look for ways to cut expenses in your operation: reduce salaries or staff for a period of time, cut back on long distance calls or travel, make do with that old piece of equipment for a while longer. Put the money saved toward the debt.

Now try to raise money to cover the debt. You can't get corporations or foundations to make a direct contribution toward your deficit. They simply won't do it because they are afraid they will be putting money down a bottomless hole. Most foundations state explicitly in their guidelines that they will not fund deficits. Any funding agency that asks for a financial statement wants to make sure you don't have a deficit.

You can ask individuals to contribute. Start with board members and the people who have given the longest or largest support. Talk to them about a donation before you appeal to your group's membership or the public.

If you have a paying membership, three to six months after your normal membership campaign you might do a special campaign for funds to pay back your debt. It's a bit embarrassing, but with a lot of tact you can succeed. Show the total you need to raise to cover your debt and how much each person needs to contribute to put your organization "in the black" again.

It's important that the tone be appropriate for your membership, and that you discuss the deficit in a businesslike manner. The tone should be, "The organization that you and I love has a problem. This is how we're going to solve it. This is what we need from you to help solve it." It is essential that you be firm and confident in your approach to your members. Don't cry on their shoulders. Keep the emphasis on what happens to the people you help — the work your organization was created to do.

Sample 6 is an example of a letter to members asking for contributions to a debt.

You can also try to pay back your deficit by allocating a portion of it to each project. If you have a 2 percent deficit, write into your project budget "contribution to deficit" and make that figure 2 percent of the total project cost. In this way you are being honest about it. Some people try to pay back a debt by padding budgets. That practice is dishonest and unethical and it offends donors.

Running a group with a debt is depressing and demoralizing. *Don't ignore it because it won't go away.* Confront the problem. Figure out a way to get out of it, then follow through with your plan.

Once a group projected a deficit in an attempt to pressure potential donors to contribute. The line was, "If you don't give now, we are going to go under," and it wasn't really true. To make matters worse, this tactic was being used in an approach to a bank! There is no real temptation to try such a tactic: it doesn't even work. Don't cry wolf!

5. Sole-Source Funding

Some organizations have the mixed blessing of receiving all their money, or most of it, from one source. This occurs most often with government funding agencies (particularly in Canada and Europe; less so in the United States or elsewhere), although some foundations and individuals will provide substantial support to one group for a few years.

Government funding programs may provide the seed money for new, innovative groups. Unfortunately, many of these groups come and go because they don't plan their financial future and don't try to broaden their financial support base

SAMPLE 6
LETTER TO RAISE DEFICIT FUNDS

The Society to Save Dead Elm Trees
1 Elmsvale Crescent
Elmada, MI 04309
Phone (555) 362-DEAD Fax (555) 362-1234
Email: fundraising@deadelm.com   Web: www.DeadElm.com

Tuesday, Oct. 16, 2001 (UN World Food Day)

Dear Mr. Snow,

I think you'll be pleased to hear that over 500 people have now committed themselves to saving the dead elms by taking out memberships in the Society. That includes a record of 94 new members so far this autumn!
As an active member, you are committed to preserving the natural heritage of the rural Ontario landscape by helping to preserve dead elm trees.
It costs only $100 to purchase a dead elm tree and prevent its ruin. Last year the Society to Save Dead Elm Trees purchased 90 dead elms, thanks to you and supporters like you. Their locations are mapped in the enclosed brochure so you can visit or photograph them.

It appears that we were a little over-enthusiastic in our purchases last year. The Dead Elm Tree Purchase Fund fell $1,000 short of its goal of $9,000. We are currently operating with a deficit of $1,000 — not a large amount, when you consider how <u>urgent it is to take action before the chain saws rip into the heart of another tree</u>. Now new controls on spending have been instituted to prevent any future deficits, and we are making a special appeal to you and others who care, for donations to cover this deficit.

As you know, dead elm trees provide —

· food and shelter for woodpeckers,

· scenic perches for hawks, and

· much-needed homes for wayward racoons.

Of the ten trees that are not yet paid for, three are particularly significant, as they are located along Highway 401 and are viewed and enjoyed by thousands of people every day. As a loyal member for over three years, Mr. Snow, we are asking you today to contribute $25 (or more) to the Dead Elm Purchase Fund.

The woodpeckers, hawks, racoons and I would be very grateful if you could give a little extra support now, before the snow flies.

Please use the enclosed reply form and the postage-free envelope to rush your donation.

As always, you will be able to deduct your gift from your taxes.

And thank you again for your continuing interest in saving the dead elms.

Sincerely,

(signature)

Dr. Jane Woods, MD
Chair of the board

P.S.: Lumberjacks are getting ready to cut down the dead elms for fire wood, so it is especially urgent that you make your gift today, before they get out their chain saws. What nice Christmas present this will be for the animals who call these trees home.

until their grant has almost run out. Groups that have been solely funded by one agency for a few years are often unwilling to face up to reality when they are informed that they will be on their own. Often, much time is wasted in fruitless lobbying — time that would be better spent developing and implementing a new funding strategy.

Occasionally, a wealthy individual or member of a board of directors will provide the bulk of the funding for a group. You may think, "We should be so lucky!" But this person could end up having far too much control over the policies and direction of the group because he or she controls the purse strings.

If you depend on sole-source funding, take a careful look at the situation, weigh the pros and cons, and consider developing a broader base. You need to be sure that your funding source does not have a controlling role in determining your direction and does not restrict your ability to carry out your mandate. Before that source of money dries up, you had better be prepared if you are to survive.

Top Ten Reasons to Hold an Annual Campaign
(even though your organization just inherited a million)

by Ken Wyman © Ken Wyman & Associates Inc., Toronto 2002

(The following article first appeared as a reply to a question posted on a www.charitychannel.com listserv discussion group. It is reproduced here with the permission of the author.)

When a YMCA in a mid-size city inherited a million dollars from a generous donor, their board debated stopping their fundraising campaigns.

What a delightful problem to have. But a very real problem, nonetheless. Here are some tongue-in-cheek and simultaneously very serious reasons to keep fundraising:

1. A million is never enough

The excitement of having the money leads people to develop creative ways to invest that money in the community. Soon the volunteers, the staff, and the neighbors discover the community has enough opportunity for good work that it could use two million. Or ten. *Wyman's law of budgets:* The need for good work always exceeds the funds available.

2. The million will eventually be all gone

It may be a year. It may be a decade. But it will not last forever, no matter how wisely invested. Sooner or later you'll need a campaign again. If you haven't done any fundraising in the meantime, you'll forget how. You'll have to start all over again to find friends, volunteers, and donors. That will be hard. In Canada there are many charities that were 100 percent government funded for 10, 20, 30 or more years. They are now losing some or all of that government money due to cutbacks. It's like watching a junkie try to quit. Don't get addicted to easy money — it's a bad drug!

3. An organization that does not fundraise is a dead organization

Outreach, contact with the community, debates, demands for accountability — these activities are life's blood to a real community group. The world has too many dead churches, sustained by endowments, going through the motions until the last elderly parishioner dies off — and then there is a trust fund looking after the cemetery in perpetuity. *Better to give the money away than die rich.* This not only makes good organizational sense, but it is also one of Carnegie's principles of philanthropy.

4. A million means you can invest in proper fundraising

What a joyous luxury to plan a fundraising campaign with true long-term vision, instead of a short-term panic to make enough for this month's bills. Too many groups are scrambling for cash and offend donors because they don't take time to say thank you and build strong relationships.

5. Money attracts money

A million now will be like honey to the bears. Fundraising will never be easier, provided everyone knows what the money will do for the community. Potential donors might decide that if someone believed in the YMCA enough to leave it a million, there might be a good reason.

6. Fundraising is never just about money

When people give, they feel ownership. If they don't give, it is disempowering. The bad old image of fundraising is of the white-gloved lady bountiful from the rich part of town dispensing little blessings on the poor little crippled children. Yuck! No wonder people with disabilities rebelled. And many other people, once portrayed as needy and pitiful, are rebelling against demeaning handouts. What's needed is self-help. That includes asking people to give whatever they have (time or money) to their own organizations.

7. Fundraising builds leaders

That's part of your organization's mandate. People learn how to think, how to speak, how to organize, how to overcome shyness. People make new business contacts and new friends. Fundraising campaigns are a community service to many of the volunteers.

8. Fundraising builds communities

People discover they can get money, and they feel empowered. They learn to work in teams. They go on to tackle other problems.

9. People need to give

Stewardship means we all have something to give, and if we don't use our gifts, we are poorer for it. The people who use your services need to know they aren't getting something for nothing.

10. Fundraising is fun

This is especially true when you are not frightened that failure has terrible consequences. This cushion means people can enjoy the ride.

CHAPTER 5
DEVELOPING A FUNDRAISING STRATEGY

1. Strategy Is the Key to Success

A large number of organizations still function without a strategy of any sort — either a strategic plan for the whole organization, or simply a fundraising strategy. A strategy is critical to the organization's effectiveness; operating without one is like going on a trip without a road map.

Joyce once worked with a social service agency to help them develop a fundraising strategy. Working with a fundraising committee of the board, she assessed the organization's needs, strengths, and weaknesses and tried to match that to funding sources and fundraising techniques.

The consultation had a dramatic outcome. It was as though the fundraising strategy development process had held a mirror up to the organization and given it a full and accurate picture of itself. In the previous year, it had undergone some major changes, including —

- hiring its first full-time staff,

- merging with another organization, and

- increasing its annual budget by 700 percent.

In one year, the organization was proposing to —

- host a national conference for the first time,

- double the annual budget,

- begin fundraising outside the government sectors, and

- move from 100 percent government funding to 100 percent funding from other sources.

When that picture was presented to the board members, they understood why they were feeling exhausted and overwhelmed. They were quick to lead the discussion about what they could give up or put on the back burner. They realized they couldn't do all that in one year with limited resources.

The first step in developing a strategy is to answer honestly the following questions:

a) Where have we been?

b) Where are we going?

c) What do we have to work with?

d) What's going on outside the organization that's going to affect us?

e) What is our best course of action?

A strategy can be developed at the program or project level for a function such as fundraising, or on an organization-wide basis. Just keep in mind that it needs to be done. You will never feel that you "have time" for working out a strategy. It will always seem like an abstract, academic exercise. So why bother? Because it is one of the smartest things you can do for your organization. It will give you a way of thinking about your organization that will enhance your ability to survive and it is an essential tool for organizations committed to quality and effectiveness.

2. Fundraising Strategy Matrix

Your fundraising strategy will be the outcome of an analysis of factors inside and outside your organization that determine what you are going to sell and to whom you are going to sell it. By taking into account the strengths and weaknesses of your organization and recognizing the external factors that will influence your fundraising success, a fundraising strategy will tell you how to get the best return on your effort.

The fundraising strategy matrix is a tool to help you identify your potential funding sources and fundraising methods and to evaluate your ability to raise funds successfully from each of the sources or by using the various methods. The components of the matrix are listed below.

2.1 Fundraising choices

a) Source: Individuals

   1. Mass Market

     i. Direct mail

     ii. Telephone campaigns

     iii. Special events

     iv. Bingo, raffles, casinos, and other gambling

     v. In memoriam and celebration cards and commemorations

     vi. Door-to-door canvass

     vii. Product sales

     viii. Telethons and other broadcast direct response

     ix. Free Public Service Announcements (PSAS) in newspapers, magazines, radio, and tv

     x. Paid advertising

   2. Major donors or special names (large gifts)

     xi. Face-to-face requests

     xii. Bequests, insurance, and other planned giving

   3. Fee-for-service work

b) Source: Corporations

   4. Project proposals

   5. In-kind goods and services

   6. Matching employee contributions

   7. Joint promotions

   8. Sponsorship of events or publications

   9. Fee-for-service work

c) Source: Foundations and governments

   10. Project proposals

   11. Fee-for-service work

d) Source: Other organizational donors

   12. Service clubs

   13. United Way (as regular funders or for special grants)

   14. Employee charitable funds

   15. Religious groups

   16. Unions

   17. Seniors' and retirees' associations

   18. Professional groups (such as Business Women's Association)

   19. Other nonprofits

e) Source: productive enterprise or community economic development

    20. Consulting work

    21. Manufacturing or products

    22. Sales, shops, vending machines

    23. Services

    24. Other quasi-business income sources

2.2 Evaluation

You can evaluate each source/method's potential for your organization by considering it in relation to the following factors. Some of the factors won't apply to certain sources/methods.

a) Contacts

Are there staff or board members in the funding organization with whom your board, staff, supporters, or clients have an established relationship?

b) Market

What is the correlation between the people you serve and the people the funder serves?

c) Profile

What is your visibility within your community of interest? Will the name of your organization, your staff, your president, your programs be recognized by members of key constituencies? Are you in the media?

d) Information

Do you have the basic information on this funding source — annual report, brochures, application forms, news clippings, and names of donations officers? The information should be no more than two years old.

e) Criteria and areas of interest

How well do you fit the funder's criteria? Which criteria don't you fit? How important are these criteria? How well do your areas of interest fit the funder's areas of interest? This question is more general than the one concerning criteria. If the funder's areas of interest are not defined, try to establish this by analyzing the pattern of their donations over the past few years.

f) Skill

Do your staff and volunteers have the requisite skills for this type of fundraising — proposal writing, corporate and foundation research, meeting skills, presentation skills, event management, personal selling, or other relevant skills? Do staff and volunteers have enough time? Do they need training? Are there tasks they would never be comfortable doing? Do you need to recruit new people with skills or contacts?

g) Policy

Do any of your organization's stated policies, positions, or beliefs conflict with the funder's stated policies, positions, or beliefs? Review speeches, bulletins, news clippings, the funder's Web site (if they have one), and any other available information. This element is critical for your advocacy activities. Do your positions conflict with the stance of the current administration?

h) History

What is the fundraising history of your organization? What fundraising techniques and what funding sources and methods have been successful in the past? What was tried and failed? What has changed internally since past attempts?

i) Means

Do the prospective donors have the kind of money you are looking for? Is the money out there for what you are trying to do?

j) Projects and programs

Do you have your activities packaged into fundable projects and programs? Which of your programs and projects will be most attractive to funders?

k) Competition

What other organizations are competing for the same charitable dollar? Can you hold your own with them?

l) Lists and donor records

Do you have good, up-to-date lists of members and potential members? Do you have contacts in other organizations who would "swap" mailing lists with you? Do you have access to information on appeals to this or similar donors? If you get a sudden influx of new donors, will you be able to keep up with the work of entering information, sending thank-you letters, and making repeat contacts on time?

m) Geography

Does your location give you direct access to many of your funders? Does it make your group a priority for any government, corporate or foundation funds?

n) Budget and resources

Do you have the money to invest in this form of fundraising? Can you wait while a long-term process slowly ripens or do you need an immediate cash boost?

The cost of different fundraising techniques has been well established through years of experience. Here are costs of various forms of fundraising methods reported in a survey of Canadian charities. The figures are averages, and must be taken with a grain of salt, of course, in the same way that surveys show the average family has 2.5 children. If you are higher or lower than the figures shown here that does not mean you have a problem.

o) Donor recognition

What are appropriate, ethical methods that your group can use to give the donor extra publicity, well-deserved ego satisfaction, or a commemorative honor for a loved one?

Benchmarks for Fundraising Costs:
What Does It Cost to Raise a Dollar?*

Direct mail acquisition	90¢ to $1.25
Special events	50¢
Product sales	35¢
Telephone solicitation	32¢
Planned Giving	25¢
Gaming (bingo, lotteries, raffles)	23¢
Direct mail renewal	20¢
Corporations/Foundations	20¢
Capital campaigns	10¢ to 20¢
Work place giving	7¢
Average cost to raise a dollar	26¢

---

*Sources: Association for Healthcare Philanthropy (AHP) Librarian Erica Heftmann, reported in *Canadian Fundraiser* (July 31, 1996); and Canada West Foundation survey of 1,516 nonprofits (excluding religious groups and private foundations), reported in *Globe and Mail* (August 27, 1996).

p) Responsibilities and administration in multi-level organizations

If your group has local, regional, national, international, or other levels, how do you avoid turf wars? Will a donor activity be done more effectively at this or another level, balancing local contacts and economies of scale? Will the donor be confused by multiple donation requests from different parts of the organization?

3. Using the Matrix

The fundraising strategy matrix can be used in a worksheet format to evaluate fundraising sources/methods in relation to your organization and in relation to each other (see Sample 7). You can add to, reduce, or change the evaluation factors to suit your particular circumstances.

Work through the strategy matrix with a group such as a fundraising team. On paper (for example, a flip chart), or on a white board or blackboard, list the evaluation factors down the left-hand side. Then choose the sources/methods you want to evaluate and list them across the top. Work your way down the list of evaluation factors, discussing each one as it concerns the different sources/methods and then deciding whether it is a plus (+) or a minus (-). When you have considered all the factors for each source/method, tally the pluses and minuses, then list in order the sources/methods that got the most plus signs. Apply your judgment and decide which sources/methods to pursue.

Developing a fundraising strategy requires judgment. There is no linear formula that will give you the "right" answer. The strategy matrix is simply a tool to help you think it through logically and make a more informed choice.

4. Fundraising Strategy Think Tank

Another way to develop a strategy is through a think tank. Bring together people from outside your organization who are knowledgeable about your issues, your constituencies, and fundraising. Ask them to commit just one evening to help your group come up with a fundraising strategy.

Samples 8 and 9 are from a think tank held by the Legal Education and Action Fund (LEAF). Sample 8 is the agenda followed by LEAF. Each small work group dealt with a different source/method. To guide their discussion, each had a list of specific questions. When the whole workshop regrouped after discussion, there was a great deal of excitement and positive energy in the room. Many innovative and creative ideas emerged. From the reports of the small groups, a collective road map gradually emerged with clearly marked barriers and passages.

To close the session, we distributed the thank-you card shown in Sample 9. Inside was a short questionnaire by which people could offer to provide time, money, or contacts, or simply say they had a fun evening. These were collected at the door.

By the end of the evening, LEAF had some money, a rough fundraising strategy, and a new, high-powered fundraising committee that was ready to roll. Not bad for a night's work!

5. Corporate Fundraising Strategy

Corporate donations are an important source of income for nonprofit organizations. Don't overestimate their value, however. In the United States, a study found that only 4.7 percent of all the private sector donations come from corporations. That constitutes over $6 billion out of $129.88 billion total. More than 80 percent of the money comes from individuals. Foundations give 7.6 percent. Bequests total 6.8 percent. Another study found that in Canada charities get less than 2 percent of their revenue from corporations. Governments give 56 percent of the donations, individuals give 10 percent, and the other 33 percent come from fees and a variety of other sources of revenue.

SAMPLE 7
FUNDRAISING STRATEGY MATRIX

	INDIVIDUALS			CORPORATIONS		GOVERNMENT
	Direct mail	Special events	Canvass	Project proposal contributions	Matching employee	Project proposal
Contacts	n/a	+	n/a	-	-	+
Market	+	+	+	-	-	-
Profile	-	-	-	-	-	-
Information	+	n/a	-	+	+	+
Criteria	n/a	n/a	n/a	+	+	-
Skill	+	+	+	+	+	+
Areas of interest	+	-	-	-	-	-
Policy	+	+	+	+	+	+
History	-	+	+	+	n/a	-
Means	+	+	+	+	-	+
Projects and programs	-	-	-	-	-	-
Competition	-	+	-	-	+	-
Lists	+	n/a	n/a	n/a	n/a	n/a
Geography	n/a	+	+	n/a	n/a	-
Budget & resources	-	-	+	+	+	+
Donor recognition	n/a	+	n/a	+	+	+
Multi-level	-	+	+	-	-	-
Donor records	+	+	+	+	+	+

SAMPLE 8
AGENDA FOR FUNDRAISING STRATEGY WORKSHOP

AGENDA

LEAF FUNDRAISING STRATEGY WORKSHOP

TIME	ACTIVITY	STAFF
5:00-5:20	Reception	Everyone
5:20-5:30	Assembly	Marilou McPhedran
	Introduction of guests	
	Purpose of meeting	
5:30-5:40	Our vision of LEAF	Nancy Jackman
5:40-5:50	Achievements to date	Shelagh Day
	Current situation	
5:50-6:00	Task description	Joyce Young
	Division to small	
	work groups	
6:00-7:40	Work in small groups	Facilitators
		Recorders
7:40-8:00	Plans for follow-up	Marilou McPhedran
	Reports from	Facilitators
	work groups	
	Cards for guest follow-up	
	Thank-you and closing	

SAMPLE 9
THANK-YOU CARD

Please complete this card and leave it with a LEAF representative before you go. Thank you so much for your guidance and suggestions this evening.

Yes, I am prepared to serve on the fundraising task force ☐

Yes, I am prepared to serve on a special events committee ☐

Yes, you can call me for advice and ideas ☐

Try me; I can help LEAF with _____

Name _____

Telephone number _____

_____

5.1 Brainstorming

The first part of your corporate fundraising strategy must be to determine which corporations, if any, are most likely to consider funding your group. One good way to approach this question is through a technique called brainstorming. It's best to conduct this process with a group of people, perhaps your whole staff or board of directors as well as a few outsiders who have a broader view of the organization. Let your imagination run free and get everybody to say anything that comes into his or her minds. Record everything on a flip chart. The technique will produce some ridiculous and some clever results. A key to brainstorming is not to censor or eliminate any ideas in the first, creative phase. Censorship might make people hesitate to suggest ideas that may be perfect, but unusual. Later choose the ones you can most effectively explore now. Avoid negative comments on the ideas put aside.

When you are trying to identify potential corporate donors, there are two stages to your brainstorming (although in practice they will probably be intermingled). The first is identifying sectors of business and industry that are likely to be interested in your cause. The second is identifying individual companies within those sectors that are most likely to donate to your group.

a) Identifying business sectors

Begin with your statement of objectives. If your objectives are clear and specific, they will help you and your fellow brainstormers to consider the question: "Who does the organization serve?" For example:

- If you run a daycare center, you serve children and parents.
- If you run a rape crisis center, you serve the victims of rape, and the community at large.
- If you run a gallery or theater, you serve your patrons and the community at large.

- If you run the Society to Save Dead Elm Trees, you serve the people who love the dead elm trees (as well as the wayward racoons).

If possible, those who benefit directly from your group should pay at least a portion of your annual budget. This funding, however, is rarely enough. Otherwise, you could become a profit-making business! You need to find other sources. So, the next question you toss to your brainstorming group is, "Who has a vested interest in the people we are serving?"

- If you run a daycare center, manufacturers and retailers of children's toys, books, clothes, diapers, baby powder, and so on have a vested interest in children and parents. So do the companies whose employees would not be able to work if they had no daycare.
- If you run a rape crisis center, manufacturers and retailers of women's clothes, jewelry, cosmetics, and publishers (and readers) of women's books and magazines all have a specific, vested interest in women.
- If you run a gallery, manufacturers of canvas, artists' supplies, picture frames, and paper have an interest. You might also get support from companies trying to keep employees from moving away, or attract new ones in a tough market.
- If you run the Society to Save Dead Elm Trees, tourist industries have an interest. So does the real estate developer who can charge more for homes near a nature reserve.

In this way you will get a list of business and industry sectors that should be interested in your work since your clients form their market.

b) Identifying individual businesses

Once you have identified the kinds of businesses that should be interested in your issues, brainstorm which specific companies within those sectors are most likely to give to your group. In both the United States and Canada, companies tend to give where they do business, so identify which manufacturers or retailers of children's toys, diapers, jewelry, or other products operate in your community.

The next question is, "Do we have a contact in that company?" Many granters automatically give high priority to a group where someone they know is involved. Again, your fundraising task force may be able to name a person in that company or provide an introduction.

Look among your board, volunteers, friends, and (if it is appropriate) the people you serve. You might find people who work for the companies, buy their products in quantity, sell them supplies, or have a friend on the inside. While a high-ranking contact is the most influential, many companies give preference to charities supported by their employees at any level. Corporate employees can often get matching grants for nonprofit organizations they support with time or money. For example, IBM doubles, and sometimes even triples, donations made by its employees and retirees or their spouses. Depending on the type of organization, it will give donations of either $2 or $3 for every dollar an employee or retired employee gives or will donate IBM products of that value. IBM will also give cash or equipment to community organizations and schools where their employees and retirees or their spouses are active.

5.2 Beyond brainstorming: Researching the corporate sector

Through brainstorming, you can come up with a list of sectors of business and industry that should be interested in your cause and individual businesses within that sector that might be good to approach because they operate in your community or you have contacts in them. Through brainstorming, you can further narrow your list. Not all business sectors are equally active in philan-thropy, and not all companies are equally generous. Companies in some sectors give more than companies in others. Therefore, as well as identifying the kinds of businesses that should be *interested* in your issues, it is also important to identify which companies *like to give*. Giving tends to be related to the health of the sector and the financial health of the individual companies in the sector. In some industries, such as banks and food products, profitability is fairly consistent from year to year. Other industries such as car and truck manufacturing, oil and gas production, metals mining, and forest products are "cyclical." Their profitability rises and falls with the health of the global economy, fluctuations in the cost of their raw materials, and the balance between supply and demand for their products. You may have better results approaching companies in sectors that are booming than those in sectors that are suffering.

Members of your brainstorming group will likely have some knowledge of which sectors are prosperous and which are struggling, which companies are making money and which are not, and which companies are generous and which do not give very much money.

However, once you have obtained as many ideas and as much information as possible through brainstorming, it is necessary to go on to the next stage and supplement brainstorming with ongoing research. Although your intuition, knowledge, and experience tell you that certain sectors and specific companies should be good prospects, you need to verify this with solid information to avoid wasting the companies' time and yours. You also need to monitor developments in the business world to recognize new opportunities or identify the potential loss of existing opportunities.

Research can supplement your information, uncover additional prospects, and pare your existing list. Your existing donors, especially foundations, government, and corporations, can help identify other donors with similar interests. Ask them.

There are numerous sources of information about which sectors and individual companies are making money, where they operate, whether they are generous givers, and their areas of interest and funding criteria.

In the past, your research might have started with a telephone call or letter to a company to ask for a copy of its annual report and to find out how many employees it has in your community. You would also read the business pages of the daily newspaper and business publications such as *Canadian Business* or *Business Week*.

Today, you might turn first to the Internet. Most large corporations have a Web site where you can view — and often download — their annual report and quarterly financial reports. There is usually other useful information about the company on the Web site as well, such as recent achievements, products manufactured, awards that they sponsor, and charitable donations policies and practices, funding priorities, and projects they have recently funded.

For large companies and foundations, you can often obtain a grant application form online as well as a description of the funding criteria and guidelines for submitting. The Web site will often provide a postal and/or e-mail address where you can contact the grants officers to request further information. For example, the Canadian Pacific Charitable Foundation gives donations on behalf of a group of corporations in the fields of mining, forest products, transportation, and hotels that are members of the Canadian Pacific group of companies. On its Web site <www.cp.ca> you will find the foundation's funding criteria, application procedures, guidelines for filling out applications appropriately, and application forms.

Finding information you need on a Web site may require digging, especially in a large company Web site. Try searching the Web site for terms like corporate responsibility, community relations, charity, donation, or contribution. It is easier today to find this information than ever before.

Here are a few other handy URLs for a random sample of well-known (and sometimes controversial) international companies. (Please note their addresses may change.):

AOL Time Warner:
www.aoltimewarner.com
/corporate_citizenship/index.adp

Coca-Cola:
www2.coca-cola.com/citizenship

Enbridge Natural Gas:
www.cgc.enbridge.com/G/G04-00
_community.html

General Electric:
www.ge.com/community/

General Motors:
www.gm.com/company/gmability
/philanthropy/

Hewlett-Packard:
www.hp.com/hpinfo/community
/main.htm

IBM:
ibm.com/ibm/ibmgives/index.html

Labatt:
www.labatt.com/enhanced
/commun/com_mn.html

Merck (pharmaceuticals):
www.merck.com/about/philanthropy/

Microsoft: www.microsoft.com/giving/

Nike:
www.nike.com/canada/siteInfo
/faq.html

RBC Financial Group:
www.rbc.com/sponsorship/index.html

Sears: www.sears.ca/e/info/cause.htm

TD Bank Financial Group:
www.td.com/community/index.html

Wal-Mart: www.walmartfoundation.org/

Similar information can be found for foundations and government departments.

There is a great deal of detailed information about the financial health of industry and business sectors and individual companies available in business publications such as the business pages of daily newspapers, *Forbes* magazine, *Fortune*, *Canadian Business*, and *Business Week*, to name a few.

There are organizations that study the financial health of industry and business sectors and other organizations that track trends in giving, such as the Conference Boards of Canada and the United States, the Canadian Centre for Philanthropy and Statistics Canada. Statistics on the profitability of business sectors and corporate giving are available from these organizations. Most of these organizations also have Web sites where you can view their findings or at least find out what research they have carried out and how to obtain a copy. You will find a list of such organizations in our Appendix.

There is also a wealth of financial information available over the Internet. In addition to the Web sites maintained by individual corporations and trade associations, there are multitudes of sites that appeal primarily to investors. The information these Web sites can give you about a particular stock include quotes, news, charts, profiles, past and present earnings, and estimates of future earnings; recommendations of stock analysts; financial data, and even insider trading reports. Some of the Web sites that are most useful are EquityWeb, Zack's, Yahoo Finance, Thomson Investor Network, Microsoft MoneyCentral, BigCharts, GLOBEinvestor.com, TheStreet.com, and Bloomberg. Sometimes these sites are linked to each other. For example, most of the other sites in this list can be accessed through the EquityWeb site: <www.equityweb.com>.

By doing this research, you can discover which kinds of companies give the most and which give the least and you can update this information as it changes. For example, you can find out from the Conference Board's Web site <www.conference-board.org/> that in the United States the pharmaceutical industry continues to be the most generous of the corporate donors year after year. Drug companies gave over 17 percent of all the corporate donations in the country in 1998 (the most recent year for which information is available). That amounts to about $483 million out of $2.8 billion that corporations gave charities in the United States. You will find through research that this is up dramatically from 1993 when drug companies gave $207 million, about 10.5 percent of the $1.975 billion given that year.

The same source will provide similar information about sectors such as telecommunications; computer and office equipment; food, beverage and tobacco companies; the petroleum, natural gas, and mining sector; and utilities.

You can also find out from the same source how much of a sector's donations are in cash and how much are donated goods and services ("in-kind" gifts). For example, in 1998 American pharmaceutical companies ranked fourth for total industry cash contributions. This industry's cash contributions were exceeded by telecommunications companies; the petroleum, gas, and mining sector; and transportation-equipment manufacturers. On the other hand, if non-cash contributions such as donations of goods and services are included, pharmaceuticals still gave the most, followed closely by computer- and office-equipment companies, trailed by telecommunications companies, and the petroleum, gas, and mining sector.

Through research, you can also identify which individual companies are generous. For example, on the Web site of the Canadian Centre for Philanthropy <www.ccp.ca>, you can discover the names of 550 Canadian companies that have set examples for the rest of the corporate community by making a commitment to donate at least one percent of their pre-tax profits to charities and by encouraging their employees to give and to volunteer. These companies have been declared "Caring Companies" as part of the Centre's IMAGINE campaign. Most companies give much less. As a result, these 550 companies give 40 percent of all known corporate gifts.

5.3 Deciding which corporations to approach and what to ask them for

Please do not send a form letter to all 550 companies in the IMAGINE campaign, or to all the companies that seem from your research to be potentially interested and able to give to your group. One corporate donor estimates that they get 10,000 applications a year. That works out to one every ten minutes. This is far too much for the donors to handle. Many of the corporate donors are very frustrated at the amount of time they waste dealing with requests that should never have come to the company in the first place.

To get funding, get a realistic view of the community needs and discuss this openly in your request. Form alliances and partnerships with like groups. Trim down your list to the most likely donors before you send applications. Here's how.

Many of the larger consumer-oriented corporations have quite specific areas of interest and limit their giving to these areas. Others define several areas and allocate a predetermined percentage of their donations budget to each of those areas. Not all companies will state their areas of interest, but with a little research, you can find out where they stand. Read the list of donors in the annual reports of groups similar to yours and read the society columns in a major newspaper; both sources can yield information on who is giving funds to whom.

If you have information on corporate areas of interest for charitable giving, put those companies that contribute to your field at the top of your list.

Then decide how best to approach them. The simplest thing to ask for is a grant. However, there are other forms of giving and a variety of possible arrangements. Here are some that you might consider.

a) Joint promotions

A company may want to use your group's name in association with its product in exchange for donating a percentage of the proceeds to your group. This is called a joint promotion. The company believes that being associated with your group will give it an advantage in the marketplace. Of course, you have to decide whether you want to be associated with them! Consider your members' feelings on the subject and check it out before you proceed.

If you decide to go ahead, get a written contract laying out the details. Will you have any input on the ad campaign? How will the income to your group be calculated, and how often will it be paid? What period of time does the joint promotion cover? Even if you decide against joint promotions, you can expect most companies to want some promotional value for their contributions. Solid recognition of corporate contributions will give your group a competitive advantage in the fundraising market.

b) In-kind donations

Many companies are happy to donate their products, services, employee time, building space, and leftover supplies. Often these donations in kind total far more than cash donations. Examples include printing, computers, software, fax machines, airline tickets, office space, manufacturing equipment or supplies, food, safety supplies, paint, and just about anything else you can imagine.

Make a list of what you need. Ask your current supporters, and other businesses in your community.

Three organizations can assist you. Together, they have arranged for charities to receive goods and services worth over $3 billion. Contact them for more information:

In Kind Canada

6535 Millcreek Drive, Unit 78
Mississauga, ON, Canada L5N 2M2
Tel: (905) 816-0900
Fax: (905) 816-0870
E-mail: contact@inkindcanada.ca
Web site: www.inkindcanada.ca

Gifts In Kind International

333 North Fairfax Street, Suite 100
Alexandria, VA 22314
Tel: (703) 836-2121
Fax: (703) 549-1481
E-mail: customerservice@GiftsInKind.org
Web site: www.giftsinkind.org

National Association for the Exchange of Industrial Resources (NAEIR)

560 McClure Street
Gailburg, IL 61401
Tel: (304) 343-0704
Tel: (800) 562-0955
Web site: www.naeir.org/

Corporate Sponsorship

by Ken Wyman © Ken Wyman & Associates Inc., Toronto 2001

Don't confuse *Philanthropy* with *Sponsorship*.

Philanthropic donors support good work because it is good work. Any extra value they receive, such as public recognition, is an added bonus — and some prefer to give anonymously. If you are looking for a philanthropist, prepare to show exactly how much good their donation will achieve, and then report back to them on the results. While most companies appreciate publicity, that is not the main reason they give *donations*.

Sponsors are another matter. Sponsors are mainly self-interested. They are looking for opportunities to improve their market share, increase sales, enhance employee morale, or otherwise meet their own needs. Any good works or public benefits resulting from the sponsorship are just a bonus. If you are looking for a sponsor, show how they can receive a measurable "return on investment." Ideally you should demonstrate that for every $1 they invest in your project, they get at least $3 returned in measurable value. You must be prepared to report back to them on the results.

For example, Ken Wyman arranged a donation to a radical international development charity from a well-known Canadian company, which insisted on remaining anonymous. They felt that the project was so controversial that it could hurt them if anyone knew they had supported it. That was pure philanthropy.

At the other extreme, would be something like the Molson Indy car races. The Molson Indy does not exist because the generous people at Molson thought it was important to preserve this interactive demonstration of the inherent tension between man and machine. Nor does Molson sponsor it to explore the intersection of apparently limitless technological development and the all-too-limited realities of the frail human condition. Molson sponsors the Indy because it sells beer. Period. The day Molson finds a better, more inexpensive way to sell beer, the Indy will have to find a new sponsor. Is there even one speck of philanthropy here?

Much of the charitable world lies somewhere in between these two extremes. The donors get some good will while doing good work. "Doing well by doing good" is a very contemporary corporate motto. Enlightened self-interest. Donors don't expect as much payback as they would from, say, sponsoring the Olympic Games, and they are not so selfless as to hide their light under a bushel.

Here's how a nonprofit can do a better job of attracting these not-quite philanthropic dollars.

1. Clarify any ethical problems you may have with dirty money

Many nonprofit groups have understandably strong feelings about associating themselves with certain businesses. Examples range from tobacco and alcohol to baby-formula manufacturers, drug companies, environmental polluters, companies with poor records of promoting women or people of color, importers of products made in sweatshops, and on through a long list. Every nonprofit must decide where to draw the line. Resolve this issue before you start talking to sponsors.

2. Determine what you have to offer

What kind of payback can you provide for a sponsor? It is not enough to say you offer good will. How will you make that a reality?

a) **Events:** Are you having a special event? Events attract most of the sponsorship dollars. Sporting events get the lion's share. Be sure you know the answers to the following questions:

   1. How many people will watch the event, live or in the media?

   2. Who are those people? Age? Gender? Spending habits? McDonalds is interested in young parents, and will sponsor events that a beer company like Labatts won't touch.

b) **Publications:** Are you producing a special book, brochure, or newsletter? If the sponsor's name can appear on it, they might be interested. Pharmaceutical companies, for example, love sponsoring informative booklets that patients read. Once again, have the answers to these questions:

   1. How many people will read the booklet?

   2. Who are those people?

   3. Can you include promotional material? In one classic example, a pet food company sponsored a booklet given away to children about baby animals, which was written by the staff of the zoo. Inside were coupons for free passes to the zoo and a discount on pet food.

c) **Publicity:** Can you help the company get its name in the media along with yours? Consider the following:

   1. News coverage: Is the media going to cover your project? Major sporting events get lots of sponsorship dollars precisely because the event will be mentioned in the daily news.

     i)   What is your publicity plan? Can you cooperate with the company to issue news releases that put both the sponsor and the charity in a good light?

     ii) Do you have PR professionals helping to deliver the goods? Whether they are volunteers, consultants, or staff, the sponsor will have more confidence that you can deliver if you show that you have able personnel.

     iii) Do you have a clipping service that can prove to the sponsor how often their name was mentioned? How will the sponsor know for sure that you have produced exposure? Professional clipping services do a great job of catching references in obscure media such as ethnic and community papers. You can do this yourself and create a scrap book to show the sponsor and future prospects.

2. Media co-sponsors: Can you arrange with newspapers, radio, or TV to donate free advertising space, in exchange for the good will of being your official media sponsor? How much space or time will they give you? Then you can tell the other sponsors where and how often their name will appear in your media promotional material.

3. Signs and other advertising opportunities: Can you put up signs with the sponsor's name or company logo? This is perfect for an event, or a group with a busy facility, such as a community center, an athletic facility, a gallery, theater, or park. Small-town baseball parks often collect good revenue displaying sponsorship signs from sporting-goods stores, pizzerias, donut shops, beer halls, and similar merchants. Conferences may put the sponsor's sign on the podium so that everyone watching the speakers is reminded of who sponsored the event. Sponsors are doubly happy when photographs of the event show the sign, and triply happy when those photographs appear in the news. Consider the following:

   i)   How big will the signs be? The bigger the better, but whatever the size, tell potential sponsors the measurements.

   ii) Where will the signs be positioned? Will they stand out visually or be lost in the clutter? One company was happy to sponsor a float in the Caribana parade with a sign the full length of the float trumpeting their name. They knew hundreds of thousands of people would see their sign along the parade route, and many more would see it on TV. Unfortunately, as the parade started, supporters hopped on to the float and sat along the edge with their dangling legs hiding the sign.

   iii) Who will see signs? Show the demographics and psychographics.

   iv) How long will the signs remain up? Can you arrange year-round exposure or just a few hours?

   v)   Can you provide creative places to put the sponsor's message? Nonprofit groups have put the sponsors' names on T-shirts, hats, wrist bands, shoulder bags, note pads, drinking glasses, Frisbee® flying disks, and hundreds of other places.

d) **Naming rights:** Can you work the sponsor's name into the title? Sponsors pay more when they are strongly linked to an event or booklet. Putting the sponsor's name right into the title is worth more than putting it underneath with a phrase like "Presented by . . . " If you have many small sponsors, you can group them together in categories such as Gold, Silver, and Bronze. At the very least, list their names in alphabetical order at the end of a brochure. Examples:

   • Canada Games 2003 offer a long list of sponsorship benefits. Check them out at: www.2003canadagames.ca/site/En/sponsors.cfm

   • Air Canada Championship PGA tour www.aircanadachampionship.com

   • Bell Challenge Cup Annual Pee Wee Hockey Christmas classic www.bell.ca/en/about/sponsor/listing.asp

- National Football League Alumni
  www.nflanw.org

- The Corel Centre in Ottawa, with its WordPerfect Theatre, and the Corel Balloon Team, which raises money for nonprofit groups that sell tickets for tethered balloon rides or offer free balloon rides as raffle prizes:
  www.corel.com/events/sponsorship/index.htm

e) **Involve the sponsor:** Not all sponsors are interested in wooing customers. Some want to build morale within their work force. Get the employees involved as volunteers on a big project, and the company is happier.

f) **Product Sampling:** Can you team up with a sponsor to help them get their potential consumers to try their products? Gevalia Coffee, for example, collaborated with the Vancouver Symphony to provide free coffee, which the orchestra converted into money by selling at intermission, and packaging into gift baskets to market to supporters. This was exactly the high-end market the coffee company wanted.

g) **Dollar value of your offer:** Calculate the return on investment your sponsor will get. It must be far more than they spend. Taking on a new sponsorship property can be risky, so you have to look extra good. It once was enough to tell sponsors that they would get a lot of exposure. Then, in the era of number crunching, sponsors began hard comparisons. The value of a newspaper story is calculated based on size of the story, how prominently the sponsor's name is mentioned, circulation, page placement, and a host of factors that a consultant in sponsorship or public relations can compute. Bottom line: sponsors want to know that for every $1 they invest, they can measure a $3 return. In recent years they have demanded even more. After one Olympic sponsorship, Fuji Film calculated a return of $18 for every dollar invested, and everyone else's expectations went up.

Sponsorship is changing fast. The days are gone when a CEO's interest alone dictated that the company sponsor golf, or hot air balloons, or opera, or a gala for a women's shelter.

Big companies and big charities are much more scientific. Small businesses and non-profits are just beginning to explore the rich rewards that this offers.

Much helpful information is available on the Internet. For the most useful, up-to-date information, you may have to pay. See the Appendix for places of special interest.

6. Foundations Fundraising Strategy

There is still quite a mystique about foundations, where they get their money, and to whom they give it. Even the word "foundation" is confusing, because there are foundations that raise money and foundations that give it away. This section deals with the latter.

There are four types of foundations, including those that are —

- set up by a family,
- set up by a corporation,
- designed to serve a specific community or geographical area, and
- established to foster a certain interest.

Foundations tend to focus their funding in one or more of three ways:

- Restricting their giving to a geographical area
- Defining specific areas of interest
- Defining the type of funding they will give (i.e., capital costs or project costs)

Many foundations have a calendar fiscal year, and many meet only once a year to make decisions on funding requests, so fall is a good time to approach them.

Canada has far fewer large foundations than the United States. Few Canadian foundations have staff, so a lot of your contact with Canadian foundations will be through correspondence.

A few foundations are very innovative and will fund things that nobody else will touch. Most foundations are conservative and tend to give most of their money to large, traditional campaigns such as university research, health organizations, and hospitals. Most are quite specific about whom they will fund. Other than that, it's impossible to generalize. There are some large foundations in Canada, and there are a few very large foundations in the United States that accept requests from Canadian groups. Finding the one that's going to give to you is a matter of doing your homework.

You identify foundations that may be willing to donate to your group largely the same way as you find corporations: by brainstorming and by research. Look at annual reports from other non-profits in the same field as you to see which foundations give to them and you'll know at least that the foundation has an interest in the area (although it is possible that the foundation donated to that group primarily because someone in the group knew someone in the foundation rather than because of interest in the area). In addition, there are numerous publications and Web sites dealing with philanthropy that carry news about recent gifts by foundations and the interests of individual foundations. A list of such publications and Web sites is in the Appendix.

One of the most systematic ways of finding foundations that have an interest in your cause or are active in your geographic area is to go through a directory of foundations. Fortunately, this can be done in a fraction of the time it used to take because such directories are available online and can be searched electronically by using key words such as "AIDS," "health," or "wildlife."

The most comprehensive written source on Canadian foundations is the *Canadian Directory to Foundations and Grants*, published by The Canadian Centre for Philanthropy (see the Appendix for the publisher's address). The directory also includes a section on American Foundations and one on American Granting Agencies. It has a good bibliography of resource books on foundations around the world.

The Canadian Centre for Philanthropy also offers training, and publishes books on fundraising and management for nonprofit groups. Ask about their computer-assisted research on foundations. Their toll-free number is 1-800-655-7729. Fundraisers can also find useful information in directories published by Prospect Research Online (PRO) and Metasoft's BigDatabase. Both provide Internet information on

Canadian and US corporations, private and public foundations, employee charitable trusts, and major individual donors. For a directory of international foundations, groups can research *The International Foundation Directory*. (See the Appendix at the end of the book.)

American groups should get *The Foundation Directory*, prepared by The Foundation Center (see the Appendix for the address). The Foundation Center's libraries keep sets of IRS records (Form 990PF) for all foundations in the United States. Located in New York and Washington, DC, these libraries are open to the public and are free. Only about 900 of the 40,000 foundations in the United States publish annual reports, so the information returns are an important data source. The Foundation Center's field offices in Cleveland, Atlanta, and San Francisco keep foundation information returns for their regions.

As well, The Foundation Center operates a library network of over 200 cooperating collections in North America. All are open to the public and are free. To check on the location nearest you, in the United States and Canada, you can call their toll-free number at 1-800-424-9836. From elsewhere call (212) 620-4230. You can also access the Foundation Center's World Wide Web Internet connection, fdncenter.org. This includes *Philanthropy News Digest*, which provides summaries of articles in the major media.

You can also find directories of foundations that give to a particular cause or are active in a geographic area simply by using one of the search engines on the Web, such as Google or Yahoo. For example, using Google, we typed "foundation health funding." We found links to dozens of Web sites that included individual foundations that fund health issues, databases and directories of such foundations, and reports on trends in health funding. Entries included the Hogg Foundation for Mental Health, the Sierra Health Foundation Grants Program, Special funding initiatives of the ADA Health Foundation, and a

Trend Analysis and Report on Foundation Funding in Health Policy. And these entries were in the first ten out of several thousand entries containing these three words. We could have further narrowed the search to include only funding for mental health, for women's health, or for health groups in the south-western states or northern Canada.

Donors in many parts of the world can be researched at —

Charities Aid Foundation (CAF)
Kings Hill, West Malling,
Kent ME19 4TA United Kingdom
Tel: +44 (0) 1732 520000
Fax: +44 (0) 1732 520001
Web site: www.cafonline.org/

CAF **America**
King Street Station,
1800 Diagonal Road, Suite 150,
Alexandria, VA 22314-2840, USA
Tel: +1 (703) 549-8931
Fax: +1 (703) 549-8934
E-mail: cafamerica@cafamerica.org

Australia CAF
282 Victoria Avenue, Suite 311
Chatswood NSW 2067, Australia
Tel: +61 2 9267 9210
Fax: +61 2 9267 0544
E-mail: caf@cafaustralia.org

Bulgarian CAF
4 - A, Vesletz Str., 4 floor,
Sofia 1000, Bulgaria
Tel/Fax: + 359 2 987 1574 / 981 1901
Also: + 359 2 894 082
E-mail: bcaf@CAFonline.org

CAF **Brussels Office**
Rue Dejonckerstraat 46,
B-1060 Brussels, Belgium
Tel: +32 2 544 00 50
Fax: +32 2 544 08 80
E-mail: cafbrussels@CAFonline.org

CAF **India**

Main (Delhi) Office
25 Navjeevan Vihar, Ground Floor, Opposite
Gijatanjali Enclave,
New Delhi - 110 017
Tel: +91 11 652 2206
Fax: +91 11 656 1468
E-mail: cafindia@CAFonline.org

CAF **India**

Bangalore Office
14 Cookson Road, Richards Town,
Bangalore -560084
Tel/Fax: +91 80 547 4394
E-mail: cafblr@bgl.vsnl.net.in

CAF **Russia**

14/6 Ulitsa Sadovnicheskaya 57,
Moscow 113035, Russia
Tel/Fax: +7 095 792 5929
E-mail: cafrussia@CAFonline.org

CAF **Southern Africa**

41 de Korte Street,
Braamfontein 2017,
Gauteng, South Africa
Tel: +27 11 339 1136
Fax: +27 11 339 1152
E-mail: cafsouthernafrica@CAFonline.org

CAF **West Africa**

F-146/5 Second Soula Street,
North Labone Estates,
(PO Box OS - 2956, OSU),
Accra, Ghana
Tel/Fax: + 233 21 771 953
E-mail: cafwestafrica@CAFonline.org

European donors can be found at —

European Foundation Centre
51 rue de la Concorde
Brussels, Belgium
Tel: +32.2.512.8938
Fax: +32.2.512.3265
Web site: www.efc.be/

Once you have the appropriate directories or Web sites, decide which general categories best describe your group's work, such as health, education, welfare, or ecology, and go through the areas of interest index. Select the foundations that list your category as one of their areas of interest and write to them requesting their annual report and any other information on their funding programs or check the Internet to see whether they have a Web site. If so, the information you need may be on the Web site.

Many foundations do not publish annual reports or funding guidelines, but it is worth asking the foundation or checking the Web site.

The amount of information foundations will volunteer varies widely. Some are very explicit about how much they gave, to whom, and for what. Others will be vague or not send anything when you request information. The foundations that do respond to a request for information are your first best bet, and once you have read their information you will have a better idea whether it's worthwhile to approach them.

Read the foundation's annual report or Web site carefully. Look at the type of groups and activities the foundation is funding and the dollar range of the grants. Look for any comments on the foundation's priorities for the future and note any titles it has given to a grants program; for instance, "Social Development and the Environment." You should use all these details to tailor your funding proposal to the programs of the particular foundation.

In Canada, you have access to further information. Income tax legislation requires foundations to file information on their income, their assets, and their contributions. That information, or part of it, is public, so contact Canada Customs and Revenue Agency (formerly Revenue Canada) and ask for the foundation's Public Information Return, Form T3010. The government will fax you a few or mail them if you request several. A for-profit company has put them online so you can access them for a fee at <www.foundationsearch.ca>.

In the US foundations and other charities file Form 990 with the Internal Revenue Service. Scanned images of Forms 990 are now available on the Internet through a joint effort of the National Center for Charitable Statistics (NCCS, at the Urban Institute's Center on Nonprofits and Philanthropy) <nccs.urban.org>; and GuideStar <www.guidestar.org>, the Web site for Philanthropic Research, Inc. (PRI). Search options enable users to locate charitable organizations by name, key word, city, state, zip code, revenue size, or type of organization. The Form 990's foundations file lists what groups they have funded, and how much they gave each group.

7. Government Fundraising Strategy

Even in the current climate of cutbacks in government spending, government still gives more money to nonprofits than any other source of revenue. In Canada, government agencies gave 56 percent of all the money donated to charities in 1994, the most recent year for which information was available. Provincial governments are the largest funders. Of the money given by all levels of government, the provinces put in 84 percent, the federal government 11 percent, and local governments 5 percent. Often, although not always, your project or group has to fit into a specific funding program to obtain a grant. If you do fit their terms of reference, governments tend to give out worthwhile sums of money.

Governments reflect current social issues of high priority in their funding programs more quickly and closely than either foundations or corporations. However, it often takes much longer to get a response to an application for funds and much longer yet to actually get the promised money from government sources. Government sources also require much more detailed reports on activities and financial transactions. After all, you are spending the taxpayer's dollar.

New government funding programs and individual grants are often announced in news releases or in speeches by government officials. These announcements are often posted on the government's Web site and reported in the media. You can monitor the Internet, newspapers, magazines, television, and radio for such announcements.

Most government funding programs have brochures available indicating eligibility, criteria and guidelines, areas of interest, and application procedures. These government programs will also frequently be described on the agency's Web site. Get that information before you decide whether to apply. Government funding programs often have field officers who do have time to see you, and they will help you figure out if you are eligible and under what program. They will help you with your application. Make good use of these people and try to sell them on your project because they make the initial recommendation on your proposal. Many of these government grant officers have commented that they wish more nonprofit groups would contact them and discuss ideas at an early stage so they could help the group find the shortest possible path to the funds.

In addition, befriend the local staff of elected politicians. These people, often called constituency assistants or aids, are trying hard to track as many government programs as possible. They are always interested in projects that will help bring money into the community and make the politicians look good. They can save you much research.

Municipal government funding is often overlooked by nonprofit groups that focus only on higher levels of government. City, town, region, and/or county governments can be significant sources of funds. Depending on the group's projects, funds might come from established programs, divisions such as the public health department, the Board of Education, police, fire prevention, emergency services, parks and recreation, culture, community economic development, or many other categories. In addition, the Mayor's office and individual councilors (or aldermen) may have special funds or opportunities to propose special grants for projects not included in normal channels.

Contact sympathetic people at city hall for suggestions.

If what your group is proposing to do fits in with a policy statement made by a high official or made in a government report, point this out in your application. Don't forget to ask your local political representative to endorse your project.

8. Service Clubs

Hundreds of organizations exist for a combination of community service and fellowship. No strategy would be complete without considering asking them for support. They may be able to give an outright cash grant. They may offer volunteer labor. They may create a special event to raise money for you or with you.

Most of them prefer to provide help at the local level, which makes them good resources for small-town groups, or nonprofit organizations working in specific neighborhoods. A few will give outside their home base, and some, like the Lions and Rotary, have substantial international development programs.

Most prefer to give to projects that will directly help people, especially children. The donations they give may be smaller than corporations or foundations, but occasionally they give hundreds of thousands of dollars.

Here is a partial list to get your mind running: the Ancient Arabic Order of the Nobles of the Mystic Shrine (more commonly known at the Shriners), fraternities and sororities like Beta Sigma Phi, the Blue Knights (police motorcycle riders), B'nai Brith, Civitan Club, Club Richelieu, car-owners' associations such as the Corvette Club, the Elks (and their companion women's group, the Royal Order of Purple), the Independent Order of Foresters (which runs a giant insurance company), the Independent Order of Odd Fellows, JayCees, Kinsmen Club, Kiwanis International, Knights of Columbus, Knights of Pythias, the Lions Club International (the world's largest service organization), the Loyal Order of Moose, Masonic and Military Orders of Knights of the Red Cross of Constantine, Optimists, Quota Club, Rotary Club, the Royal Canadian Legion, University Women's Clubs, Variety Club, veterans' associations, Women's Institute, Ysmen (senior members of the YMCA), and Zonta International.

9. Employee Charitable Funds

Inside many corporations, groups of employees raise money to give to nonprofit groups. They often support the United Way. In addition, many Employee Charitable Funds give large grants to a wide variety of other groups. This is the employee's own money, not the corporate giving budget.

For example, the Telephone Pioneers of America <www.telephone-pioneers.org/> is the world's largest industry-related volunteer organization. Their membership (nearly 800,000 in the United States and Canada) includes people who work for the mainstream phone companies. Their motto: "Answering the Call of Those in Need." They have "a primary focus on education, [but] Pioneers also serve their communities in numerous other ways: from improving the quality of life for the disabled to preserving the environment to forming the critical support required during times of disaster." Altogether, they raised nearly $9 million and volunteered more than 31 million hours toward providing quality services to the lonely, people with disabilities, and the disadvantaged.

There are hundreds of similar groups. An Internet search for "employee charitable fund" will give you a good start. For details see the Appendix.

10. The United Way

Even if your group does not get regular United Way funding, you may be able to get support from the organization. Depending on the city, it may provide special grants, volunteer training, or in-kind donations. It may be willing to serve as a matchmaker and introduce you to leaders from corporations, unions, employee funds, or foundations.

All of this may be provided in a friendly manner with no strings attached. In some cases, the United Way will request that you not compete with it for the same donors at the same time of year.

In many communities, there are various alternatives to the United Way that are also worth approaching. These groups may be based on religious principles, such as the United Jewish Appeal, The Salvation Army Red Feather, Catholic Charities, Episcopal Charities, and so on. They may be based on ethnic or racial groups, such as the United Black Fund of America.

11. Religious Groups

Many churches, convents, synagogues, mosques, and other religious groups give money, space in their buildings, and other kinds of support to other charities. They support social justice programs, food banks, arts groups, health care, AIDS, alcohol and drug abuse programs, seniors, children, housing, immigrant aid, and much more. Their contributions often go to groups that do not share their religious beliefs. While some are "poor as church mice," many are well endowed and capable of substantial contributions.

Usually, the clergy have discretionary funds, but they are so worried about raising money to repair the roof or meet the budget that they are not able to think about giving it away. You may get a more sympathetic hearing from the heads of outreach committees, women's groups, men's groups, youth groups, and religious educators.

Ask your board, volunteers and, if appropriate, the people you serve where they worship. If you get a donation from one place of worship, ask them to help you make contacts with others in the same denomination. Offer to send speakers to their meetings or services. Build a long-term relationship.

12. Unions

Many unions give money to charities and nonprofit organizations. They are interested in social justice, services for seniors, health care, international development, and many other causes. Of course they will support only causes that they consider pro-union, so if you work with a large organization that is unionized, you have a better chance of getting a donation than if your management has tried to keep unions out. Unions also notice whether or not you have had your letterhead, business cards, or brochures printed in a union print shop. Union print shops can put a small union symbol, often called a "bug," on your printed material.

Document any work you do that would be of special interest to union members. Find a union member who supports your work to ask on your behalf. Then contact the largest or most progressive unions in your area. They may be listed in the phone book, often under "Labor." You may also contact the Labor Council in your area, which is an umbrella group for most unions. They may be able to provide a small donation and give you addresses and contact people at the most promising unions.

13. Joining Forces: What Have We Got to Lose?

One fundraising strategy that isn't used often enough is to collaborate with similar groups.

Many groups that have difficulty surviving ignore the obvious option of fundraising collaboration. There are several reasons for this. Grassroots organizations tend to be fiercely independent. When you have struggled so long and worked so hard to create a group and achieve public recognition for it, you don't want to give up your name or compromise with other groups about approaches and programs. It's human nature to defend your turf, even if the size of your turf keeps shrinking. Secondly, poverty has the same effect on groups as it does on their clients. When you must spend all your time and energy just trying to survive, it is hard to think and plan ahead and look at the larger picture. As the saying goes, "When you're up to your ass in alligators, it's hard to remember that you came to clear the swamp."

Ask yourself these questions:

- Are we in a nonprofit sector to which a lot of people like to give a lot of money (such as health or education) or a sector to which few people give and in small amounts (such as environmental protection and small arts groups)?
- How many other groups like ours are competing for the same funds?

If the answer is that your sector is one in which it is hard to raise money and there is fierce competition for that money, and if your group and most of the others in the same sector have been struggling for years to keep their heads above water, you might ask yourself the next logical question: What have we got to lose by joining forces with other groups to do fundraising together?

However, collaboration is not only for the desperate. Even if your group is not struggling financially, it may still make sense to collaborate with other groups on specific projects. For example, you may not have enough money to invest in creating a particular product or service or enough contacts to successfully carry out a capital campaign alone. But together with one or two other groups you may be able to carry it off.

As the success of the United Way demonstrates, joint fundraising campaigns have the potential to raise more money at a lower cost than numerous individual campaigns. People tend to give larger amounts to a campaign that will benefit many organizations than to a campaign by a single group.

Joint fundraising efforts can also be targeted towards core funding — the hardest kind of money to raise.

Collaboration need not be limited to fundraising. For example, among the largest ongoing expenses groups have are office rental, office equipment rental, and salaries. A small group will rarely have enough money to buy a building to house its offices. But two or three groups that are willing to move in together might be able to buy a building. And sharing a common building makes it easier to share expenses like photocopier rental charges and maintenance or to share staff such as receptionists and bookkeepers. Thus, by working together to buy a building, the new housemates can achieve savings that go beyond lower rent.

Organizing a joint fundraising campaign or other collaboration takes a lot of time and effort. It is necessary to work out a lot of issues before groups can work together. For example, you must decide how much staff time and money each group will contribute to the effort; how the donations will be allocated among groups; who will issue the tax receipts; who will coordinate the efforts of the team; and how will each group avoid approaching the others' donors.

If one of the barriers to organizing a joint campaign is that no one in the organization has the time to work on developing it, one solution is to ask donors to fund someone to carry out a feasibility study or to facilitate bringing your group together with other groups to design a joint fundraising campaign. Funding such an initiative may be attractive to some foundations, corporations, and government agencies because it is innovative and fosters cooperation and efficiency. They may also see the advantages to them from joint fundraising. They may like the fact that a single donation helps several groups or that they have to read fewer proposals.

According to the book *Collaboration: What Makes It Work* by Paul Mattesich and Barbara Monsey, research shows that there are several factors affecting the success of collaborations among nonprofit groups. Some of these factors are largely outside your control. The political or social climate may not favor the kind of collaboration you want to have. Or there may not be a history of collaboration among groups in your area that has provided the contacts, built up trust, and provided a framework for working together. There's not too much you can do about these external factors. You may want to take the lead in organizing a campaign, but your group may not be seen as a leader by the other groups or by the community at large. You can't change history overnight, nor can you quickly change the way governments and other donors think about funding or the way the community and other groups perceive your organization.

However, many of the factors that affect the likelihood of success are within the control of the participants, such as mutual understanding, respect, and trust; a willingness to compromise; adaptability; and flexibility.

To collaborate effectively, you should do the following:

- Choose as partners other groups that have a sufficient stake in the success of the collaboration to put a lot of effort into it

- Develop consensus on both the process and the desired outcome
- Establish clear roles and policy guidelines
- Maintain open and frequent communication among the groups
- Establish both formal and informal communication links
- Develop concrete, attainable goals, and objectives
- Choose a skilled coordinator who has the respect of other groups
- Commit sufficient funds and other resources to the effort

Realistically it can be difficult to make partnerships work. Ken has worked with several coalitions of charities that hoped to reduce costs or reach new sources of donors by working together. Many have not been able to get off the ground because of inadequate resources, conflicts over access to funders, and internal rivalries. While funders encourage partnerships, they can be difficult to coordinate, and must be approached with caution.

CHAPTER 6
HOW TO APPROACH FUNDERS

Having developed your funding strategy, you now have a list of good prospects to approach. This chapter details the steps for approaching those prospects, focusing particularly on corporations because they are often the most difficult source fundraisers must tackle. However, much of what is covered can also be applied to approaching foundations, governments, and wealthy individuals.

1. Attitude

If you hope to raise money from corporations but deep down inside you think they are corrupt, exploitative, many-headed monsters, chances are you won't meet with much success. As you learn more about the kind of decisions senior corporate people have to make, the risks they take, and the kind of jungle in which they compete, your respect will grow, at least for the exemplary companies.

One more note on attitudes. The presidential trappings of vast offices, fine art, and Persian rugs can be intimidating, especially if you have never before dealt with senior corporate management. It is useful to remember that the people you deal with, no matter how rich, brilliant, or powerful,

are just people like you and me. They may not be ordinary, but they are people, and if you remember that, it helps you to say what you came to say.

2. Setting Up a Meeting

It is very important to arrange a face-to-face meeting with the person in the organization who can do your cause the most good. When you meet with someone, you become more than just another envelope in a file full of worthwhile causes in need of more money. You become a person, an experience, and that personal contact can go a long way. You are probably more convincing in person than on paper.

2.1 Through the front door

This means going directly to the source, such as the president of the company. It's worth your effort to try to see the president in the following situations:

- You are a controversial group and without the blessing of the president you won't get anywhere

- Someone on your board or fundraising task force knows the president and can arrange an introduction for you
- The corporation is very large and conservative and you have never approached them before

The first challenge is to get the president on the phone. That in itself is a task, because almost every president has a forward guard of secretaries to protect his or her valuable time. You have to be assertive and authoritative when you make that call. The secretary will answer and say "Ms. Black's office." You can be very formal and say "Yes, it's Joyce Young calling for Janet Black." If the president is actually there, the secretary may put you right through because you sound like you know the boss. If the president isn't there, the secretary will say, "I'm sorry, Ms. Black is in a meeting. May I have her call you?" *Don't leave a message. If the president doesn't know you, she isn't likely call back.* Instead, say, "Thanks, but I'm going to be in a meeting shortly. When do you expect her back?" The secretary will tell you, and you make a note. Be sure to call back at that time.

If the secretary is especially friendly, you can try to get an appointment, but this usually doesn't work unless you already know the president or the secretary. Be nice to the secretary. She (it is still usually a woman) can decide whether or not you ever speak to the president. She may even have a lot of power to make decisions about grants. In a small company, she could even be the president's spouse! Learn her name, speak to her politely, and ask her to be your ally.

When you make this call, you have to be prepared to speak to the president and to convince him or her in three minutes to take the time to see you. In one sentence you have to say what your group does in a way that will impress, and in the next minute you have to show why he or she should be interested in what you are doing.

In response to your request for an appointment, the president may —

a) make an excuse and try to put you off for a couple of months. Accept that, but if you get put off again, understand that it is a polite "no." Either put your request to the president in writing or try to see someone else.

b) suggest that you see somebody else. Unless you can come back with, "I particularly want to speak to you because you have been involved in such and such . . . ," you will have to go along with the suggested substitute.

c) say, "What you really want is money." Acknowledge that fact, but quickly add that you also value his or her perspective as a businessperson on such and such issue. Something like, "Yes, we do raise part of our funds from the corporate sector, but we especially seek the advice and perspective of the private sector on current social issues, especially child abuse, and that's why we want to speak to you. If you could give us half an hour of your time, I'm sure we can learn a lot from you."

Remember the fundraising adage —

> If you want money,
> ask for advice;
> if you want advice,
> ask for money.

If you manage to speak to the president and you are quick on your feet during the phone call, chances of getting an appointment are fair to good. Be sure you are "up" and "focused" before you make this kind of call.

We've used the example of a corporate president, but the approach described in this section could be used for any senior official or for a wealthy individual.

2.2 The regular route

If you don't have cause to go see the president, or you can't get an appointment, you want to contact the person who handles donations. These people have various titles: "corporate affairs director," "corporate contributions administrator," "secretary to the donations committee," "chairperson of the contributions committee," "community affairs," or "donations officer."

Avoid the public relations department, however. They are more likely to evaluate your request as a marketing decision, not a philanthropic gift. Few small charities can truly offer corporate sponsors exciting results. For this discussion, we will use the example of a "corporate contributions administrator," or CCA.

The CCA is the secretary to the corporate contributions committee, if there is one. He or she is responsible for the initial weeding-out process. The CCA assesses all the requests that come in (as many as 30 per day), chooses those that fit the company's areas of interest, and summarizes them on one or two pages for the committee to discuss and make decisions.

The committee is usually made up of three or more people from the company. If the company has defined certain areas of interest, they will try to find an in-house expert to serve on the committee. For example, if the company has a budget for funding the arts, somebody with interest and experience in the arts will be on the committee. A contributions committee will usually meet at least every six months and, in some cases, quarterly.

The CCA will make an oral presentation and answer questions on the requests that made it to the committee level. That's why it is important to get to see the CCA and get him or her on your side.

To get the name of the CCA, phone the switchboard and ask, "Who handles donations to nonprofit groups?" If the switchboard operator doesn't know, ask to speak to the director of public affairs. Most PR directors will be nice to you and quite patient because that's their job. Ask the PR director to whom you should address a request for funds. Get the correct spelling of that person's first and last name and their official title. Then write a one-page letter to the CCA introducing your organization and explaining that you would like to arrange a brief meeting to discuss such and such and you will call in a few days. Enclose your objectives sheet and annual report. Make it clear that this is not — yet — a request for funding.

Don't enclose a funding proposal at this stage. You can introduce that topic at the meeting. In your approaches in the works log, note the letter, the date you mailed it, and the date you should phone back.

3. The Meeting

You've cleared the first hurdle: you've got a meeting with someone in the organization. You need to prepare to make every minute in that meeting count for you.

3.1 Before the meeting

If you haven't already done so, read or skim the company's annual report and Web site. If your group has dealt with the company before, re-read the correspondence. If they have given you money before, know how much, when, what it was for, and the results of the work they funded. If you asked and were rejected, know that too. You want to have this information at the tip of your tongue. Funders may keep good files, so you should too.

Decide what information you want to get across and what information you want to get from them. Put a scenario together in your head, and then be prepared to ad lib. Bring your objectives sheet and your annual report if you haven't already sent them. Don't put all the paper on the table when you arrive. Keep it in your briefcase, out of sight, unless the CCA asks for it. Focus on a conversation instead.

It is very important to take somebody with you to the meeting — a staff member, a board member — whoever is appropriate. You can be the businessperson and your partner can be the expert. That takes some of the pressure off you during the meeting, and it gives you somebody with whom to compare notes afterward. You should be able to communicate well with your fundraising partner so that the meeting will be a smooth, three-way discussion.

3.2 At the meeting

Be on time! Punctuality is very important to corporate people.

Be appropriately dressed. Blue jeans or green hair aren't allowed when you are on their territory asking them for money. You might get away with wearing something other than normal business clothes if the company is known to value eccentricity, as is the case with some dot-coms or ad agencies. Even then it probably won't hurt to be dressed conservatively.

If you dress casually at work, it's a good idea to keep a suit, dress shoes, etc., in the office for meetings on short notice.

When your contact comes out to greet you, shake hands, introduce yourself, your organization, and your partner. Then begin the discussion. You might start by asking if he or she is familiar with your group, give a very brief history about how and why your group was formed, and then get to the point — the project you would like funded. Try to get your listener involved and asking questions about your group. Encourage a real discussion and try to establish rapport.

Keep an eye on your watch. If you said you only needed half an hour, get in and out in that space of time.

Should you discuss money in the meeting? Certainly you shouldn't discuss it until your meeting is almost over. Get your contact warmed up first, and don't discuss money at all unless it feels right. Your contact assumes you are there to get money.

If you don't know that you've sold this person on your cause and you want to find out where you stand, try this approach: "Perhaps you can tell us a bit about your areas of interest for funding. We are a registered charitable group, and we do depend on contributions from organizations like yours. Could you tell us the kinds of activities you fund and if you would be amenable to an approach for funding from our group?"

If you feel the person might respond to a very specific approach to fund a specific project, you might say, "The total budget for our project is $40,000, which will cover salaries, travel expenses, and printing. We were considering asking your company for $4,000 toward our project. Would that be appropriate?"

In one fundraising effort, we were driving in the president's car back to his office after a superb luncheon at his private club. The president had commented on the power of positive thinking and expecting good results — just cheerful and friendly chitchat:

> *President: "Well, I've really enjoyed talking to you, but I don't think you've put all your cards on the table. Don't you want to ask me for some money?"*

> *Fundraiser: "We're not going to ask you for money, Don, we expect some money. The only question is how much!"*

He burst out laughing, but we got the money.

3.3 After the meeting

Immediately after the meeting, go have a cup of coffee with your partner, compare notes, and write down new ones. Summarize the discussion. Make a note of any requests for further information and questions or comments that were raised about your group. If the meeting was exploratory — not a specific approach for a specific project — decide which project or aspect of your activities you think that organization would like to fund and how much money they might contribute.

Make some comments about your contact: "friendly and interested" or "bored and preoccupied." What kind of rapport did you establish with the CCA or the president? Were you on a first-name basis by the end of the meeting?

This list of information is called a profile sheet. It is worth doing because you won't remember all the details about that meeting, and next year when you or your successor approaches this source again, you will have a record of your relationship. Staple this to the inside of your file on the organization, as well as adding it to your computerized donor-tracking system.

3.4 Back at the office

a) Follow-up letter

When you get back to the office, or within a couple of days at the very most, write to the person with whom you met. Thank him or her for the meeting. Answer any questions or resolve any concerns that were mentioned. Add any new information relevant to your discussions. Introduce the funding proposal you enclose by reiterating the objective of the project in one paragraph. Mention the total budget and name the amount you would like that person or organization to contribute. For requests for small amounts of money, a letter with your annual report and objectives sheet may be all you need to send. Larger requests require a detailed funding proposal.

Should you name a price? Definitely. You should ask for a specific sum of money that you feel is reasonable. That removes a lot of guesswork for the donor. It makes the expectation clear. The donor can and will cut down your price if they think it's too high. Once a donor contributed $600 more than requested because they thought the project was under-budgeted. It was.

How much money you can expect one corporation or foundation to contribute depends on the size of the corporation or foundation and its policies on contributions, the size of your group,

how well known and established you are, how popular your cause is, and the nature and popularity of the project you are trying to fund. For instance, in a capital campaign, you can ask for much larger gifts than you can for an operating budget.

Some companies and foundations give in dribs and drabs (from $50 to $500) to a lot of groups. Other companies have a policy of giving larger sums to fewer groups. A donation of from $1,000 to $5,000 from a large corporation to a project run by an innovative or controversial group with an annual budget of $300,000 would be about par. That's a big generalization, but it will give you some idea what to expect. In the United States, many of the larger consumer-oriented corporations have defined specific areas of interest for funding and will give larger sums in those areas.

Many of the larger companies will require the approval of their board of directors for larger donations. That means it will take longer to get a decision on your request because you have to wait for a board meeting. That's the general climate for corporate giving to innovative group projects.

b) Keeping track

Enter the date of your letter and the amount you requested in your log (see chapter 13). If you don't hear from the organization within three months, call the person you dealt with and see how your request is coming. One good way to check is to call and say, "I'm planning my cash-flow for the next few months and I was wondering if we can count on a donation from (name of organization)." They understand cash flow and will respond to it. If there is no decision yet, try to find out when they will make a decision, as this will indeed help you to plan cash flow. Note any new information in your log.

4. What To Do When a Check Arrives

When you are a fundraiser, you watch the mail like a hawk. On a good day you get a few checks or one big one. That same day you must write a nice letter or send an e-mail confirming that you have received the check in the amount of $____ and enclose their receipt. You can say a bit about the progress of the project they have funded and enclose copies of any recent news clippings about your group. If you send an e-mail initially to confirm receipt, it is probably best to follow up with a letter.

Don't let this duty slip or get behind on it. The funders need that receipt to keep their accounting up to date. It's best if they get your thank-you letter before they get their canceled check.

Stamp the back of the check with the name of your group and the words "for deposit only." Put the check in a safe place until you can get to the bank. Do this as soon as you record the check. Take the check to the bank as soon as possible. Checks, like scraps of paper with phone numbers, can get lost. They can also be stolen. It's very embarrassing to have to contact the company and have them cancel and reissue a check. Get into good habits about handling checks.

In Canada, you need to issue special tax credit receipts for donations. Businesses may not require you to issue a tax credit receipt, since they can deduct the donation as a promotional expense, whether or not your group is a registered charity. In fact, corporations never claim tax credits for half of all the receipts charities issue.

You need an original plus one copy for each Canadian tax receipt. If the donors live in Quebec, they need two copies of their tax receipts, one for their federal tax form and one for Quebec. The receipts will have your charitable registration number and will be numbered sequentially. If you make a mistake in filling out a receipt, don't destroy it, just cancel it. The auditor will want to see it to make sure you aren't writing out receipts for yourself.

5. What To Do When They Say No

If you are working hard, you will be getting "no" letters every other day. Don't tear up the "no" letter in anger and disgust. If you can't bear to read it closely, set it aside until later. It is important that you read these letters and learn from them.

Follow up on rejection. Corporations, foundations, and other organizational donors often turn down grant requests with a letter that says something like "Our funds are committed for this year." Too many groups interpret this as a permanent rejection.

They may be willing to give. Perhaps you applied too late. If you have received support from them in the past, they may have a policy that limits the number of years in a row in which they will donate to the same groups. Potential donors might welcome an application in future. Follow up any such letters with a note to ask if you should reapply, and, if so, at what time of year.

In turning down your request, a corporation might say something like —

- "Your group does not fall within our mandate." (Get lost.)

- "We would really like to give you some money but we simply don't have any more." (Come back next year.)

- "Your group looks interesting but we are not able to fund you at this time." (We are waiting to see if your group will survive. Try again next year, earlier in the year.)

Enter the "no" in your log and record it in your donations card file. Make a note of when you got a response. Since many companies make decisions on requests only once or twice a year, you don't want to miss the deadline next time.

Now sit down and write that company a letter. It may seem like an utter waste of time, but it's not. Sometimes you can find out why you were turned down without coming right out and asking. There must be no hint of sour grapes in this letter. You are just writing to say "Thank you for your consideration. . . . This is what our group is up to and we will keep you informed of our activities." Why should you do this? It is a courtesy. The company will remember you for it. Sometimes it can help you discover how that company regards your group. It can be worth its weight in information and rapport.

Don't let the "nos" depress you; they are part of a fundraiser's job. And don't give up on a source after one negative response. Unless you are clearly told to get lost, keep trying each year for three years before you give up. Keep that company, foundation, or organization on your mailing list to receive information such as announcements, annual reports, and newsletters.

6. The Old Buddy Route

Most of this chapter assumes that you, the fundraiser, are approaching the corporation yourself. You may have had a member of your board or fundraising team help you get your foot in the door, but once you're in, you're on your own.

Rather than taking this approach, more traditional groups tend to rely heavily on the "old buddy system" approach. In that method, members of the board recruit other members of the business community to assist with soliciting corporations and wealthy individuals. These volunteers then directly approach their peers, the corporate presidents and vice presidents, and seek a contribution for your group.

With the old buddy route, the fundraiser's job is very different. The fundraiser does a lot of the work but is always behind the scenes. The fundraiser helps to identify and recruit fundraising volunteers, coordinates their approaches, provides the brochures, drafts follow-up and thank-you letters, and makes sure the tax receipt is sent.

If your group uses this approach for some of its fundraising, or if you are in a position to try it, here are a few words of advice.

Don't overload your volunteers; if you do, you'll lose them. The rule of thumb is that each volunteer should be given no more than five prospects to solicit. If they do well with those and will take more, give them another five.

Offer them training in face-to-face fundraising. You can teach them how to do it and get them to organize their prospects in one four-hour session. It's a great morale booster too! See chapter 7 for an outline of a training session in face-to-face fundraising.

Be prepared to accept the judgment of your volunteer as to whether it is appropriate for him or her to approach a certain individual. If he or she doesn't feel comfortable about it, it won't work anyway. At the same time, you have to distinguish whether the volunteer is exercising good judgment or is just timid about asking. Nobody likes asking for money, and very few people find it easy.

Your volunteers are probably people of influence and affluence and, no doubt, very busy. Respect their time, use their time efficiently, and make it as easy as possible for them to do their end of the job.

Sometimes you will have fundraising volunteers who don't come through for you. They may put you off for months on end, promising and promising but never actually doing the job. Try a one-year rule: if a volunteer doesn't produce in the course of a year, look for a replacement.

The old buddy route for fundraising may not be acceptable or available to public interest groups. If your organization is in a position to use that approach, use your own judgment as to what would be acceptable and appropriate.

CHAPTER 7
FUNDRAISING IN SMALLER COMMUNITIES

Matching wits with corporate presidents and trying to convince them to fund you is fine for groups located in big cities. But what if you are based in a small town?

If you live outside the major centers and you serve primarily the local community, your fundraising strategy and approach will be quite different. In this case, your potential base of financial support includes wealthier individuals in the community, local branch plants of major companies, support industries, local small businesses, members, and local government.

As a fundraiser in a small community, educating community leaders about philanthropy is an important part of your job. Try to speak on the topic of philanthropy at a chamber of commerce or business club luncheon. Make a case for the importance of nonprofit groups, volunteerism, and giving. That investment of your time doesn't produce a quick return, but it usually pays off in the long run and it gives your group visibility.

1. Approaching Individuals

Begin by identifying noteworthy individuals in the community — people of influence or affluence — who might be sympathetic to your cause. If your issues or activities are very controversial, this may be difficult or impossible. But you should at least try to identify a few sympathetic influential people, and try to persuade them of the importance of your work. Like it or not, these people can affect not only your success in fundraising, but your success in fulfilling your mandate.

Smaller cities and towns tend to have a small and clearly defined local establishment: the smaller the community, the greater the control exerted by this group. If you are able to get the local establishment or members of it to support your group, you will have a much easier time finding money and getting your program established. In that case, the best way to proceed with your fundraising will be through the "old buddy route" described in chapter 6. Because smaller communities are so tightly knit, fundraising peer pressure is all the more effective.

Here are a few basic principles for raising money from wealthier individuals. First, recruit as many "fundraising volunteers" as you can. These people will themselves be wealthier, prominent, respected members of the local establishment. They may be members of your board, or they may be volunteers recruited by your board. It is important that these individuals contribute financially to your group because they are then in a much better position to invite their friends and associates to contribute.

In a small-town setting, a fundraising task force structure would be effective. Team meetings provide your volunteers with an opportunity to socialize and that makes their involvement more prestigious. If your fundraising volunteers end up competing with each other to see who can raise the most money, you're set! That won't happen if they never see each other.

Researching prominent families and individuals in the community will be your job. You need to identify those people who are capable of making a contribution in the dollar range you are seeking. Sources for your research include plaques on the walls thanking recent donors to hospitals, churches, community centers, colleges, recreation facilities, art galleries, park benches, tree planting, or any other past fundraising campaigns. These are people who are proven to be generous, and they are your best source.

Second best are people who are affluent, but may or may not be generous. To find them, research membership lists from golf clubs, country clubs, and the chamber of commerce, old-timers who know the life history of prominent families, and the local newspaper. The newspaper is a terrific source because in smaller towns a lot of the news is about people. You need to learn "who's who."

People who have moved away from the community are an excellent source of funding in many small towns. (Ken knows one man who sends an annual donation to the church his parents attended, even though he left town more than 50 years ago, and never goes to church himself.) They often feel warmly about the old place, especially if they have friends and family still living there. They may be willing to give even though they have not been in town for years and may have no intention of returning. This group includes younger people who have moved away to find work, seniors who left after they retired, and people who worked there for a while, such as teachers, doctors, nurses, clergy, and so on. Ask people in town to assemble a list of "exiles" who might be able and willing to donate. Contact them in person if you are traveling to their new town. A telephone call is second best. Mail is a distant third.

These people may need special cultivation to reawaken their old sentiments. Add them to your newsletter mailing list, invite them to visit if they are in town, and use all the other methods of cultivation.

When you seek major individual donations, try to get the largest contribution first. This is called "the pacesetting gift" in fundraising jargon. If you can secure it first, you will have peer pressure working for you. Others in the community will want to donate in like measure. It will take a lot of work to get that first large gift, but that single donation might amount from 5 percent to 10 percent of your total budget, so it's worth it.

Remember that face-to-face solicitation is the most effective method for raising money from individuals. Telephone solicitation is the next most effective, and letter writing comes in a slow third. It is very important that prospective donors be approached by someone they know. The better they know each other, the better your chances of success.

Nobody likes asking for money, and few people can build up the courage to do it often. For these reasons, you shouldn't expect your fundraising volunteers to solicit more than five prospects each, whether the prospects are individuals or corporations.

An important part of your job as a fundraiser is to build up the morale of your fundraising volunteers so that they are confident about going to meet their prospects. You also have to be prepared to take a leadership role with your volunteers and encourage them to come through for you. Otherwise you are wasting your time, and so are they.

It is essential that you recognize and honor both your volunteers and individual donors. Volunteer and donor recognition can range from a sincere, personal thank-you letter to a banquet honoring volunteers, to a hospice wing named after a generous donor. How you provide that all-important "thank you" really depends on what would be fitting for your group, your volunteers, and your donors. Just be sure you do it on time, in good taste, and at a low cost so donors don't feel their money is squandered.

Although this is written in the context of fundraising in a small community, the principles for soliciting individuals apply anywhere.

2. Training for Face-To-Face Fundraising

The following section outlines a two-hour training session to use with your board of directors, fundraising task force, or any other group you want to train in face-to-face solicitation. It teaches how to ask for money and uses role-playing to develop confidence through practice. The greatest barriers are people's fear of asking for money and their fear of failure. The training described here is also useful for door-to-door fundraising and telephone fundraising or telemarketing.

2.1 Introduction

Open the session with good news or a recent achievement of the organization. You might bring in a guest to talk about the importance of a new issue. Discuss positive news that will make the group feel motivated and involved. Reassure them that no names they choose to share will be pursued without their consent.

Next, explain the overall fundraising program and how much you expect to raise from each sector, including individuals. Your volunteers need to see how they fit into the overall plan. Point out that approaching individuals is the fastest, easiest, and least expensive way to raise money. More than 80 percent of all charitable dollars raised in Canada and the United States each year comes from individual donations. Stress the need for your organization to raise funds from individuals.

2.2 Methods of solicitation

Ask the participants to recall times when they have been approached for a donation and answer the following questions:

a) How were you approached?

b) By whom?

c) Where?

d) When?

e) Did you contribute?

f) Why?

Have the group discuss their responses to each question. From this, each person will recognize how he or she responded to different types of solicitation. Talk about the effectiveness of the various approaches. Face-to-face is most effective, followed by telephone and letter, but many people are initially uncomfortable with face-to-face solicitation. By the end of the training session, most people will feel more comfortable about it, but if not, ask them to use the method that they can handle best. Better this than to lose them as fundraisers.

Participants should consider their own financial commitment to the organization. It's easier to ask for money if you are supporting the group financially yourself.

2.3 Dealing with fear

Ask how many people feel reluctant or afraid to approach somebody for money. Tell them to take a few minutes to think about that privately and to write down what they are afraid might happen. Then facilitate a group discussion about these fears. Don't pressure anyone to reveal what he or she wrote. Approach this discussion with an attitude of understanding and respect, and stay away from guilt or put-downs.

Simply having your volunteers identify and articulate their fears will go a long way toward resolving those fears. Some more experienced group members may say they used to feel that way too, but once they started fundraising, they found their fears were groundless. The key is to help your volunteers work it through to a point where they are comfortable and ready to go. Once you get them talking honestly, it will be very clear what kind of support they need.

2.4 Three steps to approaching donors

Introduce your group to this three-step process in approaching potential donors: identify, inform, and involve.

a) Identify

Who would you think about approaching for money? The people most likely to give are current and past donors. Draw up this list:

i)   People who have made one or more unusually large donations.

ii) People whose total amount donated over the years is unusually high.

iii) People who have given much more frequently than most, even if their gifts are smaller. Include people who attend events.

iv) People whose total number of donations or length of time as a supporter over the years is unusually high, even if the total amount is not.

v)   People who give less than you think they could.

vi) People who give an odd amount of money, like $27 or $358. "An odd dollar amount," says Chicago fundraiser/author Joan Flanagan* "can be a clue the donor is allocating his or her total annual charity budget among several nonprofits. This suggests the donor plans his or her charitable giving and your group is already on the shortlist of good organizations."

vii) People with titles and degrees, if donors on your lists are professionals such as doctors, lawyers, dentists, university professors, or accountants. Also shortlist people who have important job titles at work, such as president, vice-president, or manager.

viii) People who live in upper-income neighborhoods. A second address for their winter or summer homes is a sign of potential.

ix) Supporters who are known to be affluent and/or celebrities. Scan your donor list for familiar names. Are there well-known people who have given you a donation — even a small one? Look for business leaders, authors, artists, athletes, and politicians — any sort of celebrity. You may not know all the names. It may help to have one or two knowledgeable friends go over the list with you, in strictest confidence. If time allows, check *Who's Who,* the *Directory of Directors,* or similar books. (See Appendix.)

Now you have your shortlist of top prospects. Ask your board and volunteers to go over this list. Their job is to find the five people whom they feel most confident in approaching.

If there are other people your board and volunteers think are better prospects, discuss them. If there are not five people on this list the volunteers feel good about approaching, brainstorm an additional list, possibly from their personal contacts.

---

*Joan Flanagan has written several excellent books, including *Successful Fundraising: A Complete Handbook for Volunteers And Professionals, The Successful Volunteer Organization,* and *The Grass Roots Fund Raising Book.*

Ask current or past board members, senior friends, and volunteers for donations. Even if your board members aren't wealthy, getting their financial support will impress other donors.

It's not enough for board members to give their time. Their financial contributions show leadership, even if the amounts are not large. Their gifts begin the campaign with success, proving their commitment.

It is reasonable to expect your organization's board members to give a bigger portion of their income to your organization than to any other (with the possible exception of their place of worship).

People who use your services are prime potential donors in most, but not all, cases. Watch your lists for any who are already donors or volunteers. This is essential for groups in the arts, where audience members or families of young musicians are among the best supporters.

It is also key for religious groups, sports, education, and many health organizations. Even those who help poor people may find that clients feel greater self-respect when invited to contribute toward the cost of services. However, this may be a very low priority for some groups.

Studies have shown that people with ordinary incomes and lifestyles have given major donations. Major donors are not only the super-wealthy or those with famous names. They do *not* even have to be what is commonly called rich.

The most generous donors to non-religious activities in Canada are most typically —

- age 30 or older,
- married, with children or have children who have left home,
- from two-income families,
- professional or managerial in occupation,
- earning $50,000 annual household income,
- university-educated,
- regular religious service attenders,

- donors to religious organizations,
- residents of Canada's prairie provinces,
- active in the community,
- members of at least two associations, and/or
- volunteers.

The two most important factors are religion and community involvement. The most generous donors to religious organizations are often —

- age 60 or older;
- married, aged 30 to 50, with children;
- married, aged 40+, with no children;
- single, age 50+, with no children;
- two-income families;
- professional or managerial in occupation;
- earning an annual personal income of $40,000+;
- university-educated;
- residents of Canada's Atlantic region;
- very religious;
- regular religious attenders;
- active in the community; and/or
- members of at least two organizations.*

Part of identifying donors is discovering your web of contacts. Only after exploring your contacts should you consider approaching strangers.

Build a cold list based on research. Discover promising strangers among the following:

i) *Donors to similar organizations.* Look in annual reports, programs at events, newsletters, and plaques.

ii) *Neighbors of community groups.* List owners and employees of nearby businesses by asking the Chamber of Commerce, City Hall, or business improvement councils. Find the more well-to-do residents from real estate agents, developers, and directories.

---

*This data is from "The National Survey of Giving, Volunteering and Participating," 2000 <www.nsgvp.org> and *Canada Gives: Individual Canadian's Attitudes Towards Charities*, by Allan Arlett, published by The Canadian Centre for Philanthropy, 1988.

iii) *People known for generosity.* Watch the news, *Who's Who*, and other directories. Check the lists of donors to political parties.

iv) *People who can't say no.* Who you know is important. Many prospects will give to a nonprofit group they do not support because of the person who asks them. Similarly, business people often give to a customer's favorite nonprofit group to get more business.

v) *People who can benefit.* Some people and businesses want public recognition. They may want to honor someone they love. Offer them benefits they cannot get otherwise.

Now you are ready to brainstorm with the board, volunteers, major donors, and staff. Kim Klein, publisher of the *Grassroots Fundraising Journal**, suggests asking everyone to check their personal and professional address books or card files and put a check mark beside the name of anyone who might share their interest in the nonprofit group. Finally, ask them to note how much they would be willing to ask for.

Ken's firm developed a webbing exercise that reveals your hidden network of connections: people you didn't know you knew. Get people to delve into themselves to uncover long-lost connections to people now in a position to provide help. Even when you do not have direct contacts with prospective major donors, you may know someone who knows someone. See the boxed text, "Webbing Exercise," for more information.

Webbing Exercise

Here's how to run your own webbing exercise:

1. Gather supplies.

You'll need lists of all your current donors (marked confidential) in alphabetical order and ranked from the largest donations to the smallest; lists of known donors to other nonprofits in your area, collected from nonprofits' annual reports and newsletters, programs from performing arts groups, and plaques on the walls of hospitals, schools, and community centers; *Who's Who, Directory of Directors,* and similar books; and phone books.

You should also have available large sticky notes — a stack for each participant; big marking pens — one for each participant; a meeting room large enough to hold up to 20 people around a table, with lots of empty wall space; and refreshments.

2. Invite people who know people, and who believe in your purpose.

Explain that you are asking for two or three hours of their time to help discover new contacts. Include board members; volunteers; staff; your top donors; and knowledgeable friends, such as business leaders, fundraisers from other nonprofits that are non-competitive, politicians, etc.

3. Explain how the webbing exercise works:

a) Everyone will be asked to come up with names of possible supporters (usually donors, but the webbing exercise can be used to find new volunteers too).

b) No one named will be contacted without the permission — and, ideally, the active participation — of the person who suggested the prospective supporter.

c) All names and information shared are confidential. No names are to be taken away to be used by other nonprofits. No gossip about people should be engaged in.

---

*www.chardonpress.com

d) Everyone should focus on possible donors with whom the participants have a personal contact. It is fine to suggest your nonprofit should ask Bill Gates to donate, but unless one of the people actually has a contact with Bill Gates or a Microsoft executive, this approach is not likely to be successful.

e) As participants think of the names of possible supporters, they should write them on the sticky notes with the large marking pen. They should neatly write only one name per sticky note, and write it large so it can be posted on a wall and read across the room. They should also put their own name on each sticky note so it is easier to connect people later.

f) Encourage participants to flip through the resource materials for ideas.

g) Encourage interruptions. If someone thinks of a name, he or she should get it out and on the list before it is forgotten.

h) Encourage lateral thinking. One person may suggest someone named Kim Low. That might remind someone else of Jean Kim. It does not matter how you get to the names, as long as you get useful names.

4. **Warm up to the webbing exercise by playing "Six Degrees of Separation."**

This game demonstrates that the group is better connected than it might think. For example, as part of the game, Ken will often ask if anyone in the group knows the pope. This does not mean they have seen him on TV, but that they have met him personally, and if they called the Vatican they might actually get to speak to the pope.

Surprisingly often there is one person in the room who does have a personal connection. If not, ask if anyone knows someone who knows the pope. If this gets blank stares, ask if they know someone who knows someone who knows the pope. By this time, a contact has usually been found, with only three degrees of separation. If no contact is found, ask the group how they could easily meet someone who can begin the connection. Point out that anyone can go and talk to a local Catholic priest, who will know the bishop, who knows the cardinal, who knows the pope.

Try it again asking if anyone knows the president of a major bank. If necessary, point out that they could walk into any branch, meet a bank teller, who will introduce them to the branch manager, who can make a contact with the regional manager, who knows the district supervisor, etc.

5. **Ask if anyone will start by suggesting possible major donors to your group.**

Remind them to write the names on the sticky notes, and put them on the wall. When they run out of ideas, move to the next level.

6. **Suggest connections that might start the group thinking.**

For example, tell them that the Canadian Customs and Revenue Agency (Canada's equivalent to the American Internal Revenue Service) analyzed the tax returns of everyone who paid taxes to find out what occupational group donated the most to charity. The group that gave the largest percentage of their taxable income to charity were accountants. Ask if anyone in the group knows an accountant. Most people will put their hands up. Ask if anyone knows, on a personal basis, an accountant who just might — if approached correctly — make a big donation to your nonprofit. A few people might put their hands up. Get them to write the names on their sticky notes and get them on the wall. The goal is simply to stimulate the participants' thinking.

Other occupations noted for giving are farmers, doctors, lawyers, and dentists. In each case, ask the participants if they know anyone in these occupations who might give a large contribution.

7. Use other connections to stimulate more names.

For example, religious people give more than those who do not take religion seriously. In addition, the older people are, the more they give. (People over 55 give five times more than people under 35.) Ask your participants to think of the older or religious people they know. Can they think of anyone who might give an unusually large amount?

Use the list below for more stimulus. The asterisk (*) indicates groups that research shows to be particularly generous:

- Accountants (self-employed)*
- Association members
- Banks*
- Big companies
- Clubs
- Colleagues
- Community leaders
- Dentists*
- Donors to other groups*
- Entertainment industry
- Farmers*
- Foundations
- Hospitality industry
- Land developers
- Local businesses
- Medicine
- Nurses
- Older people
- Politicians
- Places of worship
- Professions
- Real estate
- Retailers
- Service clubs
- Small business*
- Suppliers to your nonprofit group; companies where your board members work; other nonprofit group; others in your field
- University-educated*

- African Americans*
- Automotive industry
- Beverage industry
- Clients/customers of your nonprofit; companies you know; other people in your field
- Doctors*
- Donors to your group*
- Employers (past/present)
- Family
- Food distributors/producers
- Friends
- Insurance
- Law
- Media
- Neighbors
- Oil and gas
- People you met recently or long ago
- Pharmaceuticals
- Printing
- Publishing
- Religious people*
- Seniors*
- School friends
- Sports
- Textiles
- Transport
- Trust companies*
- Unions
- Volunteers*

8. Prioritize the list of names before the webbing session ends.

Ask people to look at all the names on the wall and choose —

- the ten who would give most quickly,
- the ten who would give the most,
- the ten who would be easiest to ask, and
- the ten who require and deserve cultivation over the long-term.

9. Verify your list quickly.

The next day, type up the complete list of all the names suggested and who suggested each one. Send the list to all the participants. Ask them to double-check spelling, add any information they can about the prospects, and confirm which prospects they would be willing to approach personally and which should be handled by someone else.

10. Prepare for the next steps

Now you must —

a) research the prospective donors;

b) warm up the relationship with the prospects;

c) decide what part of the nonprofit's projects would excite the prospect most;

d) estimate how much to ask the prospect to give, based on the prospect's past donations to your group (if any); known donations to other nonprofits; available information about their likely income range, life style and expenses; connections to your projects; and contacts with your team;

e) rehearse the way you'll ask;

f) prepare any documentation needed;

g) ask the prospect for support;

h) thank the prospect.

b) Inform

How could your participants inform the people on their list about your group? They might —

- pass on a newsletter or news clipping to them,
- invite them to an open house or special event, or
- mention involvement in a conversation.

Participants should write down one or more appropriate actions they could take to inform each of the five people they are responsible for cultivating and contacting.

c) Involve

How could your volunteers involve these people? The reaction volunteers receive to the informing step is the best clue. If people aren't interested, they should be left alone. If they are interested, asking them to contribute or asking them to volunteer is a logical next step.

2.5 Playing the role

Have participants form groups of four or five: a pair of fundraisers, a prospect (or two if they are playing the role of a couple or business partners), and an observer.

Ask them to improvise and act out a solicitation for 20 minutes. They should select an appropriate potential donor and act accordingly.

In preparation, ask them to think about —

- how the askers will open the visit;
- how they will encourage the donor to talk about the important issues;
- what part of the organization's work might interest this donor in particular;
- what other factors might motivate this particular donor, such as special recognition, appeals to their values or religious beliefs, emphasis on how the gift will help their business or strengthen the community, connections to their families' tradition of giving, an opportunity to give back in thanks for what they have received, or any other motivations;
- how they will bring up the subject of a donation;
- how much they will ask the donor to give;
- how they will deal with any tough questions;
- what signals the askers will use to silently communicate between themselves; and
- how they will close.

The askers should also consider where they will be when they ask for the contribution. The supporter's home is best for a personal or family donation. His or her office is a good site if you are approaching a business or foundation. Your nonprofit's facilities may be appropriate. Avoid restaurants, however. There are too many distractions and social graces to worry about, and deciding who pays is awkward. Also, avoid asking for money at parties. But if you do happen to meet a possible donor at a function, Joan Flanagan suggests that you make polite conversation, trying to listen and learn as much as possible about the prospect. The next day, send your prospect a brief letter — one paragraph on how much you enjoyed meeting him or her and one paragraph on how you would like to have an opportunity to tell more about your project. Include one recent clipping and one brochure. Send a copy of your letter to the host or hostess with your thanks for making the introduction.

When volunteers make an appointment to approach a real donor, they must say that they want to discuss their volunteer work and an exciting opportunity to help make something good happen. Don't pretend that it is a purely social call, hoping to sneak up on the subject. If the potential donor would refuse to see you knowing that this is a fundraising call, cultivate the relationship first. Don't rush.

In the meeting, after a small amount of socializing, participants should focus the discussion and carry it through without going off on major tangents. In their role-playing scenarios, volunteers should practice following these steps:

a) Mention the organization, their role in it, and some detail about why they became involved. They should let their feelings about the organization show; sincere emotion lends weight to words.

b) Ask the donors what they think about the issue that is most relevant to the organization's fundraising. By asking the right questions, the volunteers can help the donors to talk themselves into giving generously. The donors should do 70 percent of the talking. The fundraising team (volunteer and staff) should spend 10 percent of their time asking leading questions, and no more than 20 percent of their time trying to persuade the donor. Use open-ended questions that cannot be answered "yes" or "no."

c) Depending on what the donor says, selectively describe the organization, what it does, and why it is important. The asker should say what makes him or her proud to be involved.

d) Outline the group's budget and what parts of it need to be raised from individuals. Mention a specific project that meets the donors' interests, and explain how much needs to be raised.

e) Keep printed information handy to help respond to any request, but only offer it if asked, as printed materials can distract the donor and the asker from the discussion.

f) Ask the donor to help the organization by making a financial contribution.

g) Name a specific dollar amount or a range that they think is appropriate for their friend to donate. Ideally, tie this amount to the work it will fund.

h) Stop talking, smile, and wait for the donor to react. If he or she asks a question, answer it briefly, and then ask for the dollar amount again. If the donor is silent, wait. Give him or her time to think. Do not interrupt. In particular, do not "down sell" by saying, "If that's too much any amount you can give will be fine." A fundraiser from an Episcopalian school in Texas told Ken of his experience waiting nervously after asking a prospect for $10,000. The donor sat looking shell-shocked, and as the pause lengthened, the fundraiser was sure he had asked for too much. Just as he was about to back-peddle, the donor said, "You want $10,000? I ain't got but $7,000 on me right now. Can you wait 'til Monday for the rest?"

i) After the donor makes a commitment, sends the pledge form or writes the check, thank the donor, of course. Ask if the donor wants a receipt for tax purposes.

j) Thank the donor, and say how much this contribution will help the group.

After this role-playing enactment, have the observer and the prospect give the fundraiser feedback about what was effective and what wasn't. When the whole workshop regroups, initiate a discussion about what was effective and what wasn't. Ask what was hardest, and how they felt.

2.6 Action

Before the role playing, have each volunteer decide which five people he or she will approach, how, when, and where. These names should be put before the whole group so there will not be duplication. Set a date when the team will meet again to report its results. This will boost follow-through.

2.7 Follow-up

Call your volunteer fundraisers to see if they have approached their friends and how it went. Provide support and coaching. Praise the successful ones; encourage those who are shy or tardy.

3. Approaching Local Major Industry

Often smaller cities are dominated by one major industry, and this situation can cause problems for the fundraiser. There may be only a few companies that you can approach for a substantial donation.

If your local major corporations are subsidiaries or branches with head offices in a major center, you may face a second problem: the local industry may have a very small regional donations budget, or no budget at all. In some cases the local manager (or franchise owner) has authority to make small donations without requesting permission from head office. These are usually up to about $500. Bank branches, supermarkets, retail stores, restaurant franchises, and gas station chain outlets are just a few examples.

These may be part of a big business, but they want to have a hometown feeling.

The larger donations budget would be allocated by head office. It's also quite possible that the local general manager needs head office approval for donations over a few hundred dollars. On the other hand, there may be a growing tendency for industries to strengthen local donations budgets — companies become decentralized and make larger contributions in the "company" town. Certainly in head-office/branch-plant operations the management trend is toward greater local autonomy, and this applies throughout government and business.

Your first task is to approach the general manager and convince him or her of the importance of your group. If you have a business volunteer friend who can make this approach for you or with you, so much the better.

In your meeting, ask what the company's policy is regarding donations to local groups from both the regional budget and the head office budget. Try to persuade the general manager that it would be good public relations for the company to increase its donations budget in the communities where it operates. Give whatever support, ideas, and ammunition you can for getting more of the company's charitable dollars into your community. Unfortunately, in a national company, the head office budget is often allocated to national groups. In that case you will have to settle for what you can get from the regional budget.

If that's not the case, or if the general manager isn't entirely certain how it works, try to get him or her to work with you to approach head office for a contribution. Here's the best way to do this.

After you have met with the general manager, follow up with a two-page letter explaining what your group does, what you need the money for, how much you need, and why that particular company should contribute. Try to get the manager to make a commitment from the regional budget.

Ask the manager to forward your request together with a covering letter to head office. The covering letter should say why the manager thinks you are a good group, why head office should contribute, and how much they should give. In other words, you convince the local manager, he or she donates, and then convinces the head office to give also.

It may be that the general manager takes a very dim view of your group and has turned you down before. Should you try to approach head office directly? In most cases the answer is no, because the people at head office are going to be very, very reluctant to go over the head of the local manager on a local matter. In fact, head office might well send such a letter back to the general manager to draft a reply! Then the general manager will take an even dimmer view of your group.

Matching employee contributions is the other common technique for soliciting local major industries. For every dollar you raise from the company's employees, the company contributes the same amount or, perhaps, twice as much. Often such a plan is in place for well-established charities, but it won't automatically apply for your group.

To set up a matching employee contributions plan, approach the union leadership first, if there is a union. The union leadership will be much more effective than you in soliciting its membership and persuading management to match employee contributions. Once you persuade the union leadership to support you, try to get the company's agreement to match the funds. Get this before you solicit the union membership. The members will feel that their donation is accomplishing more if they know the company will match it.

4. Approaching Local Small Business

The industrial base in your community may consist of small industries and businesses. You may find plant managers and independent proprietors who have little or no experience with philanthropy. Outside of political contributions and a yearly gift to the United Way (if you have one), they may have never even been approached before. They won't have a specified donations budget, let alone funding committees, policies, and areas of interest.

To solicit local small business and industry, you could either use the old buddy route or try going yourself, which might work with the owners of small business because they are entrepreneurs and will admire initiative.

A lot of the corporate giving is done at the local level in the form of $200 to $500 donations. Cultivate this source because once you get on the list, it's renewable money.

5. Organizing Special Events

Charity art sales, auctions, swim-a-thons, raffles, concerts, fundraising dinners — all of these activities are fundraising special events. They tend to be popular methods of raising funds in smaller towns and cities. In some places, a special event is the only form of fundraising people know.

Special events can be effective for promoting your group, getting publicity, and broadening your volunteer base, but they are not always the most efficient method of fundraising. They are very labor intensive, require money to start, and can burn out your volunteers. Be clear about your own objectives and recognize special events for what they require and what they achieve. If your top priority is to raise money, your time might be better spent asking very generous individuals for large personal donations.

5.1 Be clear about your goal

Special events can have several different purposes. Choose one or at most two from this list — more than two purposes at one event can lead to confusion and disaster. The possibilities include —

- raise as much money as possible, after expenses
- get names and addresses of new supporters (either volunteers or donors)
- encourage current supporters to give more time or money (which includes thanking and recognizing them)
- raise your group's profile or build awareness with a target audience who will support you with time or money, or use your organization's services

5.2 Make sure you have enough people

To make any special event work, you need good people. You need people who are organizers and leaders, people who do all the different volunteer jobs, and people who come to the event and spend money.

5.3 Plan your finances carefully

Be certain you can afford to hold the event. Do you have enough investment funding? If you are having a concert or holding a dance, for example, you may need to pay out many of the expenses before you collect the income. If you don't have any "up front" money to spend, certain events will be impossible for you.

Before you decide to go ahead with a fundraising event, try to calculate how much money you will make from it. Figure out exactly what your expenses will be, then estimate how much money will come in from the event. Over-estimate expenses and under-estimate revenue to minimize nasty surprises. When you subtract your expenses from the revenues, you get net income.

For example, if you are holding a raffle, write down the names of all the people who will sell tickets and how many tickets each person will sell. Be realistic about ticket sales. Many people hate selling tickets and won't do it despite pep talks and the promise of rewards. Ask people if they really will sell tickets, and if they say 'no' or 'not many' believe them. On average, those willing to sell tickets will sell about ten tickets each. Try to get each person to agree to sell a certain number of tickets: give each person a quota, but don't fool yourself into believing they will sell more tickets than they will. Figure out the total number of tickets that will be sold, multiply that by your cost per ticket, and that will give you your total revenue. Then subtract your expenses and you will have your net income.

Some fundraising events generate more money for less work than others. You will only find out which methods are "most profitable" in your community by experimenting and keeping careful records. It's important to compare different events to see how much money you make for how much work. People like variety, so you may need to keep trying new kinds of events to keep people coming out.

5.4 Keep costs low

Sometimes you can't avoid expenses, but as a general principle, you should try to get everything you need donated. Give generous credit to donors in announcements made by the master of ceremonies during the event, in the program for the event, and on signs.

5.5 Hold several money-making activities at the same event

If you are showing a movie, you might try selling tickets for a raffle at the door and sell popcorn, drinks, cookies, T-shirts, and posters at a concession stand. If you are having a concert, you might have a break and hold a dance contest in which people pay to enter the contest and there is a prize. During a fundraising dinner, hold an auction. It takes a lot of work to get people to come out to an event, so once you have them out, give them many different ways to spend money!

If you want to sell T-shirts, posters, or buttons, remember economy of scale: the more you

have made up at one time, the less each one costs you. The lower your costs, the greater your profits. Therefore, if you can get a large quantity of T-shirts printed at once, it will be more profitable for you. You can continue to sell them after the event on other occasions and you can give them to volunteers as a way of saying "thank-you" or to visiting dignitaries as a way of helping them to remember your organization. But don't get more made than you feel sure you can sell or use wisely!

5.6 Pay attention to timing

You don't want your date to conflict with major sports events or other local attractions.

5.7 Types of events

The following is a list of ideas, tips, and warnings on how to successfully organize several common events. Many of the tips will apply to other types of events as well.

a) Film/video night

Get the free film rental catalogues offered by companies who rent films or unusual videos. Order your films several months ahead in case there are transportation problems. You don't want people to show up and find out that your film is lost in the mail. Planning early will also give you a lot of opportunity to promote the film on radio and put up posters. About a week before the film night, get someone to review the film on radio or TV. This will generate more interest.

When the film comes in, preview it. Run the film or video all the way through once to make sure that the technology is working and there are no tears in the film or (as has happened) pornography recorded over part of the video. Be sure to have an extra projector bulb on hand. Get somebody who knows a lot about the technology to act as your volunteer "projectionist."

Get volunteers to make popcorn, brownies, cookies, and get donations of juice or soft drinks to sell at the concession stand during intermission. Set the prices to make some profit. The concession stand can be a good money-maker, especially if you have good food and you are running a double feature!

Insure the film or video for its return journey: if it gets lost in transit, the dealer can charge you for the cost of a new copy.

b) Auction

Auctions may be the most lucrative type of event. They also require hard work, and they can fail. Before you decide to have an auction, check that people have things to donate. Make sure you have enough items to make a good auction.

Be imaginative about what you can sell. Crafts, pies, jams, and preserves can be auctioned. Besides selling material items and products, you could sell a ride on someone's boat or horse, a music or poetry lesson, a diet dinner, the first peek at a new baby, six weeks of yoga lessons — whatever you can think of and people will agree to donate.

Among the most lucrative objects to auction are fantasy items, the value of which is not restricted by marketplace costs. These include unique experiences, nostalgia, and/or celebrities. The following are examples:

- Dinner cooked by a volunteer fire fighter who has a talent in the kitchen, and served by a local celebrity, such as the mayor.

- A day of gardening by someone with a green thumb

- A ride in a hot air balloon, perhaps owned by a local brewery, pizzeria, or real estate company

- A week in a private cottage or cabin, a city apartment, or on a boat, donated by someone who will be away

Here are a few real-life examples of celebrity items that have raised money for charities:

- A walk-on part on "Seinfeld" fetched $15,000 at a rain-forest charity auction.

- Baseball player Pete Rose's good-behavior voucher from an Illinois minimum-security prison raised $770.

- The Toronto Humane Society's dinner and auction raised about $38,000, including items donated by actors Betty White, Elizabeth Taylor, and other celebrity animal lovers.

- Tony Blair and his wife, Cherie, auctioned photos of their new baby, Leo, taken by Mary McCartney, daughter of former Beatle Paul McCartney, to help British cancer charities.

Beware of art auctions, however. While they are sometimes lucrative, too many are disasters. If your audience members are not art-lovers, they may balk at paintings that don't match their living room furniture. Bargain-hunters may bid so low that the artists who donated the works are insulted and may even find the perceived value of their paintings is damaged in the wider market place. Even well-known artists have been frustrated with the results when they donated valuable works to inexperienced nonprofit auctions. Better to ask artists you know to contribute *experiences*, such as lunch at the artist's studio, a guided tour of a gallery, custom-made pottery, or a special sketch or portrait painted of the highest bidder.

Get a good auctioneer — somebody who is funny and not shy — who will give the audience a good time. Radio and TV personalities will often do this. Politicians are often good volunteer auctioneers, because they are used to both public speaking and fundraising.

Put starting prices on the larger or more valuable items, to make sure somebody doesn't buy a couch for fifty cents just because nobody else wants it. A "reserve bid" keeps items from selling too cheaply. For artwork, the artist may be offended if people appear not to value the art highly. But do not show the normal retail value of the item; this encourages bargain hunters to stop bidding below the retail price, which becomes the maximum bid.

Organize a dinner, or at least a food concession and bake sale to be held the day of the auction. Always charge at least a small admission fee to the auction. If people don't want to pay an entry fee, they are not the sort who will make your auction a success by bidding high.

Set the items out at least an hour ahead of auction time so that people have a chance to look at them up close before the sale starts. It's handy to do a list of the items and give each item a number and then sell them in order. A good description in a printed program sheet helps bidders understand what is being offered, especially for intangibles.

Delegate one team to write down who bought what for how much. Make a little card for each person's name, and when the time comes to pay, add up that person's card before he or she gets to the cashier.

Organize the cashier so that the line-up to pay at the end of the sale won't take long. Many people will want to pay by credit card for more expensive purchases. Set up your own credit card arrangements with a bank, or ask a friendly local business to run purchases through their system. Be sure to get a full mailing address and phone number for each person who attends, so you can approach them in the future for a straight donation.

Silent auctions can work as an addition to another special event such as a fundraising dinner, dance, or concert. Unlike a regular auction no auctioneer is necessary. However, silent auctions usually raise less money than an auction with the excitement generated by a skilled auctioneer. Use a silent auction if your event's agenda is already crowded or you have items to sell that will not fetch much money.

Display the items near the dining or dancing area. Put a pen and paper in front of each item and invite people to bid on the items by writing their names and the amount they are bidding. For example, Joe Smith writes his name and $50. Mary Jones then comes along and writes her name and $75 on the line under Joe's bid, and so on. Periodically throughout the evening, especially during breaks in a performance or between dinner and desert, the master of ceremonies for the event reminds people to put in a bid.

Establish one or more cut-off times for final bids. The MC gives everyone a last opportunity to bid before closing time. Around the end of the festivities, the winners are announced, everyone applauds each announcement, and everyone goes home happy — especially the group, which has supplemented the income it raised by charging admission to the event.

Online auctions are becoming popular, but are not always successful. For more details, read the story at <www.fundraising.co.uk/examples/events/auctions.html>.

c) Dance or concert

Get good entertainment. Some entertainers will donate their talents, but even then there are costs that your group must cover. In a small community, it may not be possible to attract famous groups to come and play because it might be too expensive, but if a few communities get together to book a tour by a band, and if the band is interested in seeing your part of the country, it might work out.

Consider adding a dance contest or at least a concession to your event to bring in more money.

d) The fundraising dinner

Fundraising dinners range from church-basement suppers, pancake breakfasts, and potluck dinners to black-tie events with prominent guest speakers at fancy restaurants or hotels. Dinners held at hotels, convention centers, or expensive restaurants are more likely to be held by groups based in large urban centers than grass-roots groups in small communities. To succeed in charging a fee large enough to justify the work and expense, the following tips may help.

Hold the event to celebrate a special anniversary, such as the 10th, 20th, or 25th anniversary of your group's existence. Everyone likes to celebrate a birthday, and people who may not be willing to pay $100 every year to attend a dinner will do it once every five or ten years to celebrate a special occasion. (However, groups that can attract a more affluent crowd may successfully mount an annual dinner.)

Offer several ticket prices. Nonprofit groups too often lower the admission price for an event to suit the poorest people. By all means, provide a few discount tickets to those who cannot afford more. Also offer premium ticket prices for those who can — and will — pay at stellar levels. Pricing begins by estimating your full costs for the event. The regular ticket price should be twice the cost per person to attend. That way you get to keep at least half the money you raise. Then offer bronze, silver, and gold tickets. For example, if your event costs $25 per person, ticket prices must be $50 if the event will be worth the work. A discount ticket might be $35. Premium tickets could range from $75 to $125. If more than 10 percent of the people attending buy the highest-price ticket, increase the top price next time.

What do people get for paying more? One or more of the following things:

- Nice warm feelings because they helped so much

- Bigger tax charitable credit

- Bragging rights that they are among the elite

- Their names prominently mentioned or displayed

- The opportunity to sit near the front, or at a specially decorated table

- Invitations to a special reception before or after the event, at which they might meet the guest of honor

- Photos of them with the guest of honor in your newsletter, and perhaps in the media, if you can arrange it

- Special loot bag of donated goodies from local businesses or crafts people

- Anything else you can dream up that does not cost you more money than it raises

You can also ask people to purchase a table. Instead of buying one ticket, a corporation, consulting firm, law firm, or accounting firm may buy a table for 6, 10, or 12 and send several of their members. Charge more for a company to buy a full table. For example, let's assume tickets are $100 each, and there are 10 seats at a table. Many nonprofit groups mistakenly assume the price for a table should be $100 times 10, which equals $1,000. Some groups even offer a volume discount. Instead, charge a premium, perhaps $1,200 for a full table. Prominently display the names of those who buy tables: put signs on their tables, a special mention in the program booklet, and/or signs on the walls. You may be surprised how many companies will happily pay extra for this.

Choose a guest of honor who is a powerful local businessperson. Many other business leaders will buy tickets to your event because they must be seen in the company of your guest to further their own financial interests. If there are no businesspeople you like well enough to honor, ask them if they will let you roast them with good-natured digs at their imperfections. The more powerful this guest is, the more successful your event. Beware of honoring people who are merely genuinely good but not powerful. Experience shows that not as many people buy tickets to events celebrating the saintly person. Nor are celebrities, politicians, clergy, teachers, health professionals, or retired business leaders a good substitute. Find a businessperson who has clout and connections, such as an investor, the head of a construction company, or the manager of the largest business in the area. This may seem cynical, but it works well.

Have a prominent and preferably entertaining as well as enlightening after-dinner speaker. He or she should be one who is familiar with your cause and can inspire people to get more involved with your group. Such a speaker will draw people who might not otherwise attend. Some nationally and internationally known celebrities charge high fees to give a motivational speech. Avoid them unless you are very confident you can raise enough money to pay the fee and still come out ahead financially. However, other prominent people, including some celebrities, will speak for free in support of a worthy cause.

e) The awards ceremony

Does anyone give awards for the kind of service your group provides to society? If not, perhaps you should create one and hold a ceremony to present the award to deserving individuals or groups.

The awards ceremony has fundraising advantages. It is likely that friends and colleagues of the person given the award or members of the group being honored will pay to attend; it is a recurring event rather than a one-shot idea; and it gives a focus to the evening. But an awards ceremony has benefits beyond the funds that can be raised by selling tickets to it. It provides an opportunity to recognize and support unsung heroes, educate the public about your cause, raise the profile of your organization, and attract media attention.

f) Conferences

Does your group deal with issues of such profile and urgency that people will pay to be educated about them? Is anyone else providing that education? If the answer to the first question is "Yes" and the answer to the second is "No," the time may be ripe for your group — perhaps in conjunction with kindred organizations — to organize a conference. You may be able to obtain grants to do so and also charge a substantial attendance fee — a financial double whammy!

If there is sufficient interest in the first conference and enough new developments each year, this can also become an annual event.

Like awards ceremonies, conferences also have spin-off benefits: publicity, public education, profile, and identification of potential allies and supporters. However, like concerts and many other special events, the risk of losing money is high. Planning a conference should be approached with caution.

g) The no-event event

Hold a non-event and invite people to stay at home! This tried-and-true technique is sometimes called a No-Tea Tea or a Dinnerless Dinner. *Warning:* This does not work if your people are party animals. However it is perfect if you have very few volunteers and/or your supporters are too busy to come to an event.

Tell people how much you save by not renting a hall, arranging catering, and hiring a band. All the money they give goes to good works.

Remind them how much they save by not hiring a baby-sitter, getting their hair done, buying party clothes, and paying for parking. Attach a tea bag (donated of course) to the ticket and encourage the donors to throw their own tea party.

You can send clever invitations announcing a non-reception, not to be held anywhere, followed by people not scheduled to perform. Send reply cards with a note like the following:

Gee, thanks for letting me stay home.

Here's my contribution to ensure that I will be invited NOT to attend again next year!

❑	$15	I will not attend.
❑	$25	Neither I nor my companion will attend.
❑	$50	No member of my family will attend.
❑	$100	I will keep the neighbor away.
❑	$250	I will keep my politician away.
❑	$———	I will have my own party and send you the proceeds.

CHAPTER 8
DIRECT MAIL

Before beginning any discussion of direct mail, please understand that this type of mail is directed to people in their homes for their personal donations. This is not the way to approach companies or foundations or any other organization for a donation. Occasionally a letter directed to an individual will result in a donation from a company or another institution — perhaps because the nonprofit group wrote to someone at their work address, or because someone received the letter at home and took it to work. That is not a problem. Most of the time, however, it is a bad idea to send direct mail letters, of the sort we describe here, to institutional donors, because they result in smaller donations than you might get by approaching them properly with a grant proposal.

With that warning, let's explore the world of direct mail — one of the most effective techniques nonprofit groups have to get support from large numbers of people. Despite concerns that there is too much mail, that it is bad for the environment, that it invades peoples' privacy, direct mail remains a reliable part of most fundraising plans.

To successfully solicit funds from individuals by sending them a letter in the mail, you require a strategy, a mailing list, a package, and some money.

Think through your direct mail campaign very carefully before you launch it. Figure out the cost of the mailing, and the percentage of success required to break even and to make a profit. Direct mail has become extremely popular, and many seasoned fundraisers feel the market is becoming saturated. However, if the package is good and the issue and timing are right, direct mail still boasts a good enough response rate to make it worth considering.

However, direct mail has become harder in the last few years. More people are throwing mail away without opening the envelope. Costs are rising and response rates are plummeting. It can still be effective, but a few of the rules have changed. More than ever, a nonprofit has to know what works and what doesn't.

1. Strategy

It is best to use a direct mail campaign for a specific issue that is high profile, easily understood by the general public, and compelling. A "cold letter" (a letter to an individual you have never contacted before), asking for a contribution to your operating expenses is boring, and will quickly land in the garbage. However, a letter asking for money to house the homeless, protect abused children, or save a scenic gorge is something everybody can relate to. In other words, emotional issues with broad appeal or high-profile political issues — issues most people are aware of or affected by — are most likely to bring in direct mail money.

Direct mail has an annual cycle: your campaign has a better chance at certain times of the year. Summertime is generally poor because people are on holiday. September to November is the best time, and February to May is the next best time to do your campaign. Late August can be effective for groups with a "back-to-school" theme. Mailings a month or two before Christmas will usually do very well.

2. The Mailing List

Once you have focused on an issue that has the right characteristics, you have to identify a target group that is sensitive to this issue and that can afford to contribute.

If you wanted to raise money for an inner-city playground, you might want to focus on parents and teachers. When you have your target group, you will know what kind of mailing list you want and can begin to look for a list or lists that will serve your need. For the example above, you might try to get a home and school association list, a teachers' federation list, or rent the list from a children's magazine.

It is common and accepted practice for groups to exchange their mailing lists for a one-time use. Although it may sound suspicious at first, experience has shown that both groups keep their existing donors and gain new ones this way. However, if you sell your mailing list for commercial use, you will likely incur anger and possibly extremely negative publicity. In addition, if you trade your mailing list to numerous other groups, people on your list may soon turn against your organization as well as similar groups that are bombarding them with requests for money.

Is It OK to Exchange Mailing Lists?

by Ken Wyman © Ken Wyman & Associates Inc., Toronto 2002

Concerns about trading lists range from ethical issues on invasion of privacy to pragmatic concerns that donors will be angry. There are solutions to these problems.

Fear 1: Other groups will use our list over and over forever

The norm is to exchange mailing lists for a single use only, not for repeat mailings. This is called "one-time, reciprocal-use only." You don't want your list used again unless you find the other group's list useful to you and you agree to a second trade.

This is not only a good ethical practice, it also makes good sense. You want a fresh list each time. Organizations constantly update their lists as people move and add new supporters. In fact, there is about 25 percent turnover on a list each year, on average.

Fear 2: There is no way to prevent rip-offs

Build an "alarm system" into your list so you can detect any unauthorized uses. This requires no special skills or computer tricks. It is completely foolproof.

To protect your list, simply add a few false names at several addresses where you will be sure to receive mail. Whenever other groups use your list, you will receive their letter.

Tell any groups with access to your list that you have the system in place. Encourage them to add false names to their own lists, too, so they can be sure you will not steal from them.

Although this method does not fully prevent abuse, it does enable you to catch any offender, and that knowledge can be a powerful deterrent. Violators can be cut off from any future list trades, which will have a serious effect on their mailings. You might also sue them for breach of contract.

List thefts are quite rare, and these precautions are an excellent form of crime prevention.

Fear 3: Donors object to trading

Before you trade your donor list, inform your donors that you will be doing so. Allow those who may object to have their names removed from the trading list. This is called opting-out. Here's how it's done.

In a normal mailing, such as for a newsletter or a fundraising appeal, include a note on a reply device with wording similar to this:

> ***Mailing list preference survey:*** Occasionally, on a very selective basis, supporters' names are exchanged with organizations that might interest you. This is the most effective way to find more supporters for [describe the cause here, not the organization's name].
>
> *Your confidentiality is respected — only names and addresses are shared. A professional mail service handles the letters. The list cannot be used for any other purpose. Although we screen the groups carefully, we feel the decision about receiving their information should be yours. If for any reason you don't want to receive information about these groups, please let us know.*

In most organizations, from 2 percent to 15 percent of donors request not to be traded. Put a simple code beside their names on the mailing list. Omit them from any trades.

Repeat the message at least annually, to be sure everyone has seen it.

If a donor later objects that his or her name has been traded, apologize. Note that they must not have seen the survey. Immediately offer to add their name to the no-trade list.

Fear 4: Donors hate all junk mail

Although there is growing anger over "junk mail," some people actually enjoy it. It keeps them in touch with new developments and provides opportunities for new contacts.

Some people resent receiving junk mail and let you know it. Explain that it is an effective way to reach and educate people and to raise funds. It's far less wasteful for nonprofits to attract donors through the mail than through advertising in newspapers, magazines, radio, or TV.

Inform people of the "Do Not Mail/Do Not Call Service" run by the Direct Marketing Association (www.dmaconsumers.org/consumerassistance.html) or the Canadian Marketing Association (www.the-cma.org). This allows people to specify types of mail they don't want to receive. They can even request more of what they do like, such as seed catalogues or information for new parents.

Fear 5: List trading is an invasion of privacy

Never exchange any information about the donors except name and address. No one else needs to know how much they have given, how recently, what their favorite causes are, or any similar information.

The group to which you've traded your list seldom even sees who is on it. A neutral third party handles the mailing in most cases — usually a professional mailing house that applies the labels to the mail. The only people added to the other group's mailing list are those who choose to respond to their appeal.

Donors don't belong to you. They give to others, subscribe to magazines, have a phone, and so on. You can't protect their privacy.

If you don't trade, only one thing happens. You prevent your own mailings from reaching potential supporters in the most efficient manner possible. Your donor will still receive appeals from other organizations. If they are ready to leave you for another group, they'll go whether you trade or not.

If you have to rent lists instead of trading, it will cost you two to five times as much to find the same donors. Exchanging lists is the best way for you to attract more donors.

Fear 6: We'll lose our supporters to the groups with which we trade

When two nonprofits swap lists, both gain new supporters in most cases. The majority of people provide financial support for a wide variety of causes. Your donors are probably already on multiple lists, and you can't hide them from exposure to others. If their interest in your cause is waning, you'll probably lose them anyway.

If they like both nonprofit groups, they will give to both. You are not competing for a portion of fixed budget. Few people plan their giving. Most make spontaneous decisions about to whom they will give and how much. Only 17 percent of people set up a donation budget, according to the Canadian Centre for Philanthropy Decima Research Study. The remaining 83 percent have no set limits. Interestingly, the study found that 63 percent of people budget for other expenditures, such as groceries, clothes, and vacations.

Fear 7: We don't have any/enough names to trade

Even if you don't have any names to trade, you may be able to scrounge lists from other nonprofits. Sympathetic groups may share lists with you because they want to support your work. They also might loan lists on the condition that you reciprocate later. Some will expect nothing in return for this. Others will advance names "on credit" to be repaid when your own list has grown.

In difficult cases, you may even offer to pay "interest" by returning more names than you get. For example, for use of a list today, you might offer 25 percent or 50 percent more donors a year later.

Fear 8: Trading lists might endanger supporters of controversial causes by revealing their identities

Some groups fear that revealing the identities of people on their list will cause problems for their supporters or members. Advocacy groups, political organizations and those involved in controversial subjects such as alcoholism, AIDS, or abortion share this sensitivity. They are concerned about persecution, and sometimes the harassment is real and deadly.

There are certainly circumstances where trading would be unwise. Some lists should be kept confidential, even internally, lest they create problems. For example, a battered women's shelter should not send appeals to their clients, even in a plain brown wrapper. Most groups' lists are not that sensitive, however. The precautions recommended above are sufficient to protect people from accidental disclosure.

In extreme cases, groups suspect the involvement of a determined and professional counter-intelligence-style opposition. If that is the case, those who want your list will likely use other methods to gain access to your it, if they want it badly enough. Trades may be one of the less probable methods.

Be duly cautious. Avoid over-protectiveness.

Exchanging Mail Lists Saves Thouand

Exchanges are six times more efficient than rentals.

So, they waste only 1/6th of the trees and money that rentals do.

To raise $1,000:

Assuming the average gift is $25, You'd need 40 gifts.

Source of List	Reply Rate	# of Letters Needed	Cost Per Package	Cost Per Name	Total Cost	Gross Income	Net Profit (Loss)
Rental	1%	4,000	60 cents	10 cents	$2,800	$1,000	($1,800)
Exchange	5%	800	60 cents	NIL	$480	$1,000	$520
Savings							**$2,320**

If you do exchange lists, put all the details of your agreement with the other group in writing, including their agreement not to give your list to anyone else, because any misunderstanding about the use of another group's mailing list is hard to overcome after the fact.

In large cities, you can also rent lists from direct mail brokers who make it their business to keep and build lists that are very specific. This increases the cost of your campaign because renting a mailing list will cost anywhere from $75 to $150 per thousand names, depending on the list. You can find companies that rent lists by contacting the Direct Marketing Association <www.the-dma.org> in the United States, or the Canadian Marketing Association <www.the-cma.org>. You can also search the Internet for "mailing list brokers." Ken's favorite is Stephen Thomas Lists and Data Services in Toronto <www.stephenthomas.ca>.

Here's how to build your own mailing lists:

- If you have a special event, get the names of everybody who buys tickets and everybody who attends (please note these two groups may not completely overlap). One of the best ways to get names is to offer a free draw, as people will print their names and addresses neatly if they have a chance of winning a nice (donated) prize.

- If your organization has a facility where people come and go, such as a public building, a park, or a pool, hold a free draw. Give people a place to deposit their business cards or fill in a form to enter a contest. This is the same as many restaurants that have a box or a bowl near the door offering a free meal for the lucky winner.

- When you attend a conference, get the conference mailing list.

- When you are invited to speak to a gathering of people, you might be able to circulate an attendance record. Ask people to write their names, addresses, and phone numbers and state their special interests and whether they would like to receive more information on your group.

- When people phone or write to you for information or order a publication, get their names and addresses.

Since these people have already been exposed to your group, you have a better chance of getting money from them.

Sometimes, established nonprofit groups in your field will send out your fundraising letter with their regular mailing to their membership. This is called "piggy-backing" your mailing. There is a limit on how often an established group can do this as they don't want to exploit their membership. For a very special issue or an emergency, you might try approaching a group with a large membership for this favor. While it does save money, it can dilute the response both groups get, as people decide which is the most important to them at the moment. Piggy-backing can be effective when it is noncompetitive. For example, utility companies (gas, oil, electric, water, and telephone) have included messages from a nonprofit group in their bills and newsletters, asking for donations.

3. The Package

The package is what you put in the mail. There must be four key pieces with an optional fifth part:

a) Interesting exterior envelope

b) Self-addressed postage-paid reply envelope

c) Reply card

d) Letter

e) Optional: Other background material, such as a brochure, fact sheet, newsletter, a pen or something else that adds thickness, address labels, greeting cards, and so on.

3.1 Exterior envelope

The outside envelope may be the single most important part of the package. If people throw the package away without opening the envelope, it does not matter if your letter is sincere or brilliant, as people won't see it. Here are some tips that apply to letters to individual supporters in their homes, not to organizational donors in their offices.

The envelopes that are opened most rapidly have a real, live stamp, not a printed permit or a postage meter. Special commemorative stamps are better than the regular ones. Unfortunately, these cost more and are more difficult to apply by machine, so many organizations can't do this except for small mailings to their most important individual donors.

A hand-written address is also more personal, and more likely to be opened. Again, this is possible only for small quantities. Second best is an envelope with the donor's name and address typed (or laser printed) right on the envelope. For large volumes, most organizations settle for a window envelope with the donor's name and address on the reply card — this makes it easy for them to reply, and you can be sure that the name and address match your original list. Avoid sticking a mailing label on the exterior envelope. This not only looks like junk mail, it lacks the convenience.

The great debate is whether or not to add a "teaser." This is a phrase or artwork designed to capture the reader's interest. Sometimes a completely blank envelope will work, but usually people balance their curiosity about the contents with their anger at too many solicitations. If your cause is popular, the name of your group may be enough. If you have the support of a celebrity, his or her name and/or photo may do the job, or it might look like another sweepstakes. If you work with kids, their artwork may work well. A few words that ask an intriguing question or state a startling fact might work well.

However, avoid at all costs the kind of misleading "teasers" that some direct mail marketers use, such as words that imply that the receiver has won a prize, that this is an official government document, or that make it look like there is a check in the envelope when there is not. Certainly these methods will ensure that people open the envelope to find out what is inside, but no matter how badly you need money, it is unethical to use trickery.

Whatever your solution, work hard on the envelope; don't just leave it to the last moment as an afterthought. Make sure the envelope and the letter are consistent. Test a few to find which style works best for you.

3.2 The reply envelope

It's always a good idea to enclose a self-addressed, business reply envelope. The return envelope makes it that much easier for the donor to drop a check in the mail. The extra work and expense of a business reply envelope will be repaid with a higher return on your mailing.

Business reply envelopes that are postage-paid are expensive, but not as expensive as you may think. It generally increases the reply rate and the average donation, so it is a good investment. One common practice is to provide the reply envelope and let your donor pay the postage. However, this does not produce such good results. Many people cannot quickly find a stamp at home, and by the time they do, their commitment to write your cause a big check may have cooled. Contact the post office for information on postage-paid envelopes.

If you decide to use postage-paid envelopes and you are doing a large enough mailing, you can apply for a business reply mail number from the post office. It may take a few weeks to get

one, so don't wait until the last minute to apply. With a reply mail number, you don't have to waste money on stamps: you will be charged postage for only the reply envelopes that are used by donors. Both the Canadian and American postal systems have business reply mail numbers, but these numbers cannot be used for a mailing that is going out of the country, and there are other requirements. The post office is the best source of information on this.

Go to a printer and have envelopes printed with your address and the business reply mail number. Make sure that these reply envelopes fit inside the envelopes you will be using for sending out the whole package. Get extra ones printed at the same time. The cost of printing envelopes drops rapidly with volume.

You can use the extras in future mailings. Tuck them into newsletters, annual reports, and brochures. The more you hand out, the more money you will raise.

3.3 The reply card

The reply card gives the donor the opportunity to write on something saying, "I have contributed." In the trade, this is called "interactive marketing."

Keep track of your responses by coding the reply card. For example, if you were doing an experimental direct mail campaign for an environmental group, you might use 1,000 names from each of five lists (perhaps hikers, bird watchers, dog lovers, bicycle enthusiasts, and health food store customers). To find out which is best, code your reply cards 001, 002, 003, 004, and 005 for each list, then analyze the incoming mail to decide where to focus your next campaign.

The reply card also lets you ask for a specific dollar range of contribution. The choices can range from $25 to $500 and include an "other" category. You can also ask one or two survey-type questions or promote a product on the reply card, but don't overdo it. For one example of a reply card, see Sample 10.

SAMPLE 10
REPLY CARD

STOP THE CRIES OF TORTURE...

I want to help save the lives of men, women, and children detained in prison, tortured, or executed because of their political or religious beliefs.

I'm enclosing my tax creditable donation of:

❏ $25 ❏ $35 ❏ $50 ❏ $100 ❏ $150 ❏ Other $ _____

In addition to my financial contribution, please send me information about membership in AI. ❏

AI occasionally exchanges names of supporters with other non-profit organizations. If you do not wish to receive information from groups other than AI, please indicate here: ❏

Amnesty International 214 Montreal Road, 4th Floor, Ottawa, Ontario, K1L 1A4

3.4 The letter

This must be one of the best letters you write. Tell an exciting human-interest story that will engage people's hearts. Speak directly and personally to the reader, as if you were writing a one-to-one personal letter. Provide a clear and simple description of what you want to use the money for. If the donor has not supported your work before, or if it has been more than a few months since you were in touch last, a background paragraph or two on your group are required.

The letter should be two pages, or even four or more. Contrary to common belief, a one-page letter does not raise more money — it almost always raises less. While people protest that they are too busy to read long letters, the real issue is not length but interest. People will skip over a five-word newspaper headline if they are not interested but will stay up late reading a 300-page book that they just can't put down. We are not suggesting a 300-page letter, but do take two pages or four pages or even more to tell a great

story, not just a set of cut and dried facts. At the end of your letter ask for the donor's support — and do not be afraid to talk about money. You might say: "If you contribute $52.37, that will help preserve another dead elm tree and the baby woodpeckers that make it their home. Of course, anything you can contribute will help and will be appreciated."

When you are using figures in a letter, odd numbers, such as $52.37 emphasize the real costs of achieving the goal — not just a round number. This results in more people giving. If you are using a round number, the amount looks like less if you don't use the cents column. At first glance "$50.00" looks larger and therefore more intimidating than "$50" does.

Make your letter as personal as possible. If the person has donated to you before, or you are asking for a big donation, the donor's name should be added by computer using mail-merge. Using your computer to full advantage, you would do well to add a phrase like this: "Thank you again for your last donation of $[amount] which arrived on [date]. Because the bulldozers are about to plow into the Dead Elm Forest right in the middle of the woodpeckers' nesting season, preserving more trees has never been more urgent. Could you donate $[amount] again or even stretch yourself to donate $[amount times two]? The birds, like little Woody, Tweety, and Conrad, will thank you with their every chirp."

Software with a mail-merge function is common on most computers these days. Personalization is not usually economically justifiable for mailings of several thousand, but that may change as the cost of computer work continues to go down and the cost of postage increases. The donor's name can even be written in by hand if you are sending a small mailing.

The letter should be signed personally in a small mailing, or a famous person who supports your group can sign it.

Sample 11 is an example of a simple yet effective direct mail letter.

3.5 Other background material

Beyond the letter, reply form, and reply envelope, use other enclosures with caution. Such items can increase or decrease responses and donations, and only by testing your package will you know how it performs. Packages can include —

- brochures,
- newspaper clippings,
- lift letters (mini-note with an extra message),
- endorsements from clients or professionals,
- maps,
- photos,
- stickers,
- seeds (e.g., Forget-me-nots), and
- free admission passes.

4. Cost-Benefit Analysis

In Canada, a 0.5 percent response rate* is normal for a prospect mailing to acquire new donors. A 1 percent response is good, 2 percent or 3 percent is very good, and more than 3 percent is fantastic. That is the rule of thumb, but it varies according to the strength of your strategy, your list, your package, and the locale. It also depends, of course, on the dollar amount of the donations from the respondents. If you get a 3 percent response but the checks are small, you might lose money.

Given the costs involved, donor acquisition mailings generally just break even. The pay-off comes when the newly acquired donors give again, and again, and again. *Repeat* donors should produce a 20 percent response rate.

When you plan your fundraising campaign budget, plan to break even financially with a small response on a donor acquisition mailing. By breaking even, we mean recovering the actual cost of the mailing, not including labor. If your organization is on a tight budget, you should use volunteer labor to stuff envelopes.

In the United States, the direct mail situation is quite different. Some groups feel that the market is saturated and say it takes two years to begin to break even with "prospect mailings" (the mailings with which you try to capture new donors). For the first two years, you have to re-invest all the income in the direct mail program itself. If you are thinking about getting into direct mail, assess it carefully, and consider it a long-term proposition.

Certain categories of tax-exempt US groups get subsidized postage rates for second and third class mail. Inquire about a third-class nonprofit mailing permit at your local post office.

Canadian postage rates offer a complex array of discounts depending on the number of pieces you mail, the size of the envelope, the weight of each unit, the postal-code order in which you sort

---

*"Response rate" means the number of people who reply, not including letters returned because of bad addresses or complaints from people who do not want to be on your mailing list. To calculate your response rate, divide the number of replies by the number of letters you mailed out. For example, if you mail out 5,732 letters, and get 29 replies, your response rate is 0.51 percent (29/5732).

SAMPLE 11
DIRECT MAIL LETTER

**Fred Victor
Centre**
145 Queen St. E. Toronto, ON M5A 1S1
Tel: (416) 364-8228 Fax: (416) 364-4728

> Feeling hopeless about homeless people, panhandling, and wel-
> fare? That was once MY life - and I know one very good way to
> break the cycle.
>   - Frank O'Dea, Co-founder of The Second Cup coffee chain

April 16, 1999

Dear Friend

Maybe you gave me your spare change a few years ago. Back
then, I was a homeless person trying to bum the price of a jug
with my buddies.

Or, considering what I looked and smelled like, maybe you
walked by sadly. Nobody'd blame you if you did.

Who knew I could or would straighten out?

That I would go on to start The Second Cup coffee chain and
several other successful businesses. In those days, you'd never
have believed it possible.

October 23rd was the date my life changed 1971.

1999? More homeless people than ever are hurting. You see
them everywhere in Toronto. Street corners. Heating vents.
Park benches.

But today there is a much better way to help break the cycle

An organization you've heard of before has completely re-in-
vented itself, and the results are exciting!

People have trusted the Fred Victor Mission for over 100 years.
Generous people trusted it with their donations. Frightened people trusted it with their lives. They all made the right decision.

You may have warm memories of tuning in to their radio
broadcasts. The "Mission of the Air" with Harry 'Red' Foster and
the Reverend Wesley Hunnisett ran for 30 years. In those days,
soup and salvation was the theme.

They would have loved to see what the Fred Victor Centre has
become. You would too:

(over, please)

2

Soup? Anyone can still get a hot, tasty bowl-full. Welcome to the "Friends Restaurant!" Now they dish out pride with the other nutritious elements.

Homeless people worried over how to make a little money stretch to last all month long. They invented a system that would help, and the staff listened. People - community members, they call themselves here - can pay in advance, and know that they'll have nourishment even if their money is stolen or lost.

And for those flat-broke, a meal ticket credit system allows up to $5 credit. That's enough for a couple or three meals. When they pay that back, they can get more credit - and most people do pay it back. Dignity. Self-reliance.

Help getting a job is on the menu, too. Julie is just one of the community members who had a break-through thanks to the Fred Victor Centre.

"I was out of the full-time work force for six years, and at the end of my rope," Julie says.

Thanks to a program at the centre, she got six months of job training, five-days-a-week, 8-hours-a-day. Then she started sending out resumes. Over one hundred of them!"

Julie was hired full-time by one of the largest stock broker companies in Canada.

So many ways to get people out of the cycle of poverty and despair. Long-term supportive housing where people can actually get their lives together. This is a big change from a temporary hostel bed for the night. I slept in places where I had to tie my shoes to my feet so they wouldn't be stolen.

I wish programs like this had been available when I was living on the street - maybe some of my old buddies would have survived. Here's a perfect example:

After living on the street and panhandling, Ron moved in to Fred Victor's Keith Whitney Homes.

(next page please

3 –

"After moving in I became involved in helping put together an Emergency Services Handbook for the housing committee," Ron said. "This got me interested in the Fred Victor Computer Centre, where I became a volunteer shift manager."

"This new interest in computers gave me ideas, too, like writing and printing cookbooks."

If it weren't for the facilities here, I'd probably be back on the street and down in the dumps. I'm grateful to the people there for giving me the opportunities I needed to get me back on my feet."

Isn't it great to see an old reliable institution with such fresh, practical ideas?

This really works

Now you know this leads to asking you for your charitable donation. But I don't want to go back to the old days begging you for spare change.

As a business person, I've learned a good investment when I see one. Fred Victor Centre will give you tremendous 'return on investment'.

Measure it in lives changed. In a city you can be proud to call home. In the satisfaction of continuing a century of good work in a new way.

Real change instead of spare change   Here's how you can help

Send $103 if you can, to mark the number of years Fred Victor Centre has been helping people in need.

Send $30, to commemorate the radio years

Send $28 for the 28 years since I turned my life around. You'll make it possible for others to do the same.

Send $15 for a week of meals for a hungry woman or man at the Friends Restaurant.

Give an amount that is meaningful to you. Perhaps a dollar for each year you've lived?

over, please)

- 4

Give more if you can, or give less. In fact, if you would like to hear more about this wonderful story but can't afford to give, just let us know.

You even have the choice of receiving a little extra something in appreciation for your generous support.

If you can give $125 or more, you have the option to receive a wonderful hard cover book "From Charity to Social Justice" with a foreword by Bruce McLeod. Would this provide the perfect present for someone you love?

You can receive the soft cover version of the same fascinating 176-page book if you give over $75.

And every donor will receive that warm feeling in the heart that comes from only one place. Because you know you have done the right thing.

Please make your donation today. Government fiscal restraints mean more people than ever are coming through the doors at Jarvis and Queen. It is urgent.

Just check off the amount you'll give on the reply form, and send it back with your donation. You can even donate by credit card for convenience. Use the postage-paid envelope enclosed, to make it easy. Please, do it now.

And if you were one of the people who long ago helped me when I was on the street, or someone like me, I hope it's not too late to say "thank you." You may have saved my life.

Bless you.

Frank of O'Dea

Frank O'Dea
Co-founder of The Second Cup, Proshred and other companies, and former street person.

P.S. A glance at the news. A short walk almost anywhere down-town. The chill of a winter night. It takes little to let you know people need your help. The work of the Fred Victor Centre is all it takes to let you know there is still real cause for hope. Please give as generously as you can today.

the envelopes, and where you drop off the mailing. Unfortunately there is no discount for charities. Consult one of Canada Post's special direct mail representatives for assistance.

The cost-benefit analysis is different for mailing to people who have already given you a donation at least once. This is much more effective than the donor acquisition mailings discussed above; otherwise, there would be no point in doing donor acquisition in the first place. For every hundred you mail out, you should expect at least 20 to 40 donations. If the letter is very exciting, you might even get 60 replies. However, that still means from 40 percent to 80 percent of your proven supporters have not sent a contribution.

To get more of them to give, ask more often. You may have just reached them on a bad day. Another mailing might reach them when they feel generous. Good mailing campaigns go to proven donors much more than once a year. Send fundraising requests at least three or four times a year. Write more often if your cause deals with a situation that changes rapidly, or if your group handles many different issues, or if your organization really needs money urgently. Many groups successfully mail seven to twelve times a year.

Some donors, inevitably, request that you send them letters only once a year. Most donors need several reminders just to give once. Many will give more than once a year, if you catch their interest.

Within two or three weeks of sending a mailing, you will know how successful you have been. If nothing arrives in the first three weeks, your mailing has been unsuccessful. About 50 percent of the total response will come in during those first three weeks. After that, a few checks may dribble in slowly.

You can increase your return by doing telephone follow-up to those in your locale who have not responded. A simple call from a volunteer saying, "Did you receive our letter?" or "Can we count on your contribution?" will improve your return. (See the next chapter.)

5. Summary

Direct mail can be a very effective fundraising tool when used by the right group for the right issue. When you have to raise funds for an emergency such as a court case, or you need money to repay a deficit, direct mail can play an important role. It is, however, expensive in materials and labor. It is also a high-risk form of fundraising because the initial investment is high. Be sure you have thought it all through before you make the investment. To be successful, direct mail requires a special savvy — knowing who your target group is, what turns them on, and how to motivate them to reach into their pocketbooks. Direct mail can bring in a huge amount of income, even after the considerable expenses. The real payoff, however, comes from upgrading these direct mail donors. Ask them to give more than last year, give more than once a year, give monthly, have donations automatically deducted from their checking account, credit card, or paycheck, or get their employer to match the contribution.

CHAPTER 9
TELEPHONE FUNDRAISING AND DOOR-TO-DOOR CANVASSING

Telephone fundraising and door-to-door canvassing both have a bad name. Too many people have been irritated by annoying calls. The phone or doorbell always seems to ring when you are in the shower, at dinner, or changing a crying baby's diaper. Sometimes the call or visit is about a cause you have never heard of before. Worst of all are the robot-like voices of weary callers reading a boring script for the hundredth time, or the over-aggressive callers who won't take no for an answer. In some cases, phone and door-to-door canvassers are actually fraudulent.

Nevertheless, telemarketing and door-to-door canvasses can be effective in certain circumstances.

1. Telephone Fundraising

1.1 When does telephone fundraising work?

The telephone can be more effective than other forms of communication. It is a cost-effective way to renew the support of lapsed or past donors who have not responded to letters. Reply rates can be five times better than mail, and average donations are two or three times higher.

When calls are made to your current supporters, the telephone is one of a number of reliable techniques to increase their giving. When funds are needed to cope with an emergency, or a major breakthrough needs to be announced, the phone is a fast way to reach people, build their excitement, and get their support.

When telephone calls are made asking for a donation on a credit card, the number of paid pledges increases and the average donation goes up, probably because the donor is saved the hassle of mailing a check.

When you send people a letter first, announcing that a phone call will follow, they are usually more receptive and donations usually increase.

1.2 The dangers of bad telephone fundraising

Although telephone fundraising may be worth considering, you must beware of certain dangers.

First, telemarketing is not for corporate donations. Avoid telemarketing calls to big businesses when you want a grant. Such calls are not only ineffective, they can also be counter-productive. The calls may offend corporate donation officers who prefer the written approach. Worse yet, they may result in small contributions, undermining your ability to get a larger donation from the corporation. Restrict telemarketing to individual donors.

Also, beware of unscrupulous telemarketing shops. Some nonprofit organizations have allowed high-pressure telephone canvassers to raise money in their group's name. Many of these bad telemarketing promoters work on a commission basis*. They provide all the labor, and guarantee a minimum level of return. This sounds very attractive on the surface, but in reality, it is often costly and damaging for the nonprofit. After the telemarketers have deducted their expenses, telephone charges, salaries, and commissions, the nonprofit often gets less than 25 percent of the money raised. Ken's consulting firm worked with one Canadian organization for which a telemarketing firm raised $360,000. The charity only received $60,000.

Several years ago, a study by the Attorney General of Massachusetts showed that the average nonprofit ended up with only 29 percent of the money after telemarketing firms made calls. In nearly one-third of the cases they studied, the return was less than 16 percent. State and provincial governments became so upset at these abuses that a number introduced laws regulating telemarketing. (For more on this, see *The NonProfit Times,* February, 1994, page 12, <www.nptimes.com> or <www.ftc.gov/bcp/menu-tmark.htm>.)

In fact, costs like these are not out of line compared to other donor acquisition costs. Direct mail campaigns to acquire new supporters often only break even financially, which means the immediate net proceeds to the nonprofit's work is zero.

A more serious problem with bad telemarketing shops is that the nonprofit often does not get access to the names, addresses, and phone numbers of their new supporters. The telemarketing company may keep these lists and may even sell them to other clients without permission.

It took one Canadian charity more than a year of legal letters merely to get the copies of the tax receipts with the donors' names. Then the charity had to retype the list onto a computer database before they could send a second request for funds. A relatively small portion of these expensively acquired new supporters became long-term donors. The delay before the charity could contact them again was just too long.

Commission payments for telemarketing callers are a special problem. The telemarketers often become pushy in order to increase their income. Carefully approved scripts are forgotten as they say whatever they think will produce a donation. The result may be long-term damage to the good name and reputation of the nonprofit organization. Donors may give to get rid of the caller, but vow never to support that nonprofit group again.

Telemarketing shops like this often ask donors to buy tickets to send disabled kids to the circus or a concert. There's nothing wrong with sending kids to a show, if that is the purpose of your organization. If not, it may be misleading. Worse yet, in many cases donors contribute enough to send many more kids to a show than actually go. That's fraud.

Legitimate telephone-canvass firms do not work on a commission basis. This practice is prohibited by the Code of Ethics of the Association of Fundraising Professionals. The Canadian Centre for Philanthropy has similar prohibitions <www.ccp.ca>. If commission-based telephone promoters approach you, do not participate.

---

* To protect nonprofit groups, commission-based fundraising is prohibited by the Code of Ethics of the Association of Fundraising Professionals. See <afpnet.org/ethics>.

Legal requirements in many jurisdictions require professionals and even some charities to register before calling donors. This has been introduced to protect the public from fraudulent calls. Check with your lawyer and with the government before you get started.

If you plan to use an outside telemarketing company to make calls, investigate several firms before working out a contract. Look for one that has experience with other nonprofit organizations like yours and understands the special attention required. Compare notes on cost, results, their ability to move quickly, and the services offered. Also note the following pointers:

a) Be wary of companies that claim to have secret lists. These lists are often compiled while the firms conduct campaigns for other nonprofit organizations, without the other group's permission. Your donor list could suffer a similar loss of confidentiality.

b) Talk to the actual telephone operators as well as the firm's salesperson. Decide if the callers can convey your group's message properly. They represent your organization to your donors. Can they answer difficult questions intelligently?

Are the callers recruited from students with a good understanding of your issues, or are they used to selling products like aluminium siding or subscriptions to magazines? Do they sound like they are talking or reading a script? Would you hire them yourself?

c) Make sure callers are paid a salary, not commission. Commission payments encourage the callers to push too hard. People who are paid a commission know that their paychecks depend on getting the donors to give at once. This ignores the value of the donor's long-term relationship with the organization. Callers have been known to distort information in a manipulative way; this angers the donors if and when the truth comes out. Commission-paid callers have been known to use abusive language toward people who do not give.

d) Make sure the script callers use is submitted for your approval and that no changes to the script are allowed without your approval.

e) Monitor calls periodically to make sure the script is being used as written. Don't hire a firm that won't let you listen. Ask to observe another campaign in progress before you sign a contract.

f) Make sure you receive all the names and addresses of donors within one month of the campaign conclusion. This must be faster if you are sending the donors a charitable receipt. If you keep your own donor list on a computer, specify that the list be given to you in a computer format that is easy to use and compatible with your existing data base format.

g) Make sure callers are carefully selected, trained, and rewarded, whether paid or volunteer.

Remember, professional telemarketing is expensive. Staff, telephone lines, rent, long-distance charges, and all the other costs add up rapidly. Many firms will charge an advance start-up fee of several hundred dollars to create the original script and train their callers.

Professional telemarketing costs about four to five times more than sending a letter. In many cases the results are well worth the cost. Only testing will determine for sure.

1.3 How a telephone campaign can benefit your organization

If it is done properly, telemarketing can recover lapsed donors because it opens the door to dialogue — provided you have good telephone volunteers. They can probe for the reasons the donors stopped giving and gently woo them back.

Knowing why you lost a donor may help you reduce the number of other donors lost.

If they still support your work, but can't give financial aid right now because of their economic circumstances, you may be able to find another way they can support you. Perhaps they would like to volunteer time. Maybe they can give again later. Perhaps a small donation on their credit card of $3 or $5 a month would be easier to give. Perhaps they plan to remember your organization in their will.

You can upgrade current donors. Telephone your middle-level donors. Begin with donors in the $50 plus range. Do not make calls to the very top donors; visit them personally if you can. Also, don't call donors who have given under $50 if you have a shortage of volunteers.

You can also solicit emergency contributions by phone. Many groups exist primarily to cope with emergencies. Examples include the Red Cross, Doctors Without Borders, and St. John Ambulance. For them the telephone is a logical tool.

Even organizations that are not created to handle emergencies might have to act fast if an unexpected situation develops. For example, the furnace at your school or church or theater might die in the middle of the winter. Pipes might burst. Fires, storms, and natural disasters might affect any group's facilities. In such circumstances, an organized telephone campaign can help.

If you are prepared, you can begin making phone calls within hours. Sending letters takes too long.

Prepare for an emergency in advance. The donor's responses might be immediate and generous within a few days of a disaster. Their willingness to contribute might fade fast once the media has moved on to a new story.

In a rapidly changing situation, a letter may be out of date by the time it arrives. Telephone scripts can be changed instantly. During an emergency appeal, organizers must analyze the results of the calls daily to decide when to stop calling.

However, while telephone fundraising can be effective with donors who know your organization, phoning people who have never supported you before is seldom cost-effective. There are a few exceptions to this:

a) A group has many members or people who have used their services (such as attending a concert or sending kids to a sport), but has never before asked them to give.

b) A group has names and phone numbers for people who signed a petition for an important cause, and phones to give them a news update and ask for support.

c) A group is raising money to help in a situation that has received a lot of publicity.

d) A small-town organization reaches out to neighbors.

e) A well-known organization approaches people who have heard of it and have similar interests.

Calling people out of the phone book is usually not worth the time, even if the calls are restricted to wealthier neighborhoods or to executives or professionals listed in directories.

Calls sometimes work with a list of donors rented or borrowed from another nonprofit. They might even work with a rented list of subscribers to a magazine, provided the magazine's topic and target audience is narrowly defined to include your supporters. However, such lists may not include phone numbers. As a result, you might have to do extra work or pay extra charges to look up the numbers.

If you want to try recruiting new supporters over the phone, test the process carefully. Compare it to the time and money required to acquire new donors through the mail, through special events, and/or through personal contacts.

1.4 How much could you raise?

Let's assume you start with 100 supporters on your list for whom you have phone numbers. (We won't count those you can't phone.)

Typically, you might actually get through to between 40 and 60 of those. The rest will be out or you will get busy signals.

Of those you reach, 10 percent to 50 percent will pledge. The rest will say no. This leaves you with 4 to 30 people who promised support.

Of those who pledge, from 50 percent to 90 percent will actually send in their contributions. The rest will never get around to it. Now you have from 2 to 27 real donors.

Average donations will be in the same range as a mail fundraising campaign. For most groups this is from $15 to $35. For a university it might be $500 or more, pledged as $100 a year over five years. For a major health charity, the average gift was $200. For a grass-roots group it could be lower. Let's assume at the low end you will actually receive two donations of $15, totalling $30, before expenses. At the high end, you might receive 27 donations of $35, totalling $945 before expenses.

Callers can make about 20 to 25 calls each during an evening session lasting three to four hours. Each call typically lasts less than five minutes. The average caller completes about ten calls per hour (not counting busy signals and phones that are not answered). The most effective callers talk to fewer people, talk longer, and get bigger donations. Completing these 40 to 60 calls will take from four to six hours.

If you have a volunteer calling, expenses will be low. If you are paying the caller, you will almost certainly lose money at the low end. It is not unusual for professional telemarketing firms to charge $25 per hour, plus $500 start-up costs to develop a script and set up the team. Four to six hours of calls would cost $100 to $150.

These results vary depending on your community, your cause, your callers, your script, and many other variables. You can lower costs by collecting telephone numbers of all donors ahead of time. Even if you are not planning a telephone campaign right now, prepare ahead. Finding phone numbers can be time consuming, costly, and frustrating.

1.5 How to get donors' phone numbers (and e-mail addresses)

Unless you use the methods below, you may never find the phone numbers for many of your donors. Some have unlisted numbers, some are listed under someone else's name, and some have moved away.

There are several ways to get donors to give you their phone numbers — and e-mail addresses — or to find them yourself. Use all of these methods. No one technique will succeed in every case.

a) Request phone numbers on reply coupons used in letters, raffles, events, brochures, and anywhere else you contact donors. Ask the donors directly. Add a line below the space for the donor's name and address on the reply card for the donor's phone number. Add another line for their e-mail address. Many donors will fill this in.

b) Check their checks. Many people have their phone number printed on their checks. Make sure the people processing donations check for this and collect phone numbers for your database.

c) Use volunteers or a paid service bureau to look up numbers for you, using phone books and/or computerized directories. Some service bureaus charge for the service, often about 10¢ to 20¢ per phone number. Some do it free for clients who are using other services.

1.6 How to approach donors

Send the letter a week to ten days ahead. In it, tell donors that in a few days they will receive a phone call asking them to give more than they have ever given before. Make this letter long and persuasive. Do not include a reply envelope or reply card. The purpose of the letter is not to get them to give right away, but to set the stage for the phone call.

Sophisticated campaigns will even send two letters. The first, a short note, says "You will receive a letter in a few days." It is from the highest staff person whose name appears at the top of the organization's letterhead. It may include a brochure. The second letter is two to five pages long, from the chairperson of the campaign, on his or her own personal letterhead. It may say the amount the nonprofit hopes the donor will pledge.

1.7 How to choose and manage your callers

Should you pay callers or use volunteers? This is not an easy question.

Using volunteers keeps costs lower and can be more effective, because the sincerity in a volunteer's voice is rarely matched by professionals, no matter how well trained. When staff or paid telemarketers call, the implication is that they are raising money to pay themselves. A call from a volunteer also pleases the donors more, since they feel you are being a good steward of their contributions.

Yet using paid callers also makes sense. You may not be able to get enough volunteers. Your volunteers may not be comfortable raising money on the phone. Paid callers tend to raise more money per hour and experienced callers get significantly better results.

Volunteers will usually work only a few shifts, while paid callers may work for weeks or months, or even years. You may find it too much trouble to repeatedly train new volunteers.

In either case, choose callers with good telephone manners. Make sure that callers are carefully selected, trained, and rewarded. Whether volunteer or paid, good callers often have a connection with the group. Universities often use students to call alumni, of course. Theaters may use actors or performers. Children's groups may get parents to call. A health-care group might get patients, nurses, or social workers to call. Look for callers among people who have sales experience. Receptionists and office workers may also be comfortable talking with people on the phone. Do not use introverts.

Paying callers may mean hiring your own team or retaining an outside company. You may wish to hire callers on your own and run the telemarketing operation without using an outside firm. This is particularly easy for organizations such as schools that have access to skilled labor. Their inside knowledge of the situation makes them good callers.

Have your callers work two or three evenings a week. A shift should last four hours with no break. Any less than that and they can't keep up their skills. Any more than that and they may burn out.

Borrow an office and keep callers close together. Don't send callers off to phone on their own from their home or work. They may never get around to calling, or children or colleagues at work may interrupt them during a call.

Instead, keep the callers in one big room while they make the calls. For a short campaign, you can often borrow an office with many desks and phones close together, thereby avoiding the cost of rent and phone installation.

Ask real estate firms, accountants, lawyers, insurance companies, or any big office. Arrange in advance for keys, security, and payment of any long-distance charges. Ask that their employees clean off their desks that day and put papers away so your callers don't accidentally disrupt work. Clean up afterwards, and leave a low-cost gift and thank-you note for every person who loaned you his or her desk. If this is not possible, you may need to rent an office and pay to have phones installed and furniture set up.

Why keep callers together? The telethon atmosphere keeps callers motivated. Put up progress charts and signs. Set off bells or flashing lights for large donations, or milestones reached. Experienced team members can also stand by to help deal with complicated calls.

Encourage friendly competition among callers. Give prizes to those who get larger contributions, or credit-card donations. You may be able to get prizes donated, such as dinner at a local restaurant, a book, or a movie pass.

Start the evening about 5:30 p.m. with training and a light supper. Finish by 9:30 p.m. or 10:00 p.m. Avoid calling on the nights of popular major events, such as sports finals.

Provide callers with the information they need to succeed. Prepare the following information to share with the person making the phone call:

a) the amount of the donor's last gift

b) the date of the last gift

c) what motivated the last gift (a letter? what was it about?)

d) any special connections the donor might have with your group (It would be embarrassing not to know that the donor was a past board member, a former active volunteer, or a current participant in a program.)

e) any other information you have about who the person is (for example, president of the Widget Corporation, a nurse or doctor, a judge or politician, an author or a celebrity — don't assume everyone will recognize the name)

Provide callers with scripts and train them in what to say and what not to say. Don't let callers decide what to say on their own. While no one should actually read a script word for word, having a set of phrases helps keep the calls short and effective. Some approaches do work better than others. Have the callers do the following:

a) Smile and say hello and ask to speak to the donor by name.

b) The caller should give his or her name and the name of your group. (In some areas the law requires this.) If the caller is a volunteer or has a special connection to the group, he or she should say so.

c) Ask if this is a convenient moment to talk. If not, arrange a time to call back.

d) Tell the donors why they were selected. It may be because they are past donors, or attended an event. Thank them for their past support.

e) If you sent a letter ahead, ask if the donors remember receiving it. If so, ask for their reaction. If not, summarize the key points.

f) Tell them what their donation could do to help people.

g) Ask for a specific donation. For example, "I see that in the past you gave $50. A number of supporters who gave a similar amount last year have chosen to increase that to $75. Are you comfortable with that?" If they agree, ask them to contribute on their credit card. If they don't want to use credit cards, offer to send a volunteer to pick up the contribution immediately or send a pledge reminder letter the same evening. Put a postage-paid business reply envelope in the pledge letter. Tell the donor on the phone this is coming and ask them to use it.

If the donor does not agree to a specific donation, callers should ask, "What would you be comfortable giving?" If the donor refuses or has questions, listen and discuss it. If possible, ask again for the gift. Don't be pushy. The long-term relationship with the donor is more important than an immediate gift.

h) Confirm the donors' addresses and the spelling of their names before you hang up. They may have moved but kept the same phone number. Double-check the amount of the gift and any other details.

i) Say "thank you" whether they give or not. Be polite. Say a friendly good-bye. Keep the relationship warm for next time.

When you call a donor, you may get a busy signal, no answer, another person who says your donor is not available, or an answering machine. (Callers still debate whether or not to leave a message: some consider it polite, others consider the message unproductive time.)

Call back in the next hour, or a few days later. Call back up to three or four times before giving up. In any case, until you have spoken directly to the donor, the call cannot be considered complete.

About 40 percent to 60 percent of your list will not be reached. Send them a letter. This is essential if you have told people in advance that you would call. It is a good idea even if you haven't, because they may hear that a friend was called and wonder why they were not. You might say "Sorry we missed you when we phoned. Your help is needed to . . . "

1.8 Following through on pledges

Send a pledge reminder letter the same evening the call is made. Give the amount the donor pledged, and an emotional explanation of what the money accomplishes. Add a heartfelt thank you.

Only about half the people who pledge will send back their contribution after this first letter. If the pledge has not been received in three or four weeks, send a friendly reminder. About 15 percent to 20 percent more will respond. A third reminder will bring in another five to ten percent.

1.9 Donors who give

Send thank-you letters to all who actually give. These should go out within a day or two of their contribution.

When people say "I'll think about it," it could be a polite brush off, or a serious statement of intent. Thank them for giving appropriate consideration to such an important decision. Provide them with additional information, and offer to talk with them if they have questions.

Many people will not give to a phone appeal unless they receive written information. Others will have specific questions they want answered. Prepare a form letter in advance to simplify responding to them.

1.10 People who say no

Thank people even if they turn you down on the phone. Include a bit more information, in case you can still convince them, but don't be a pest. Maybe they will give next time.

2. Door-to-Door Campaigns

Door-to-door campaigns must be carefully designed because they are costly and because — let's face it — they invade people's privacy. There is no doubt that it can be annoying to hear a loud knock on the door while you are in the middle of getting supper on the table for a starving family, then dealing with an aggressive canvasser who won't take no for an answer.

However, people are more willing to give at the door than they are with any other fundraising method (with the exception of fundraising by religious organizations), according to the Canadian Centre for Philanthropy. In fact, people told the Centre that their gifts at the door averaged $43. We suspect that some people must have exaggerated their donations. Some charities that do door-to-door campaigns report the average donation as being in the $10 to $20 range; an amount we feel is closer to the mark.

In a new trend, several well-known nonprofits with strong causes have sent canvassers door-to-door asking people to sign on as monthly donors, with $10 or $20 a month taken directly from their bank accounts or credit cards, in perpetuity (unless the donor cancels). This obviously produces far more income.

In typical door-to-door campaigns, volunteers visit 30 to 60 houses a night; professional canvassers visit up to 100. In the evening, you may expect to find people home at 50 percent to 60 percent of the houses visited. Groups set goals for their canvassers that range from $100 a night to near $1,000 a night. Success rates appear to vary greatly. Some charities say that they obtain donations at between 50 percent and 90 percent of the houses where someone answers the door. Typical success rates were 12 percent to 15 percent in 2000, according to Kim Klien (www .grassrootsfundraising.org/titles/feature19_6.html).

Door-to-door campaigns compare favorably with telephone campaigns in some respects, and less favorably in others. For example, they are less useful for reviving relationships with past donors. However, the door-to-door canvasser can receive a check or cash and hand over a receipt on the spot. Compare this to receiving a pledge that may or may not be honored and having to mail a receipt after the donation is received.

Door-to-door campaigns can provide significant income for some groups. They can also be a way of acquiring new donors who may give again if they are later approached using other methods, such as letters, phone calls, or invitations to special events.

2.1 Organizing a door-to-door campaign

Organizing a door-to-door fundraising campaign is similar to organizing a canvass in an election campaign. It involves preparing written material to hand out, training canvassers (including preparing a "script" and providing them with answers to frequently asked questions), organizing a route for each canvasser, and keeping track of donations. Many of the suggestions regarding training and preparing scripts for telephone callers in the section of this chapter on telephone fundraising apply to door-to-door campaigns.

In a small town, deciding which streets to canvass may not be difficult. In a large city, you might want to carry out demographic research to learn which neighborhoods are most likely to have donors, then test those areas to see if you were right.

2.2 Volunteers or paid canvassers?

Earlier, we discussed whether it is better to use volunteers or paid canvassers for telephone campaigns. Most of the same considerations apply when deciding whether to use volunteers or paid canvassers for door-to-door fundraising. If you have a small budget, paying canvassers may not be an option. If you have a larger budget, you will have to decide whether to use volunteers or paid canvassers. Obviously, using paid canvassers is very costly and could consume all the money raised. Also, donors get angry if they find out canvassers are paid, and even angrier if they find out the canvasser is paid a commission. (In fact, the Association of Fundraising Professionals and the Canadian Centre for Philanthropy both have codes of ethics that prohibit all fundraising on commission. See <afpnet.org/ethics> and <www.ccp.ca>.)

On the other hand, as the statistics above illustrate, paid fundraisers can be more efficient than volunteers.

2.3 Follow-up after a door-to-door campaign

As soon as the donation is received, you should send the donor a thank-you letter or e-mail so they will be sure the donation reached you; add each donor's name to your mailing list; and start sending each donor material such as your newsletters and information updates.

You will have to decide how much information to send them, how long to consider sending it, how to approach them for further donations, and how often. This may depend on factors such as how much money they gave at the door; whether they signed up for membership (if this was an option), and how they respond to subsequent appeals.

Depending on factors such as these, you may follow up with further letters, repeat visits, or telephone solicitations at appropriate intervals; and invite them to buy tickets to special events. Depending on their responses to follow-ups, you may start sending them more frequent information about your activities, step up the frequency of solicitations, change the method of approaching them, or drop them from your lists.

3. Assess a campaign's effectiveness

Analyze the results of each campaign, and compare them to the results you get with other techniques. For example, you should examine the following:

a) Average size of donations (usually $15 to $25 for telephone campaigns)

b) Percentage of calls completed (usually 40 percent to 60 percent for telephone campaigns)

c) Percentage reached who pledge (usually 10 percent to 50 percent for telephone campaigns)

d) Percentage of pledges who have paid (usually 50 percent to 90 percent for telephone campaigns)

e) Number of completed calls per hour (usually about ten per hour for telephone campaigns)

f) Percentage of lapsed donors recaptured (usually about 30 percent to 40 percent for telephone campaigns)

g) Average amount of increase in upgrades

h) Cost per dollar raised

i) Hidden costs, such as staff time and overhead

j) Number of complaints received compared to the number of donations

CHAPTER 10
FUNDRAISING ON THE INTERNET

We live in a fast-moving, information-hungry society. The uses of e-mail and Web sites described below can help your group organize and educate as well as cultivate deeper relationships with all your constituencies.

This chapter is designed for two purposes:

1. To help organizations who are not yet using the Internet for fundraising learn what it can and can't do for them;

2. To give groups that are already on the Internet ideas about opportunities and creative ways to use the Internet for fundraising.

This is not a technical guide to using e-mail or building a Web site: there are many good computer books and courses to help you to do that. Our aim is to help you to make online fundraising an integral part of your fundraising strategy, when and if that makes sense for your organization.

1. Should We Take the Plunge?

People respond to new technology in three different ways:

- Some are seduced by it, embrace it, and dive right in

- Others head for the hills and have to be dragged kicking and screaming to learn it

- Then there are those who sit back for awhile, wait for manufacturers to iron out the kinks and bring down the price, and decide when the time is right for them

If you are reading this you are probably Type 2 or Type 3, and we want to help you make an informed decision about leaping into cyberspace.

There are several things you can do if you are on the Internet:

- You can send and receive messages by electronic mail (e-mail)

- You can build and maintain a Web site

- You can surf the 'Net looking for information posted on other people's Web sites

- You can participate in online discussions with fundraisers and nonprofit managers.

Sending and receiving e-mail is the most popular online activity. More than 80 percent of the people who buy Internet services do it to use e-mail, so let's start there.

2. E-mail

2.1 An introduction to e-mail

Today, e-mail is the fastest and cheapest way to move information between and among people who are on the Net. E-mail allows you to send words, graphics, digitized photographs, and even video footage to your colleague in the office down the hall or to your friend (or donor) on the other side of the world, as long as you both have computers and are on the Net.

This makes the use of e-mail almost indispensable. Not only can you ask and answer questions by e-mail (just as you can in person, by telephone, fax, mail, or courier), but you can also send and receive lengthy documents as attachments to your e-mail message, edit those documents on your computer, and give or receive access to Web sites through an e-mail message. You can print out the e-mail message itself, and in most cases, you can print out the lengthy documents attached to the e-mail and the information on the Web sites that you accessed through the e-mail.

This makes e-mail an important management tool, communication device, and cost-saver.

To get on the Net, you need a computer, a modem, a phone line, and an Internet Service Provider (ISP). The ISP is a business that provides your computer with access to the Internet in exchange for a monthly fee. Monthly fees vary depending on the type of service but they are well within the budget of even a small organization. Free ISP services are available in some areas, often supported by ads. A few nonprofit ISPs also exist, often under the name "freenet."

When you send an e-mail, it goes first to your ISP, which then sends it out over the Internet. Your mail lands at the ISP of your friend or colleague, and that ISP then sends it to your friend or colleague. This often takes only a few minutes, but sometimes it can take several hours.

Your e-mail address comprises several parts. The first part is your name or your organization's name, followed by the symbol @, followed by the domain name (which is your ISP or the organization, business, university or government institution for which you work.) This is followed by a period (or "dot"), which is followed a two-, three-, or four-letter abbreviation describing the type of organization sending the e-mail. For example, ".com" indicates "commercial" (i.e., a business); ".org" connotes a nonprofit organization; ".net" means a network resource; ".ca" means the group is located in Canada; and ".gov" connotes a government. There are no spaces between the letters and all letters are lower case.

Give some thought to the address that you choose. If your organization is well-known by an acronym (such as "PBS" or "CBC", that's a good way to go. But if the name is long and doesn't lend itself to a short form, try to work with the most important noun in the name and add one or two identifying letters that make it specifically yours. You want your address to be easy to remember, easy to type, and to have a nice ring to it.

If you have not registered your domain name yet, do it now. It is very inexpensive. Even if you do not have a Web site, you might want to make sure other groups do not use your group's name or acronym. Ken recently helped a nonprofit that wanted the domain name "cprf" — only to discover that several other groups already had registered cprf.com, cprf.org, cprf.net and cprf.ca.

2.2 How can we use e-mail to improve our efficiency and effectiveness?

You can use e-mail to —

- communicate with board members, staff in other locations, and sister organizations;
- distribute your newsletters, brochures, and reports;

- organize lobbying campaigns, demonstrations, or board meetings;
- publicize an event on short notice;
- educate your members on issues of special interest;
- recruit volunteers for special activities on short notice;
- collect signatures for a petition and forward the petition electronically to its target; and
- give readers of your e-mail message direct access to a Web site.

E-mail software has an address-book application. This is a database in which you can keep an electronic list of individuals or organizations to which you want to send e-mail. The address book may list your members, work teams, and supporters. Once the data, including the e-mail address of each person, has been entered into the address book, you can send reports or bulletins to the whole address book or select portions of it with just a few keystrokes. There is a start-up cost to entering the data, but it's a good investment.

When you receive an e-mail message, you can send a reply to the person who sent it or to that person as well as all the other recipients of the message. If you receive important information by e-mail from a sister organization or a board member, you can then distribute that information electronically to interested parties in your organization or around the world by another keystroke or two.

When you are replying to messages or forwarding them to others, do consider privacy. It is easy to accidentally send a reply to everyone who received the message rather than just the message's author, and to pass on the e-mail addresses of others who may not want to share their e-mail addresses with numerous strangers.

You can also use e-mail to edit someone else's work, and vice versa. Suppose you are drafting a fundraising proposal or preparing your annual report. You type a draft on the word-processing application of your computer. Then by a keystroke or two, you attach the draft to an e-mail and send it to your colleague. Your colleague downloads the draft into the word processor, revises it, attaches it to an e-mail, and sends it back to you electronically for further changes, until a final product is produced.

You can send the final version by computer to anyone who has given you an e-mail address. The importance of this for fundraising is not only that it enables you to prepare solicitations more quickly and efficiently, but also that you can respond to a request for proposals or submit a grant application or fundraising proposal by e-mail.

You can use simple e-mail for some of your fundraising activities even if you don't yet have the resources or sophistication to build a Web site. E-mail is especially appropriate for sending out an appeal for funds on short notice for urgent matters and for membership renewal.

Sounds wonderful, right? So why would anybody hesitate?

There are two issues you must think through:

a) What percentage of your members and constituencies want to connect with you by e-mail?

b) How much staff time and computer resources will you need to devote to e-mail?

a) Online supporters or members

Not everybody has e-mail yet, although the number of e-mail users is growing rapidly. Many people have e-mail only at work, and it may not be appropriate for them to receive information from you at their workplace. If much of the information you send out is written, people may prefer reading hard copy to reading your newsletter on the computer screen. Some organizations now offer members or subscribers the option of receiving newsletters and bulletins by mail, by fax, or by e-mail. However, e-mail has now become so widespread in some circles that some organizations offer their newsletters only by e-mail, to save printing and mailing costs.

Before taking the plunge, try to determine what percentage of your members would *prefer* to communicate with you by e-mail and what kinds of information they would like to receive by e-mail. Sending out unsolicited e-mail (sometimes called "spam") is seriously frowned upon. Having a member's e-mail address is not good enough: you should also have their permission to use it before sending unsolicited e-mail attachments. Until a quarter or a third of your members tell you they want to receive a particular kind of document by e-mail, you should not use e-mail to distribute it (except to individuals who have specifically requested it).

b) Resources

While the cost of an Internet hook-up is minimal, staff time for checking and replying to incoming e-mail can consume several hours a day. Some people complain that they receive so many e-mails that they have little time left to get their work done. The immediacy of e-mail is one of its most appealing characteristics, but the downside of this is that many people expect a same-day response. If you can't commit to reading and replying to e-mail at least once a day, maybe it isn't for you.

Of course, volunteers can handle a lot of your e-mail work, once they are trained. If your volunteers have home computers with Internet access, you can simply forward routine requests to them electronically, and they can handle the replies. Still, someone has to screen, sort, and distribute the e-mail.

Remember, too, that since all of your members, directors or constituents don't have e-mail, you should still expect and be willing to send documents to some by mail or fax. You will have to maintain lists of directors who get minutes by e-mail, directors who want to receive them by fax, and directors who will get them by ordinary mail; as well as a list of members showing who receives newsletters on paper and who by e-mail.

E-mail saves labor such as photocopying or printing documents, stuffing and stamping envelopes, and taking them to the mailbox or post office. It saves materials such as paper, envelopes, and stamps. But it also requires reorganizing your office procedures to keep track of who gets what by which means.

3. Fundraising

E-mail has several uses as a fundraising tool:

a) *Membership renewals:* If you have determined that at least one-quarter of your members *prefer* to communicate online — and you *must* get their permission to routinely send them documents by e-mail if you don't want it to backfire — then it is efficient to conduct that portion of your membership renewals online. It is simple to send out reminders by e-mail, too. However, it is not so simple to *collect* funds using electronic credit-card transactions. Review the section **3.2** of this chapter, on credit-card fraud and privacy, before you decide to take this route.

b) *Emergency Appeals:* By virtue of its immediacy, online fundraising is also very well suited to raising funds for time-sensitive issues. Requests for donations for disaster relief, high-profile legal and political issues, and other urgent needs can be sent out online to current members and supporters for quick response. Using the Net for this purpose is just as quick as telephone solicitation and far less intrusive (which is not necessarily a good thing when it comes to raising money). But review section **3.2**, on credit-card fraud and privacy issues before you launch an emergency appeal on the 'net.

c) *Special Events:* In addition to telephone, mail, and fax, you can invite people to special events by e-mail and they can respond by e-mail.

3.1 Avoid spam

It is one thing to send a fundraising request to members and supporters by e-mail. It is quite another to send thousands of unsolicited e-mails to complete strangers. There are companies that will do this for you for a fee. And just as you can buy mailing lists for a price from other organizations or from commercial list suppliers, you can obtain lists of e-mail addresses. Just because you can, doesn't mean you should. This junk e-mail, or spam (as it is often called), is not only objectionable; charities that have tried it have found that it is also ineffective. Moreover, if you send it yourself, you may find that angry recipients send it right back to you, since they can do this with one or two keystrokes. This can jam your e-mail or even shut down your whole system. "Spamming" is still legal in most jurisdictions, but several US states have passed laws regulating Internet users who send thousands of unsolicited e-mails. Under the Virginia law, spammers whose e-mail causes a computer system to crash can be fined. Several anti-spam bills have been introduced in Congress. Canada will likely follow suit.

3.2 Credit-card fraud, security, and privacy

You should understand that information transmitted over the Internet is not necessarily secure or private. There is a difference between "privacy" and "security." Privacy deals with the expectations of people who give information and those who receive it. There may be an expectation or agreement about how information will be used and with whom it may be shared. Or the expectations of the sender may be different from those of the receiver. Privacy concerns arise whenever information about people is collected online or is given or sold without knowledge and consent to a third party. As a nonprofit, your organization has an ethical, if not a legal, obligation to the people with whom you deal to seek their consent before you give information about them to anyone else or use it for any purpose other than the purpose for which it was provided.

This is particularly important in the digital age for two reasons. First, you have the ability to collect information about people electronically without them knowing that you are doing it. Second, digital technology gives you the ability to manipulate data in ways that were impractical in the past. Several information databases can be combined electronically to create a detailed record of a person's history, health, financial position, interests, and activities; then that information can be sent to others.

In addition, the person or organization for whom information is intended is not the only one that can collect further information secretly or manipulate it without permission. Complete strangers can intercept your e-mail or hack into a Web site and obtain information about visitors, including credit-card numbers and e-mail addresses belonging to your members, as well as confidential information about your organization.

Security depends on the steps taken to preserve whatever degree of privacy is expected or has been promised. As an Internet vendor of sorts, you have a responsibility to secure sensitive information, and you can incur liabilities if you don't.

Brian Hurley and Peter Birkwood, authors of *Doing Big Business on the Internet* (published by Self-Counsel Press) make the following statement: "If you intend to conduct electronic transactions over the network, you should be aware that you are ultimately liable for all charges that are disputed by customers or incurred due to fraud." If that gives you pause, it should, because you rely on the goodwill of your members and donors.

There are a variety of techniques for verifying the identity of people who deal with your organization, as well as for securing information provided to you electronically and stored in your computer system. Describing these systems is beyond the scope of this book, but you should take steps to find out what is available.

Less dramatic than credit-card fraud or theft of information — but equally important — is establishing a policy on the use and distribution of your members' e-mail addresses and other personal information, and establishing procedures to implement these policies. Joyce recently received an e-mail notice of a benefit concert from a longtime friend and colleague. With the notice was a "cc." list of e-mail addresses of 50 other people. Joyce could now, with electronic ease, use this address list for her own purposes, and the other 49 people who also received the list of e-mail addresses could do the same. The result: junk e-mail, which annoys people. After you have gone to some effort to *get permission* to contact members by e-mail, you don't want to go about distributing their addresses to others who don't have permission. It is a fairly simple matter to suppress the "cc." list, but you have to be aware of the issue and have a privacy protocol. If people don't take care with these matters, fundraising on the Net will soon go the way of telephone solicitation: people will hate it and they will hate you for using it.

4. Web Sites

The first and foremost reason to establish your own Web site is not for direct fundraising, but to enhance the communication that supports fundraising efforts. Actual fundraising by asking for donations on a Web site and receiving money electronically through the site is still in its infancy. However, there has been explosive growth since September 11, 2001.

4.1 Using the Web site to raise money

Here it comes — what you've probably been waiting for: how you can actually raise funds on your Web site. But don't expect money to come flowing in. Most Web sites do not yet pay for themselves through donations.

The simplest form of fundraising, which does not require an interactive site, is to post a message on the Web site asking for donations and to provide the address to which money can be sent. One step up from this is to have a donation/membership form that the viewer can print out, fill in manually, and send in by mail with a check or money order. The form may also contain a space for inserting a credit-card number and permission for the organization to use the number to withdraw funds. This also does not require an interactive site, but the Web site viewer must take the trouble to print out the form, fill it in, and send it in.

The next level of sophistication permits the Web site viewer to fill out a form online pledging a donation or giving permission to withdraw a specified amount of money from a bank or credit-card account. It also permits the Web site viewer to send in this form by clicking a button. Obviously, this requires a Web site designed for two-way communication.

The most sophisticated method of interactive fundraising permits the Web site viewer to actually transfer money electronically by clicking a button and may even issue an electronic tax receipt.

4.2 More sophisticated Web site fundraising campaigns

What we have described above are the simplest means of using your Web site to attract donations. However, there are more and more examples of other ways your Web site can be used for fundraising, often in partnership with other charities or businesses. They include selling banner advertising on your site and linking it to a company's Web site in return for a share of the company's profits from products purchased by visitors to that site.

For examples of some of the innovative projects today, visit the following:

- <www.cybergrants.com>, an interactive online Web portal that allows nonprofits to access, free of charge, research-grant guidelines and to create and submit online funding proposals to member foundations

- <www.thehungersite.com> asks users to click on a button, and each time they do, a third-party donor who has agreed to participate in this program donates a small sum of money to food programs in developing countries. The site visitor has not given money, but is made to feel a sense of accomplishment and involvement with the cause that may lead to greater involvement.

- <www.mssociety.ca/en/events/biketour>, allows supporters to sign up for a long-distance bicycle ride and send e-mail requests for support to a list of their friends who can then donate online and receive a government-approved tax-credit receipt by return e-mail within minutes.

4.3 Web site security and privacy

Once again, we must stress that any arrangement that involves a Web site viewer electronically transmitting sensitive information such as his or her name, address, telephone number, and most particularly his or her bank account or credit-card number or transferring funds electronically raises substantial privacy and security concerns. We are constantly reminded that people are reluctant to send e-mail messages because others can intercept them. People are reluctant to visit Web sites because they are aware that the owner of the Web site (and others) can secretly track their movements through the Internet and collect and sell information about them. It is also often said that the single largest barrier to the establishment of "e-commerce" (online purchasing) is the fear of credit-card fraud, identity theft, and collection and sale of personal information.

Therefore, Web-site fundraising — or "cybergiving" — requires that the organization have policies and procedures in place and use sophisticated technology to ensure the privacy and security of the information sent to it.

Even if you do not raise or transfer money via your Web site, you should still establish a privacy policy and post it prominently on your site. Users want to know whether looking at your site will result in a bombardment of unsolicited e-mails or cause unwanted solicitations to pop up on their screen every time they use the Internet. They also are looking for assurances that you won't plant "cookies" in their computers when they enter your Web site. (A cookie is an electronic tag deposited in your hard drive by an Internet site when you visit it.) A cookie can store your name, credit-card number, Web sites visited, e-mail addresses, personal preferences, and spending patterns. The cookie transmits this information to the organization that planted it. Sometimes cookies are planted secretly. In other cases, the Web site owner places a message on the computer screen notifying the visitor that if he or she enters the site, cookies may be placed on the computer.

Cookies can be useful. For example, they can allow a wildlife nonprofit to create a personalized Web page for a supporter, greeting her by name, and giving her the latest information about projects to save wombats (her favorite) in Madagascar (which she visited on her last vacation) or Moose Jaw (she grew up there) but leave out any mention of gophers (which give her nightmares).

Although there are still few legal rules about how much information a Web site owner can collect about its visitors and what can be done with the information, the best policy is to do unto others as you would have them do unto you. Don't collect information about people without their knowledge and consent. Don't use information for purposes other than the purpose it was provided except with the consent of the person who provided it. Don't sell or give it to others without the knowledge and consent of the person who provided it. If a person questions the accuracy of information you have about them, check and correct. Finally, store the information in a secure manner and dispose of it carefully. Private information about donors, such as income or the size of donation (or credit-card number!) should never be found blowing along the street because it was left in a box by the side of the road for the garbage truck or a recycling pickup.

Back up all your data and store it off site. Replacing your donor list is difficult. Many nonprofits have lost valuable donor information because a hard drive crashed or a computer was stolen. If the back up is stored in the same place as your computer, it could be lost in a fire. In fact, if you have not backed up your donor list in the last week, go do it right now. We'll wait.

It is increasingly easy to accept secure credit-card donations on your Web site. If you are not ready to set this up on your own, you can use a central Internet donation service. This area is changing rapidly. New sites are being created and a few have gone out of business. Some are operated by charities at cost; some are businesses hoping to make a profit by offering a service. Here is a list to get you started:

- www.animalfunds.org
- www.canadahelps.org
- www.changecanada.ca
- www.charity.ca
- www.charitychannel.com
- www.charityvillage.com
- www.conservenow.org
- www.createhope.com
- www.donationdepot.com
- www.donornet.com
- www.duo.org
- www.generositywithoutborders.com
- www.givedirect.com
- www.giveforchange.com

- www.giveonline.org
- www.hcr.org
- www.helping.org
- www.justgive.org
- www.lic.org
- www.womenandchildren.org

Online services come in many other forms. A short list of the ever-changing opportunities includes —

- charity auction Web sites,
- charity shopping malls,
- affinity portals (where nonprofits get a share of the revenue from ads clicked on by visitors), and
- click-to-donate sites (where Web surfers can trigger a small donation from a third-party sponsor by clicking).

For information on these and lists of web services, go to <www.nonprofitmatrix.com>.

5. Surfing the Net: Research and Discussions

You can fundraise by sending e-mails, you can fundraise by creating a Web site that asks for donations, but you can't ask for money while surfing the Net.

However, you can obtain much of the information needed for effective fundraising more quickly on the Internet than you can by any other means. In fact, much of the information that we needed to update this book we found by surfing the Net. In our previous edition, we said that the Canadian Pacific Charitable Foundation receives 1,000 grant requests a year. By searching the term "Canadian Pacific," we found the Foundation's Web site. The Web site had an e-mail address. We sent an e-mail asking if this information was still correct. The following day we received an e-mail telling us it is now 2,000 requests each year.

On the foundation's Web site, we also found the foundation's funding criteria, funding application procedures, application forms, and information about projects that the foundation has recently funded.

Knowing that Lotus, a software company, used to have a policy of matching employee donations of time and money, we searched the term "Lotus" on the Net and found out that Lotus is now a division of IBM. We also obtained detailed information about IBM's funding criteria, funding procedures, and projects that have been funded.

It would have taken far more time and energy to track down this information by mail or over the telephone.

Do you want to know who might donate a computer to your group? Go to a search engine and type in a combination of words like "donate" AND "computers" and you can obtain several lists of agencies that help nonprofits obtain donations of computer hardware and software.

By surfing the Web, we obtained, free of charge, the full text of numerous articles and even whole books on topics ranging from direct mail campaigns to running an effective board of directors.

6. Online Fundraising Discussions

In addition to information posted on Web sites, you can also engage in discussions, ask questions, and share information about fundraising and nonprofit organization management with hundreds of other people interested in the same issues.

Internet mailing lists called "listservs" permit you to send a message to an e-mail address that identifies a list of people interested in a topic. The message is then redistributed to everyone who reads this list. You can ask a question such as, "Does anyone know of a source of funding for HIV/AIDS support groups in Montana?" and anyone on the list who wants to help can send a message back to you.

To get on a list, you must "subscribe." To subscribe to a list, send a message to the listserv address and fill in a form. The same process is used to get off the list (or "unsubscribe").

There are also other formats for discussion and exchange of information on the Internet — "Usenet" or newsgroups and electronic conferences. Usenet or newsgroups are similar to many electronic bulletin boards. Special software is needed to subscribe to and use newsgroups, but it is generally included with a package from an ISP or can be downloaded from the Internet. Your ISP may provide you with a list of newsgroups. You can also search for newsgroups by name or view a large list of discussion groups and mailing lists by visiting <tile.net>.

You can subscribe to a listserv or participate in other electronic discussions through several of the Web sites listed in this book's Appendix. If you want to get a sense of what is available and how this works, look at the list of nonprofit sector forums listed at <CharityChannel.com/forums>, including CharityTalk. You can also compare notes with other fundraisers at <www.arnova.org>, <www.gilbert.org>, and <www.nonprofits.org/npofaq>.

CHAPTER 11
FREE GIFTS AND PRODUCT SALES

The reason many nonprofits have so much trouble sustaining themselves financially is that almost by definition, those who benefit directly from their services can't afford to pay for them. And those who can afford to pay for services such as food banks, shelters for abused women, or a clean environment don't need the services or only benefit from them indirectly.

The reason businesses thrive is that they sell products or services for which people are willing to pay.

One way out of this dilemma, therefore, is for nonprofits to provide a service or product for which people are willing to pay as a way of developing steady, ongoing financial support for their primary products or services, which aren't marketable.

Unfortunately, this is easier said than done and most groups will not find such a product or service. However, for the few who are successful, this is one way out of the nonprofit poverty trap.

One highly successful free gift program is the War Amps key tag program. This organization started out to assist veterans of war who lost limbs in battle and has evolved to assist physically handicapped children. Every year it obtains a list of the names and addresses of licensed car drivers in Canada and sends each one a numbered tag to put on their key chain together with an envelope for donations. If your keys are lost, the finder can drop them in any mail box and the post office will send them to War Amps, who will identify the owner of the keys from the number on the tag and return them to their owner.

Although the tags are free and there is no obligation to donate, people appreciate this service so much that they give enough money each year to fund a substantial program and pay for the following year's campaign.

Free gifts that can be sent through the mail and which may be appreciated enough to stimulate a donation include greeting cards, address labels, and calendars. These may be a glut on the market now, as more and more nonprofits try it. Donors have drawers full of labels, often with their names or addresses misspelled, and yet address labels still produce revenue. Sometimes.

Producing and distributing such products is expensive, and it is easy to lose money if you misjudge the mood of the public.

A very few nonprofits have also successfully developed and marketed their own products. One example is UNICEF Christmas cards. UNICEF not only continues to sell the Christmas cards and calendars for which they have become known, but has expanded its product list. Guides continue to successfully sell cookies (in fact they are selling advertising space on the cookie boxes). And Scouts have apple day (and in some areas, sell millions of dollars worth of popcorn each year). Greenpeace operates stores in tourist areas where it sells a variety of products.

When you design, manufacture, distribute and sell a product, you are operating a business. The likelihood of any business failing is high, so you should have a solid business plan, do market research, and test the market before embarking on such an inherently risky venture.

Many wholesalers and manufacturers love to work with nonprofits. You can purchase almost any product for resale. For a small fee you can have your group's name on it.

Ducks Unlimited found a supporter who owns a brewery, and they raise money by selling Canvasback Beer wherever fine beer is sold. (**Note:** Unlike chocolate bars, this product is not sold door to door by kids.) Ducks Unlimited has also struck deals with clothing makers, a furniture company (comfortable chairs, bookcases, gun racks), Jimmy Dean beef jerky, a boat maker, and even a major truck company for a signature product. They sell art, shotguns, luggage, collectible decoys, pocket knives, and camping equipment. For more information, see <www.ducks.org/supportdu/official_products.asp> and <www.ducks.org/supportdu/event_merchandise_2002.pdf>.

In England, The Bug Factory sells more than a million charity bugs a year, and businesspeople will buy and wear red foam clown noses to raise money for the homeless.

Smaller nonprofits have partnered with big companies to resell —

- toys and teddy bears,
- food,
- books (new, used and via Internet book vendors),
- long-distance telephone services,
- electrical power,
- clothes of every sort,
- pens,
- mugs,
- buttons, badges, and pins,
- first-aid kits,
- flashlights,
- picture frames,
- plants,
- mouse pads
- pet food,
- key rings,
- fine jewellery and glow in the dark bracelets,
- bags and sacks,
- religious items,
- candles,
- aromatherapy products,
- sports water bottles, and
- private-label wines.

Could you sell any of these? Should you? There are some issues you may need to consider.

You usually have to pay for the goods in advance. Do you have advance funds available? Goods that are not sold often can't be returned unless you buy on consignment. This means that the wholesaler or manufacturer agrees to take back unsold goods without penalty. Can you risk a loss if a volunteer shows up months after the last date for returning goods for credit and mentions that he or she has a closet full of unsold items and he or she would like you to have them back?

Delivery of the goods to the consumer presents other problems. Shipping by mail is expensive and can be unreliable. Materials can arrive late or broken. Of course, you will replace a broken item, but unless you bought insurance at the post office, that's income lost.

Packaging odd-sized items can be a nuisance too. Include shipping costs in your budget calculations.

Collecting the money is also a concern if orders are taken by mail, over the Internet, or over the telephone. You may find that you have shipped the goods but cannot get paid. By contrast, if a donor pledges a contribution (as opposed to a purchase) and the money does not materialize (which happens all the time), you've wasted time and money, but you haven't paid for and shipped a product.

In addition, dated products, calendars, and perishable goods can be a problem. If a calendar doesn't reach people at the right time, you can't sell it next year. And by mid-January there is no market for unsold calendars. John once worked for a company that tried to sell Christmas cards to corporations in bulk to send out to their clients. The cards were very attractive and innovative, and superimposed on attractive artwork was a plastic laminated recording of organ music. Unfortunately, when the company sent its sales force out in September, the sales people were told by almost every large corporation that its Christmas cards had been ordered in June or July.

Food and fruit must be kept fresh and away from pests and must pass health inspections. Food and flowers must be kept refrigerated, carefully packaged, sold quickly, and shipped expeditiously. One large charity known for its flower sales, lost a fortune when the refrigeration in a truck failed and thousands of dollars' worth of flowers wilted.

Involving youngsters as sales people raises concerns, including whether or not the product is appropriate. Does it send the wrong message to have them push candy? The safety of the children is crucial. Frankly, they often lose orders, write down the information wrong, forget to turn in the money on time, or count on their parents to do it all. Again. If the sale involves a school, the school board might decide not to permit it.

Having your group's name on merchandise is an advantage. Every time the supporters see it, they think of you. Do they think nice thoughts? If they do, is your toll-free phone number or Web site visible so they can contact you?

Finally, you need a realistic plan for how to sell them. Will stores agree to carry your product? Can you send out order forms by mail? Will you have to find volunteers to go door to door, make telephone calls, or sit at a booth in a shopping mall?

In short, this method is like the lottery. The chances of winning are very low. But for the few winners, it's a bonanza.

CHAPTER 12
GIFTS THAT KEEP ON GIVING: AN INTRODUCTION TO PLANNED GIVING

It was the classic story, the one staff and volunteers at every nonprofit dream about. A couple that always lived a modest lifestyle left an $80-million bequest, including $5 million to build a new public library in Point Loma, California, which was to be named after the couple. James and Jean Hervey made an early investment in Price Club, one of America's first bulk-item superstores. James Hervey, who was an attorney, provided legal advice to Price Club founder Sol Price and took an early opportunity to invest in the fledgling company. The investment, which was worth about $12 million at Hervey's death in 1996, ballooned recently following the chain's acquisition by Costco Wholesale. The endowment went to the San Diego Foundation (www.sdfoundation.org/).*

The world of fundraising is full of such stories. Could it happen to you? Perhaps!

1. What is planned giving?

If a person gives you money now that you can spend now, that's not planned giving. If a person gives you a commitment to provide funds in the future, that's planned giving. Planned giving can be a commitment to give money in installments over time or a promise to give money at a particular time in the future.

Planned giving ranges from concepts that are simple, such as a bequest in a supporter's will, to complex financial arrangements that require a fundraiser to have a combination of personal sensitivity and technical knowledge of tax planning and estate planning. It includes memorial gifts, bequests in wills, gifts of the proceeds of life insurance policies, gifts of limited interests in property, and gifts of stocks and bonds. It can also include gifts made in celebration of happy occasions.

There are several complex legal and financial instruments that can permit a donor to contribute throughout and even beyond his or her lifetime. These financial instruments can be attractive to wealthy donors because they can provide tax reductions that substantially lower the cost of giving.

*Source: Stetz, Michael. "Modest Pair Leave Gift to San Diego Charity: $80 Million." *San Diego Union-Tribune*, 6/24/2000. http://fdncenter.org/pnd/archives/20000718/003507.html

But don't even think about these more complex instruments unless you have sophisticated fundraising staff or volunteers, access to legal, tax planning and financial advice, and a pool of wealthy donors. Even the names of these complex arrangements are daunting: deferred charitable gift annuities, pooled income funds, charitable remainder unitrusts, and grantor lead unitrusts.

2. Bequests: The Simplest Form of Planned Giving

The simplest form of planned giving is a bequest granted in a will. It is also the most common form of deferred donation. Approximately 80 percent of planned gifts are bequests in wills. If you are just beginning to explore planned-giving campaigns, your best bet is to focus on requests for bequests.

However, this form of planned giving is not always useful for new organizations. No one who expects to die in 30 or 40 years is going to name in their will an organization that has existed for only two years, as the chances of the organization continuing to exist for the next 30 years are slim. In addition, since you probably won't see the money for decades, a bequest is of little immediate value. A group that is struggling to pay today's bills is unlikely to spend a lot of time or money on soliciting bequests.

Your group doesn't have wealthy patrons? You feel it is inappropriate to visit someone in the hospital and ask them to change their will? There are still steps you can take that require little time or money to encourage bequests and other deferred gifts.

First, put brief articles in your newsletter about planned giving. Mention a donor who has left you a bequest, and celebrate her life. Tell donors how easy it is to include a nonprofit in their wills, and point out that if they have not made a will, the government will decide who inherits their estate.

Send letters to sympathetic lawyers, accountants, and trust companies asking them to recommend your organization to clients when preparing their wills or doing tax and estate planning.

For a small group, planned giving is unlikely to be a priority. However, even a small group can begin to learn about planned giving so that it can prepare for the day when it will have the capacity for such campaigns. It may also promote planned giving in a small way. After all, if you do nothing, some potential donors may die before they have an opportunity to consider remembering you in their wills.

Consider the story of The Minister Who Forgot to Ask. An elderly member of her congregation, long a generous supporter of the church, became seriously ill. The minister visited regularly, taking the best wishes of fellow parishioners and providing comfort and support. The woman often expressed her appreciation of the work of the church and left no doubt that she valued its efforts. After her death, the minister was shocked to discover that the church was not mentioned in her will. She had left her entire estate to another nonprofit group. One day, the minister ran into the executive director of that group. "Why you?" he asked. The answer: "We asked."

3. Other Methods of Planned Giving

Please note: Laws and tax regulations vary by region and change rapidly. Please consult a lawyer, accountant, or tax specialist to see what options are available in your area at the present time.

3.1 Living annuities

A living annuity allows a donor to give a nonprofit group a lump sum of cash that is to be invested by the group. The investment pays the donor a reliable income for the rest of his or her life (or for the life of a loved one), and whatever is left goes to your group after the donor's death.

3.2 Life insurance

There are several ways to give some or all of the proceeds of a life insurance policy. They include the following:

a) The donor makes your group the beneficiary of a life insurance policy purchased specifically for the purpose of donating the proceeds of the policy to your group. In this case, the donor can deduct the premiums as charitable gifts.

b) The donor makes your group the beneficiary of all or part of the future proceeds of an existing life insurance policy that is no longer needed for its original purpose. For example, a supporter of your group may have taken out life insurance to provide for his or her spouse and young children. Once the children are adults, and possibly the spouse has departed (either through death or divorce), the supporter may no longer need the proceeds. If the premiums are all paid up, the donor may make your organization a beneficiary of all or part of the policy.

Alternatively, if the supporter is tired of paying premiums for a policy that is no longer needed, he or she may offer to make your group a beneficiary in return for your group taking over paying the premiums. To discover if this is cost-effective, you may need to obtain an actuarial analysis of how long the donor is likely to continue to live and whether or not the premiums you will pay are likely to exceed the money you will recover.

c) A donor assigns to your group all or part of a policy provided as an employment benefit. For example, you receive life insurance at work along with health-care coverage. You already have life insurance, or have no dependents and do not need much. So you assign all or part of the policy to a nonprofit in case something happens to you. If you change jobs, you may

have the option of carrying on this insurance or letting it lapse.

A word of caution: Life insurance companies and insurance brokers sometimes approach charities, offering to set up planned giving programs on a commission basis. In general, we would advise groups to avoid such arrangements. At best, they may not present all the options. At worst, they could put undue pressure on your group's donors to purchase their products. This could drive donors away. It may also leave your group open to criticism and possibly even to lawsuits by the donors' families and other potential beneficiaries for exercising undue influence over the donor.

Far better to recruit knowledgeable volunteers to promote planned giving, such as accountants, tax lawyers, or retired life insurance sales people who no longer have a personal financial interest. Or, if you have the money, hire staff with expertise in this area.

3.3 Memorial and celebration giving

People donate to charities to mark funerals as well as to celebrate holidays such as Christmas, religious festivals, birthdays, anniversaries, job promotions, and other happy events. You can encourage this kind of donation by including attractive gift cards in your mailings to members or by creating an attractive display of sample cards for your lobby or at special events and speaking engagements. You could start with cards purchased commercially and design your own cards as your program grows.

4. Setting up a Planned-Giving Program

Here is a systematic approach to designing and implementing a planned-giving program. You can be as modest or elaborate as your resources permit. Pick and choose among these components to suit your needs.

a) *Set up a planned-giving task force.* The task force will carry out all the work of creating a planned-giving program, not just recommend ideas. Its job will change over time. Initially, the job will involve creating written materials. Recruit a chair with experience in planned giving or financial management, perhaps someone who has worked on planned giving for another nonprofit group, a lawyer, an accountant, or an insurance professional. Create four work teams within the task force:

- Wills and bequests team: Encourages supporters to leave money, goods, stocks, bonds, or real estate in their wills

- Annuity team: Creates annuity programs

- Life insurance team: Creates and promotes programs to encourage supporters to make your group a beneficiary of their insurance policies

- Memorials and celebrations team: Creates and distributes gift cards for various occasions, and creates written materials to encourage the use of these cards

b) *Develop written materials on planned gifts.* Collect samples from other charities, including churches, health-related groups, and universities. This should include information about wills and bequests, life insurance, annuities, gifts of stocks, bonds and property, memorial funds, and celebration opportunities.

c) *Start by asking your inner circle to make their own planned gifts.* Ask everyone working on the planned-giving task force and working groups to commit to making their own planned gifts. Ask your board of directors, volunteers, and staff to contribute. Encourage everyone to arrange their own planned gifts, including using memorial and celebration cards, remembering your group in their wills, or making your group a beneficiary of their life insurance policies. If your organization provides life insurance coverage to staff as an employment benefit, ask staff to consider signing over a percentage of the proceeds of their policies.

d) *Actively promote planned giving.* You should actively promote planned giving in ways that are tasteful and appropriate for your group:

- Talk to selected donors directly and personally mention planned giving in your newsletter in articles in which you thank donors for their support and in your own advertisements.

- Encourage planned giving in your annual report and in special bulletins

- Create a brochure designed for this purpose. Look at samples from most major universities, health groups, United Way, or religious institutions. The content does not change much.

- Send special letters soliciting this kind of donation to all donors or to selected donors.

- Add a few tactful words to letters you send to thank people for their donations.

- Hold estate-planning and financial-planning educational events at which you mention planned giving. Invite lawyers, accountants, financial advisors, or insurance agents to speak. Topics might include minimizing taxes, protecting your loved ones, estate management, or ethical investment strategies.

5. The Ethics of Planned Giving

Before you embark on a planned-giving campaign, your organization should have policies on what kinds of donations you will accept, from whom, and what you will and will not do in requesting or in negotiating the terms of such donations. These policies and practices should ensure that you do not accept a gift that a donor cannot afford to give and that these gifts are never given under pressure.

Donors should be encouraged to discuss proposed gifts of significant value with family members and with independent legal or financial advisors of their choice. Although you might provide potential donors with sample bequest language for different kinds of gifts to put into a will or sample language for other agreements, any legally binding document should be drafted by the donor's own lawyer, not yours.

If you have any reason to believe the donor may not have the mental capacity to understand the consequences of giving away money or property, you should take steps to find out. This is not only for the donor's benefit, but also for the sake of your group. It is not pleasant nor is it good publicity to be sued by relatives of a donor who argue that you took unfair advantage of someone who was sick or elderly.

6. Practical Considerations

Develop policies on what kinds of donations you will accept, and on what conditions, because you can actually lose money by accepting some gifts. For example, if you accept valuable property, you should exercise diligence to ensure that you have clear title and to investigate any potential liabilities. If you accept a gift of land that turns out to have contaminated soil, you may be stuck with government-ordered clean-up costs.

Similarly, a donor may give you property on condition that he or she live there for the rest of his or her life. You are the legal owner, but you aren't in a position to sell it or benefit financially from it for many years. If you accept such a gift,

will the donor continue to be responsible for paying taxes, property insurance, utilities, maintenance, and repairs, or will you be responsible for these costs?

Who should talk to donors about these sensitive issues? It should be someone well informed on the technical, legal, and financial implications — but that can be learned. More important, choose someone who has already included planned giving in his or her own life; you can't ask others to do what you have not done. And, usually, look for someone who is older or has been through life-changing illness or loss. A donor should not have to cope with a young whippersnapper who thinks he is practically immortal and seems to say "Well, granny, looks like your fixing to die real soon, but before you go. . . ." Much better to be able to say "You and I are at that time of our lives when we start think about what legacy we will leave behind. Here's what I've done. . . ."

7. For More Information

For more information on planned giving, contact the following organizations:

- National Committee on Planned Giving
  www.ncpg.org/
- Canadian Association of Gift Planners
  www.cagp-acpdp.org/
- Gift Planning Resources Center
  www.cam.org/~gprc/
- The European Association for Planned Giving
  www.plannedgiving.co.uk
- Planned Giving Today
  www.pgtoday.com

CHAPTER 13
HOW TO KEEP THE MONEY COMING

Getting initial support from individuals, foundations, corporations, governments, service clubs, and all the rest is only the first step. The challenge is to get them to support you again and again. This is particularly important because it takes so much time and money to find the special few who will support a nonprofit group. In smaller communities, or for specialized groups, there may be very few donors to draw upon. How do you maintain good relations for the long-term?

Keep your donors informed. Keep your promises to donors. Keep up the quality of your work. Keep good fundraising records. Keep trying to attract new donors. Do all that and — with a little luck — you should be able to keep the money coming. It's a simple formula, but a lot of hard work.

1. Keep Your Donors Informed

Donors increasingly complain about being overwhelmed with requests for help from so many nonprofits. This feeling is often referred to as "donor fatigue." The best way to overcome this syndrome is with "donor invigoration." Balance the seemingly never-ending parade of need, gloom, and despair with the good news of your group's progress, achievements, and accomplishments. Energize donors by telling them what their donation have made possible. Refresh and revitalize them with positive news, until they are willing to give again.

Government donors usually require detailed financial accounting, an interim report, and a final report. They will ensure that you report.

Corporate and foundation funders don't always make reporting a strict requirement: they just expect it. If they hear from you only when you want money, they won't be impressed.

Individuals don't have reporting requirements, but they wonder where their money went. Some will tell you not to waste precious money by sending them thank-you cards and newsletters. Honor their feelings by coding them in your donor list (see below) so you do not send what they do not want. However, do not assume that the majority feels that way. Thanking and informing donors does result in more donations. But try to get printing and paper donated, and make sure everyone knows that you have kept costs low.

1.1 Send news about all your work

If you produce a regular newsletter or magazine for your members, be sure that you also send it to your donors, including contacts at corporations, foundations, and government. Send any recent positive news clippings about your group. News clippings tell the donor that you are reaching your audience and initiating change.

A one-page professionally printed bulletin should be sent to donors quarterly if you can afford it. A news format with catchy headlines and short stories is best. It may not be read in detail, but it will show that you are producing.

Don't forget to send donors a copy of your annual report, or at least give them the option of letting you know whether they would like to receive it or not. Done properly it can be one of your most effective communication vehicles. This is especially important for the institutional donors who have given larger sums.

1.2 Projects

Once a project is completed, do a final report that includes an evaluation of the success of the project and a copy of the final product, if there is one. This report should be no more than five pages long. If the final product is a book or slideshow, send it to major contributors only and tell other funders that it is available if they wish to see it.

Send the report to all funders who contributed specifically to the project, as well as general contributors who expressed an interest in the particular project. Include a covering letter thanking them for supporting the project and outlining the enclosures. If you have plans to do further work in the same area, say so.

Donors should be invited to any conference, workshop, or film presentation that they have funded. Consider inviting them to other events organized by your group, even if they didn't fund them. They probably won't come, but the invitation is a courtesy they will respect. If they do show up, all the better: it helps to build the relationship.

2. Record-Keeping

Failing to keep track of when to approach a particular source can result in missing a funding opportunity. Conscientious donors file funding requests and then make decisions two or four times a year. Most donors, however, make decisions when they feel like it, or close to their fiscal year-end when they can predict the tax benefit of contributions.

Approach funders two or three months before the time they donated money in the previous year. Make a list of which source donated how much in which month of the previous year. Total the monthly income. Now you know whom to approach in which month during the upcoming year.

This funding approaches schedule will also show the slow months and help you plan cash flow. September through November and January through March are usually high-income months. The rest are slow months. Plan your fundraising activities with this information in mind.

To keep your records, you may wish to consider computer software designed specifically for fundraisers. Good software is essential for a group that plans to continue fundraising for several years and grow to have a few thousand supporters or more. If you have more than a few hundred, don't try to save money by keeping records in a word processing program or a homemade data base. The professional fundraising software includes useful systems you might never have considered. Other groups have also tested it, and frequent upgrades are offered to improve the system further. If something goes wrong, you have an expert a phone call away.

This software can cost from less than one hundred dollars to many thousands. As this book went to print you could still find simple programs available free for small groups. You'll find a partial list at <www.nonprofit.about.com/cs/npofrsoftware/>.

However, fundraisers from small, poor groups can get started with good paperwork to keep their records straight.

The three basic paper record-keeping systems are —

- a log book of approaches in the works,
- donor card files, and
- correspondence files.

2.1 Approaches in the works log

This log puts all the relevant information about your current approaches in one place. It saves checking through your appointment book to find out when you met with Mr. Blatz, or going through correspondence to find out how much you asked for.

Every fundraiser should have a financial target. If you need to raise $10,000 per month, you can determine how many approaches you must do weekly and monthly to meet that target. You will get discouraged when you're fundraising, and it's easy to procrastinate. From your financial goal, determine the number of letters and meetings per month you need. The log is a constant reminder of your quota. When it's time to check on the progress of your approach by telephone, the log will show whom to phone.

Fundraisers should report monthly on fundraising activities to staff or to a member of the board. The log makes that reporting easy.

A format for this log is illustrated in Sample 12.

2.2 Donor card file

Your donor card file will tell you at a glance how much a donor gave last year, when, and for which project. To set up a file, you need a card-file box with 5" x 7" (12 cm x 17 cm) file cards. File them alphabetically by name of funder. Color coding the cards according to the type of funder — corporate, foundation, or government — can save you some time.

Don't handwrite these cards — type them or put them on a computer. You may be able to decipher your own handwriting, but your successor may go crazy trying to read it.

Sample 13 shows an example of a donor card.

2.3 Correspondence files

Open a letter file for every source you approach. File them alphabetically by name of funder. Keep your filing consistent and up to date. In the same file also keep news clippings about funders' mergers, new senior staff, donations to other groups, new products or services, ups-and-downs, and any other news that will help you decide how much to ask for, who to ask, when to ask, and what their latest interests are.

3. Monthly Donors, Credit Cards, and Electronic Funds Transfer

Nonprofit groups can raise more money by taking donations on credit cards. They can raise even more with pre-authorized payments (PAP) and electronic fund transfers (EFT). A monthly-giving system can be another important source of income.

3.1 Monthly-giving system

Monthly plans are increasingly familiar to people through commercial transactions, such as mortgage payments, bank loans, and car payments. Bills for newspaper subscriptions, phone service, and cablevision can be automatically debited to your checking account or credit card. The same goes for donations.

Many donors who would not otherwise be able to give generously can do so on monthly installments. A person might find it hard to give $100 on a single check. The same person might

SAMPLE 12
APPROACHES IN THE WORKS LOG

FUNDER	DATE OF LETTER	DATE OF PHONE CALL	DATE OF MEETING	AMOUNT REQUESTED	DATE AND AMOUNT REC'D	COMMENTS
Blatz Ball-Bearings	Aug. 8	Aug. 15	Aug. 23	$2,000	Nov. 23 $1,500	Water pollution project
Conserver Foundation	Aug. 8	Aug. 15	Aug. 25	$4,000		Natural areas study
Hickle Leasing	Aug. 21	Aug. 29	Sept. 7	$250	Oct. 29 $250	General
Lambten Realty	Aug. 22	Aug. 29	Sept. 12	$500	Nov. 3 NO	Bought out by Master Realty

SAMPLE 13
DONOR CARD

Company   **Blatz Ball-Bearings Limited**
Address: 204 Widget Drive Unit 47
Address2:   Cleveland Ohio 20105

Contact: Ms. Jo Blatz
Title: President
Telephone: 216 555-4321   Cell: unknown
Home: 216 444-0987   Fax: 216 555-4322
Email: JB@blatz.com   Web: www.blatz.com

Contacts	Materials Sent	Contacts	Materials Sent
Oct. 1999	Annual Report	April 2001	Water pollution map progress report
April 2000	Water pollution report	May 2001	Invitation to special event
Oct. 2000	Annual Report	Oct. 2001	Annual report
Oct. 2000	Thank-you letter	Dec. 2001	Seasonal card
Dec. 2000	Holiday greetings card		

Donation Request History

Date	Amount Requested	Response Date	Amount Received	Project
10 Aug 1999	$1,000	15 Oct. 99	zero	general support
21 Sept. 2000	$1,234	17 Oct. 00	$1,234	water pollution map
19 Sept. 2001	$2,345	20 Oct. 01	$2,000	water pollution map 2

Our contacts:
- Maria Garcia (our board vp) works for them as a bookkeeper. MG says she can't ask ("too shy") but will make introduction.
- Kim Nguyen (volunteer on our water project) went to university with Jo Blatz. Last saw each other March 2001 at International Women's Day awards for women-in-charge. KN is willing to ask, says "Jo owes me one" for a donation I made to her daughter's school.

Other information on donor:
- Article in Cleveland Plain Dealer newspaper on ethical corporations 12 May 1999 (see file)
- Donated $10,000 to Rock and Roll Hall of Fame and Museum (wall plaque) in 2000
- Donated $7,500 to Cleveland Symphony (program booklet) in 2001
- Had booth at Gay Pride parade
- President honoured by the Mayor's Race Relations Committee
- Family has cottage on lake front in Wisconsin

not mind giving $10 a month, even though that totals $120 a year, which is a 20 percent increase.

Monthly donations provide a reliable cash flow for your organization, which can make your planning easier. The cost to raise a dollar is lower because the amount given is higher. It also evens out the income, which is often disproportionately high in the pre-Christmas period, and very low in the summer.

About 15 percent of a nonprofit group's donors will sign up for monthly-giving plans. This 15 percent gives a disproportionately high share of their total income. Some groups may get as many as 30 percent of their donors signed on.

Donors who sign on for monthly giving usually allow the money to be deducted until they request that it stop. This is known as a "negative option." The drop-off rate or donor loss may be half what it is for donors who have to take action to give again.

A negative option means it is not necessary to convince the donor to give again. This, in turn, reduces the amount of junk mail that might unintentionally alienate some people. Inertia is on your side, since the donor must take conscious action to discontinue giving.

In addition, monthly donors can be sent fewer fundraising letters, thus lowering the cost of communication and wasting less paper. You also send only a single tax receipt at the year-end. These savings more than make up for the staff time required to administer the plan and the small fees charged by banks.

3.2 Credit cards

Donors make larger contributions on credit cards than they do by checks or cash. Ken's firm has found that gifts are 10 percent to 25 percent larger.

Storekeepers and mail-order merchants know that credit-card shoppers spend more. Now charities can benefit. Maybe donors give more when they can use their credit cards because it is simpler. For some people, finding their checkbook is

hard. Then depression might set in as the donor looks over the bank account balance. Then there is the nuisance of actually writing out a check.

Credit cards are particularly helpful for people who agree to contribute over the phone, e-mail, or Internet. Typically, younger people are more comfortable with this than seniors. We explain on the following pages what arrangements you need to make to be able to accept gifts by credit card.

3.3 How to get started

Very small groups with only a few donors may find it too difficult to set up their own monthly donor and credit-card systems. Perhaps you can find a friendly business person or sister nonprofit group who will let you deposit donations through their account. However, donors may become confused when their credit-card bill arrives showing a payment to Joe's Pizza instead of your group.

For groups with more than 100 donors, it is probably worth setting up your own system. Here's how:

- *Encourage donors to write a series of post-dated checks.* Post-dated checks are an adequate system of monthly donations — though credit cards or pre-authorized checking (PAC) is better. People are unlikely to write very many checks at once — seldom more than a year. However, with credit cards and PAC the donations can continue, without further action, until the donor stops them. In addition, the bank occasionally returns post-dated checks and PAC transfers if there are insufficient funds. Credit-card donations are almost always honored.

- *Arrange to accept gifts on credit cards.* Contact your bank and ask them to set up a merchant account so you can take donations on both VISA and MasterCard. American Express has research that shows that people who donate with American Express cards donate twice as much as people who donate with regular bank cards. Groups that deal with upper-income people may also wish to accept American Express or other credit cards.

Credit-card companies do charge fees. Many people are surprised to learn you can negotiate for the best possible credit-card fees. Credit card companies usually tell you that you must pay them fees of 5 percent of the amount deposited. Many nonprofits have arranged fees as low as 1.5 percent. Negotiations will be easier if you have a board member or friend who is a major customer or employee at the bank or credit-card company, or a respectable community leader, such as a doctor or lawyer.

You also have to open a special clearing account and keep a small minimum balance in the account at all times. To protect themselves against fraud, credit-card companies may initially insist that you keep a very large amount on deposit. Ken has heard of credit-card companies expecting nonprofits to put up as much as $10,000, especially if the nonprofit will be taking donations over the Internet. Again, this can usually be negotiated. There will also be a small deposit for the card-impression device or electronic card-verification system. If you are not satisfied with your reception at one bank or card issuer, go to their competitors.

You may be able to set up arrangements for credit-card donations to be made to your group online through a service organization. For more on this arrangement, see chapter 10 section **4.3**.

- *Make arrangements for automatic monthly deductions from donors' credit cards.* Encourage donors to make monthly donations by designing a reply card or pledge form that allows you to deduct a contribution from their credit cards each month.

You do not have to have the donor's card to create a deposit slip; this is the same operation that is used in mail-order shopping. Write the donor's card number, expiry date, and name on a credit-card slip. In the spot where a signature is required, write SOF, which means "signature on file." (There will be a description of this procedure in the instruction book provided to you by the credit-card company.)

If you only have a few donors at first, you can process their monthly donations manually. Set up a simple internal reminder system so you can process these donations smoothly every month. Use a "bring forward" system to note which donors should be charged on each date. Don't be late. If you make your deposit a few days behind schedule, the donor will be irritated to find two payments to you on the same month's credit card statement.

Later as your volume grows you can automate this with the help of a bank.

3.4 Set the example

Ask the board, volunteers, special friends, and staff to give via the monthly system. This helps cover any minimum volume required to achieve economy of scale.

3.5 Ask often

Include monthly giving options in every fundraising appeal to individuals. On a reply form or in a brochure, include a phrase to allow this. (See next page for an example.)

Be sure to leave enough space to fill in the card number, which can be 18 digits long or more.

Even better, make the monthly gift the default, and other ways of giving start to seem unusual. *Foster Parents Plan** is famous for encouraging donors to sponsor a child for $31 a month (Canadian figures). Some donors may choose to pay for

---

*You can find more information on their system at <www.plan-international.org/canada>. As this book went to press, the Web site of Foster Parents Plan Canada did a better job of emphasizing the monthly donation than their US counterparts at <www.childreach.org>.

```
┌─────────────────────────────────────────┐
│  I wish to give   ❏ $5    ❏ $10   ❏ $15 │
│                   ❏ $20   $_____        │
│  to [name of nonprofit group] every month.│
│  Please charge it to my   ❏ VISA         │
│  ❏ MasterCard    ❏ American Express      │
│  Card number _____ │
│  Expiry date_____ │
│  Effective date_____ │
│  Name on the card _____ │
│                                          │
│  _____│
│  Signature _____ │
└─────────────────────────────────────────┘
```

the "adopted" child quarterly, semi-annually or annually, or just give occasionally, but most are focused on the monthly gift from the start. Can you put the emphasis on the monthly amount in your fundraising?

3.6 Expand to pre-authorized checking

Pre-authorized checking (PAC) is also called Electronic Fund Transfer (EFT). This is the same system used by many people to pay installments on car loans, mortgages, and insurance. The bank automatically withdraws the money from the donor's checking account every month and deposits it in the nonprofit group's account.

The bank will charge monthly administration fees. These are usually about $35 a month, plus 15¢ per donor (subject to local variation and negotiation). It is usually not cost-effective until you have about 50 donors signed up on monthly donations.

The banks often have complex legal forms they ask people to sign when they register for PAC. These are designed for commercial transactions, such as insurance or car lease payments. Most of the wording is irrelevant to a nonprofit group. Fight for the right to use simple, jargon-free wording.

3.7 Explore payroll deduction plans

It is increasingly easy for employers to allow employees to have contributions deducted from their paychecks automatically, thanks to new computerized pay systems. However, the hard part is convincing employees to sign on and name your group as the recipient.

Donors can also do this in many areas using payroll deduction plans already set up by the United Way and similar groups. They simply name your group as their designated beneficiary. It may be easier to convince people to do it this way, at first, rather than to set up your own system. The following steps should guide you in preparing your own donor system:

a) If your nonprofit group has employees, begin by setting up a payroll deduction plan for them. You can't ask others to do what you do not do yourself.

b) Discuss the payroll plan option with the United Way or similar groups in your community. If you receive support from them, be sure you do not endanger an important relationship. Research the methods they use and copy them. The local United Way may be willing to pass donations along to you free of charge, or there may be a small administrative fee to recognize the work they do in processing donations.

c) Ask board members to sign up where they work, or if they own or manage companies, to encourage their employees to sign on.

d) Send letters to your supporters, volunteers, clients, and members encouraging them to designate your group on their existing payroll deduction plans.

e) Approach large employers and ask if you can set up displays or send speakers to address employees.

4. Encourage Additional Donations

Do not send monthly donors all the direct-mail appeals sent to other people, but do write to them at least twice a year. This maintains their awareness and loyalty. It also gives them the option to give an extra amount because of a particular program that appeals to them. A high percentage of monthly donors do this.

Write to them in the pre-Christmas season, when donors are in their most generous mood. For those who do serious tax planning, it is also the last opportunity to give before the end of the calendar year.

Also, write to them in the spring, the second-most generous time of year. Filing tax returns (and in some cases getting tax rebates) may also remind people that they want to give more to charity.

5. Upgrade Donors

Contact monthly donors each year to encourage them to increase their gift level. Do this as part of the pre-Christmas appeal or when you have important news.

Modern forms of payment are gaining popularity among donors and nonprofit groups. Monthly donations, credit cards, and electronic fund transfers make it easy for people to be as generous as they want. They also improve cash flow and donor retention. The costs involved are negotiable, and are reasonable for a mid-size to larger group, particularly if you expect the group to be active over several years. Younger donors are more comfortable with this technology, but it is becoming more common everywhere.

CHAPTER 14
FUNDRAISING CONSULTANTS

There are two kinds of fundraising consultants: those who advise you how to raise money and those who do it for you. Some consultants do both. This chapter is primarily about consultants who give advice, rather than those who do your fundraising for you. In other chapters, we discussed some of the pitfalls of hiring outside firms to do your fundraising for you. However, there may be circumstances in which hiring an outside firm is cost-effective.

Fundraising consultants are widely used by the larger nonprofit groups in the United States, Canada, and Europe. This chapter will tell you when to consider bringing in a consultant, what a fundraising consultant can and can't do for you, and how to get value for your money. These suggestions are based on our experience both as staff and board members working with consultants and as consultants working with nonprofit clients.

1. When to Consider a Consultant

Bring in a consultant early, before a problem gets out of control. Don't wait until there is a crisis.

You should consider bringing in a fundraising consultant when you want to —

a) try a new method of fundraising,

b) increase your budget substantially by expanding your funding base,

c) establish your fundraising on a regular, more predictable, professional basis,

d) hire your first full-time staff fundraiser or train your first fundraiser,

e) deal with a backlog of fundraising materials and reports, or

f) prepare a fundraising strategy.

2. Selecting a Consultant

If the above situations sound familiar and you want to investigate using a consultant, here's how to go about it. Contact other fundraisers you know and find out if they have worked with consultants. A recommendation from a fundraiser you trust is a good starting point. If none of your peers has used a consultant, you might try contacting a larger charity or the development office of a nearby hospital or university for suggestions.

The American Association of Fund-Raising Counsel publishes a directory of members. The directory, available free of charge, lists consulting firms, their areas of expertise, and the geographical areas they serve. Both American and Canadian grassroots groups should start by approaching their local chapter of the Association of Fundraising Professionals or a similar group locally. To find a local contact, check <www.afpnet .org>, or call the professional fundraising staff at a university or hospital; chances are good they will be members. Canadian groups can get information on consultants from the Canadian Centre for Philanthropy at <www.ccp.ca>. The Centre can provide information about consultants who only advise as well as those who actually conduct fundraising campaigns. You can also check <www.charityvillage.com>. You might also like to review the discussion in the public forum at <www.charitychannel.com>; in particular, the forum on consultants (aimed at discussion among consultants) might be helpful. See the Appendix for complete contact details for these organizations.

One advantage of hiring a fundraising consultant who is a member of associations such as the Association of Fundraising Professionals or the Canadian Association of Gift Planners is that he or she can be expected to adhere to the codes of conduct developed by these associations. These codes encourage full disclosure of information, avoiding conflicts of interest, respect for the confidentiality of privileged information, and a commitment not to enter into percentage-based contracts.

Once you have the names of a few consultants, arrange to meet with each of them. The consultant should not charge you for this initial meeting, but confirm this when you call. Often, fundraisers are afraid to even phone a consultant because they think that the clock will immediately start ticking at $100 to $200 an hour. The first visit is usually free, provided that it is a sales call, and not an attempt to get all your problems solved without paying. Consultants make a living by selling their time and their ideas. A good consultant can save you untold hours of wasted work,

and will give you ideas and systems worth far more than you pay. But in our opinion, the consultant is in no position to charge you until you have a signed contract or an agreement. If it doesn't get to that stage, you should be under no obligation. However, the only way to be sure is to ask at the outset.

The initial meeting should be attended by the executive director, the staff fundraiser, the members of the board who deal with fundraising, and the fundraising consultant. Both the staff and the board should be represented; any experienced consultant will be reluctant to deal with only staff or only board members. Ask the consultant if there is any specific information you should assemble or send to him or her before the meeting.

At the meeting, you assess the consultant and the consultant assesses you. It's a two-way street, and both parties will have a lot of questions. You want to find out what the consultant's experience is, who some previous clients are, what specific expertise the consultant has to offer, and what he or she can do for your group. The consultant wants to learn about your programs and activities, your budget and your current donors, and what you expect from him or her. Both parties need to become acquainted and judge whether or not they will be able to work together.

If you decide to use a consultant, there are several ways to proceed. You could ask the consultant to submit a proposal to you, outlining the work that would be done, how long it would take, and what it would cost. Or you could decide what specific work you want the consultant to do and ask for an estimate on the job. A third option is to agree on an hourly or daily rate and set out the functions the consultant will perform over a specified period of time.

The second option is called a tender or a request for proposals. If you choose this method, do your homework first! Don't send tenders to 28 consultants! That means you are asking 27 consultants to waste their time, and in a few weeks, you will have to call all 27 and tell them just that.

Joyce's policy as a consultant is not to respond to any invitation to tender that was sent to more than five consultants.

The third option is a common billing arrangement, but, if you use it, be sure to make the consultant give you itemized invoices, indicating how much time was spent on individual tasks or functions. You should also inquire about the consultant's billing practices for travel time, expenses for travel and accommodation, evening or weekend meetings, telephone time, and secretarial support, as well as any taxes they may have to charge. The larger consulting firms will have many staff people with a range of experience, expertise, and fees. Be sure you are getting the individual you think you are getting. Some firms may send the president or a senior partner out to impress you at the initial meeting, and then send a junior consultant to do the work. Specify in the contract the person you want to do the work by naming him or her as the principal consultant.

Some consultants work for a percentage of the money they raise for your group. The advantage to you is that if the fundraising does not succeed, it doesn't cost you any money. This arrangement is controversial. For the protection of nonprofit groups, the Code of Ethics of The Association of Fundraising Professionals (<www.afpnet.org/ethics>) specifically prohibits members from working on a commission, and the Code of Ethics of the Canadian Centre for Philanthropy states that paid fundraisers, whether staff or consultants, should never be paid finders' fees or commissions. Think through how your donors might react. Find out what the consultant plans to do, and be sure *you* retain control.

3. Getting Value For Your Consulting Dollar

One of the best ways to get value for your money is to get the consultant to teach you the tricks of the trade and to train you to be a better fundraiser. The one thing the fundraising consultant has that you probably lack is broad fundraising experience. With that professional judgment, the consultant can save you a lot of misdirected time and effort. Try to tap that experience and learn as much as you can from the consultant. Make this an explicit part of the contract. Don't have the consultant do work that you can do for yourself or that he or she can teach you to do. If you need an extra pair of hands to pitch in and do the work, it is usually cheaper to hire staff than consultants.

Another cost-effective use of a consultant's time is to have the consultant develop a fundraising strategy and plan for you. The consultant can do the following things:

a) Provide an objective assessment of your fundraising capability

b) Tell you which sectors and which specific sources to approach to fund different projects, how to do it, and who to get to do it

c) Interpret the responses to requests and tell you if a new direction or emphasis is indicated

d) Determine the fundraising tools and materials you will need for the job

Researching individual, corporate, and foundation prospects is a task the consultant can do, but it is an ongoing, time-consuming job. It would be better to get the consultant to teach you to do the research yourself. There are some fundraising functions which, in our opinion, the consultant should not perform. The consultant should not recruit fundraising volunteers or do any face-to-face solicitations for you. He or she can tell you who to recruit, who to solicit, and what kind of rationale to use, but you have to do the person-to-person contact.

There are several reasons for this. If the consultant went door-knocking for you, he or she would end up on the same doorsteps too frequently. In a fundraising meeting, the consultant might have to take a position on an issue, state policy, or make a commitment on behalf of your group. The consultant is not authorized to do this and shouldn't be.

Finally, consultants are concerned about their reputations. They can't be expected to put their reputations behind every client group, especially when they don't have any decision-making power in that group.

4. Conclusion

Consultants can play a valuable role in fundraising. The right fundraising consultant at the right time can save an organization a lot of time, effort, and money. Consultants have technique and broad experience, and they should have sound judgment and good instincts. But they don't have any magic sources of money up their sleeves. They know that fundraising is a lot of hard work, and they are prepared to do it for a price. There is no great mystery about it and no reason to be suspicious. Just be sure you have a clear contract, you know each other's expectations, and you say what's on your mind every step of the way.

CHAPTER 15
VOLUNTEERS

1. Fighting Resistance

One of the few ways to expand your organization's services without increasing payroll is by developing your volunteer capability. However, developing a sound and lasting volunteer program requires care, knowledge, and planning. It may require some effort to even convince your board of directors or your staff to create or expand volunteer activity.

A common reason for resistance to using volunteers is the myth that volunteers, by definition, are not reliable, are not capable, and are not competent. You may hear statements such as the following:

- "You will spend all this time and energy on volunteers, and just when you get them trained, they'll quit."

- "You can't trust this important task to a volunteer. It's too critical for the organization."

- "You simply can't depend on volunteers."

There is a grain of truth in these concerns. To counter them, you will need to convince your staff or board that you have a workable plan to deal with these potential problems. Present actual examples of the successful and innovative use of volunteers. Demonstrate how the benefits will add up and how you will minimize the costs.

If you decide to proceed, you must educate yourself and your colleagues about working with volunteers. You need to understand what motivates and discourages them. Learn about the volunteer cultivation process, from recruitment and orientation through training and promotion, and on to retirement.

Are the state of the economy and heavier work commitments destroying volunteerism? Definitely not! Volunteerism has changed since the fifties, when stay-at-home mothers seemed to have time available for hours of volunteer work. Now, most volunteers work. Many have university degrees, and the more education they have, the more they volunteer. Women still volunteer slightly more than men do, but not much. Volunteers still put in long hours; they are also most likely to be over 35.

2. Volunteer Roles

Many groups think of volunteers as people who are willing to work endlessly at stuffing envelopes simply out of the goodness of their hearts. There are such people, but this attitude — that all volunteers aspire to nothing more than the low-level jobs no one else wants to do — limits volunteers' potential.

Volunteers now provide direct service in many social service agencies, art galleries, environmental groups, Big Brothers and Big Sisters, and thousands of other nonprofits. They may be trained to provide direct service or to work alongside a team of professionals. Previous clients who have benefited from the organization may volunteer to serve new clients. This model is used by Alcoholics Anonymous and Bereaved Families. The individual's personal experience and motivation ("to help someone who's going through what I went through,") coupled with training in counselling, produce an excellent volunteer.

Many new grassroots groups are run totally by volunteers who function in many capacities: conducting research, formulating positions and policy, making presentations to government bodies, writing briefs, and issuing press releases. The track record of the volunteers in these groups is impressive, yet volunteers are rarely given these opportunities in traditional charities.

Bringing volunteers into a policy-making or direct service role will have an impact on the professional staff who formerly had exclusive control of those areas. Not only will they have to work with volunteers, but their jobs may shift from one of direct contact with the client group to that of a trainer and manager of volunteers. The professional may be reluctant to give up the satisfaction of direct contact with the client and may feel threatened or disenfranchised. Staff may even worry about losing their jobs to volunteers, and in several unionized nonprofit agencies, the use of volunteers has been an issue for collective bargaining.

To deal with the apprehensions of the staff, involve them in the design of the volunteer development program. Ask the board to draft a policy and set of practices pertaining to the role and function of volunteers. Make a written agreement with your volunteers so that everyone understands and accepts both the opportunities for and the limits to volunteer involvement in decision making. Identify volunteers who are interested in autonomy and decision-making power, and place them in situations requiring responsibility and initiative.

The volunteer cannot and should not replace paid staff. Volunteers extend and humanize the services, provide a strong and authentic link with the community, inject new energy, imagination, and innovation into the organization. Creative use of volunteer labor should enhance the role of paid staff, not replace it.

3. Understanding Volunteers' Motives

There is a popular assumption that people volunteer out of duty or out of their desire to *do good*. While there is good citizenship in every volunteer, there are as many different reasons for volunteering as there are people. A volunteer's motives are highly personal, and you don't need to know all the reasons why each of your volunteers works for you. However, you need to understand and recognize a range of motives so that you can design volunteer jobs to fit the motives.

Most people volunteer because *there's something in it for them*. The volunteer job must fill a need. These needs may vary from a need for self-esteem and affiliation to wanting to help create change or further one's career. Within the business community, taking a position on the board or a committee of a prominent charity is a common method for improving career mobility. It is not for paid staff to judge these motives: you need only ensure that the individual volunteer does not subvert the aims of the organization to further his or her own private interests.

Some people volunteer because they care about a particular issue such as nuclear disarmament, environmental protection, child abuse, AIDS, modern dance, education, or religion. Others want to meet new people who hold similar interests and values. People who work in the home or who are new mothers or fathers may volunteer because they need a break from parenting and want contact with other adults. Some people want to be where the action is, and others see volunteer work as an opportunity for personal development. Often people are looking for an outlet that is lacking in other parts of their lives, such as a chance to make decisions or take on a leadership role.

Volunteers give of themselves because they need something. The best way to gain their involvement and commitment is to understand their motives and use that information to place them in a capacity that will meet their needs.

4. Finding Volunteers

"Sure, we could use volunteers around here, but I don't know where to find them," you plead.

Volunteers are all around you. Almost every person you know and meet is a potential volunteer. The trick is in fitting the volunteer to the job and not being afraid to ask. Personal contacts are a good source of volunteers because by knowing the skills and interests of people, you are in a better position to match them to a job in your agency. The very best way to find volunteers is to ask people you already know.

Actively recruit volunteers to fill specific jobs. Do not wait passively for volunteers to approach you. Do not merely find tasks to fit the volunteers' abilities and interests. Instead, go "head-hunting" for the volunteers with the skills you need. Nonprofit leaders often sigh, "None of the volunteers are interested in fundraising." Many people *are* interested in fundraising, of course, but it is often true that such people are in high demand and may not be knocking at your door. Go out and find them! We promise they are available.

People who are already volunteers are a likely source because people tend to volunteer for several groups. While this may need to change in the long run, calling on those who are already volunteers will likely be productive. You can find them by seeing who is publicly praised for good volunteer work by other nonprofits. Ask other nonprofits if they have volunteers they can send your way. Large agencies such as hospitals and zoos often have more applicants than they can handle at certain times of year. They may make a referral. Others with cyclical campaigns, such as the United Way, like to keep their volunteers busy in the off-season. You have nothing to lose by asking!

Many medium-size and large cities have a volunteer bureau and a community information center. Both can help you identify volunteers, and the volunteer bureau may also assist you in training. For example, one mental health center in Ontario offers groups free collating, folding, and envelope-stuffing services, with the labor provided by patients. Critics may consider this exploitation of the patients, but the patients themselves say they are glad to be doing useful work for good causes while developing work skills and relieving boredom. If this practice is not established in your community, you might try approaching various institutions to see if they would be willing to offer such a service.

Retraining centers exist in many communities to help people develop marketable job skills. These may be for women, immigrants, people with disadvantaged backgrounds, or highly skilled people who were laid off when their organizations were downsized. Many retraining centers eagerly seek on-the-job training opportunities for their students. The trainees may be paying for this training, or they may be getting a grant, unemployment insurance, or welfare while they work for you. You may get free help for days, weeks, or months. In extreme cases your group may even get token financial assistance to compensate you for the time you spend with them. Ask schools if they can help you find volunteers.

Colleges and universities often have work-term placements where students gain experience in their chosen career by working with a nonprofit group. If you need publicity, ask if a nearby school teaches courses on media relations or journalism. High school, private school, and religious school students in some areas are expected to do volunteer work as part of their curriculum. School placement centers also know that the work experience you can offer looks good on the resume of a student or an unemployed or underemployed recent graduate. Seniors' centers also help match volunteers with groups that need help. You may find people with extensive experience eager to keep busy.

People who have recently moved to your community are another good source of volunteers. They are interested in making contacts, and aren't yet over-committed. Ask for help finding them through the Welcome Wagon, the Newcomers' Club, schools, places of worship, and real estate agents. Unelected politicians are another good source. They want to build community profile, and you know a lot about them before you start recruiting. Look at the lists of people who lost recent elections for any level of government, from school board to the highest offices, and ask them. If all goes well, they'll win the next election and you'll have friends in high places. Community sentencing programs may also offer you free work, while keeping people out of jail. These programs are for people convicted of minor, nonviolent offences. Some of the people may be unskilled, but able to help you with manual labor. Others may be highly skilled, white-collar people who can help improve your systems. Contact the courts if you think this might fit your group.

Consider asking the people you serve to volunteer. While this is not appropriate in every circumstance, it makes sense for groups involved in arts, sport, social change, adult education, and many kinds of heath care. These volunteers already understand your group. They may bring a unique and helpful view of your work. It may also help build their self-esteem to be part of the helping team and not only a recipient.

Appeals for volunteers through the mass media may work if your group is well known or if you are working on a high-profile cause. There is also the possibility that the volunteer will contact you directly. Be prepared to deal with volunteers who present themselves.

5. Recruitment and Orientation

The process of recruiting is often badly neglected. First impressions are hard to change. The recruitment experience establishes the basis of volunteers' expectations. It must be done well.

Before you begin recruiting, clearly establish the need for volunteers, the types of jobs they could perform, and the skills that are required. In other words, what jobs do you have and what kind of volunteers can fill them?

Keep the tasks short at first, unless they require a lot of training or a lengthy commitment. Research shows that almost 80 percent of people are more willing to volunteer for short-term assignments. Don't assign open-ended tasks, such as handling special events or joining a committee. Ask them to work on one part of a special event for just two weeks or a month. If you make it rewarding, they may continue on to do more. Another advantage of starting with a short-term assignment is that it is easier to get rid of volunteers who prove to be poorly suited to your needs.

Create a unique job description for each volunteer task, so you and he or she know what to expect. Make sure that your concept of the job and the volunteer's description of the position match. The more explicit you are about your expectations, the better the chances your volunteer will deliver. Be clear and honest about how much time you expect the volunteer to contribute. Nonprofit groups often underestimate the workload, in part because they are afraid of scaring away a badly needed new person by telling the truth. If you tell a volunteer they are needed for less time than they will actually spend, don't be surprised if they only put in the time they agreed to, or leave. Also offer people training. About 70 percent of people are more willing to volunteer when they receive training.

If your group expects volunteers and board members to make a financial commitment, let them know about this during the recruiting stage. Don't spring it on them later! It is fair to ask volunteers to contribute both time and money, as long as they can make the choice on their own. In fact, people who volunteer give an average of 60 percent more money than those who do not.

Next, look at your potential volunteers and establish their needs, interests, and motivations. Have them complete a form like that in Sample 14. Then you are in a position to find the volunteer that best fits the job and the job that best fits the volunteer.

It is appropriate to interview and screen new volunteers. Be selective. This is not only allowable, it is a respected sign of good management. In unusual cases, such as volunteers working with children or handling a lot of cash, it is normal to do background checks and ask the police to review the volunteer's record. Make it routine to ask each volunteer for a resume or to fill in an application form. Discuss their experience and education. Explore their goals.

If you don't have tasks that match the volunteers' needs and abilities, don't tie them up with meaningless busy work. Thank them and encourage them to look elsewhere. Refer them to other groups if you can. If you think you might need them in future, keep their names and numbers on file.

Now you can plan the actual recruitment. The recruitment technique you use should suit your potential volunteers. Will they respond best to a luncheon meeting with you or with a member of the board, or would they be more comfortable at a meeting of friends of the organization? Are they familiar enough with the group to accept an approach from any staff or board person, or would

they respond better to an approach from a group member they know personally?

Some people will need to be exposed to the organization before deciding whether to make a commitment. Provide such opportunities regularly through open houses, tours, wine and cheese parties, and other events. If people are interested, give them the chance to see how they like the group and the activity before asking for a commitment. If you push them too soon, you may lose them.

Be sure to use personal follow-up at each stage. Potential volunteers need to feel needed, and to feel that the organization cares about them. The follow-up can be done on the telephone or over coffee. Follow-up is very important in attracting and keeping volunteers.

Try to find out as much as you can about your prospects' interests, what they think of your cause, what they might enjoy doing with your group. Tell them about the facets of your work and try to get them to identify what they see as their niche in the organization. These recruitment procedures are also part of the orientation process, as the volunteer is becoming familiar with the group, the task at hand, and the people with whom he or she will be working.

Once a prospect agrees to try out a job, provide a period of orientation, a chance to see if he or she likes the position and fits in. Providing the time and the process for new volunteers to check out the organization and their role in it will give you happier and more productive volunteers. Orientation should be matched to the needs of the volunteer. It need not be a long, structured process, but it should make the newcomer feel comfortable and confident in the new setting.

Before volunteers begin working, give them a tour of the organization and introduce them to people with whom they will be working. This is a time for informal chatting, a chance to ask questions and observe work, a chance to break new ground and figure out how they will fit into their

SAMPLE 14
VOLUNTEER PROFILE

Name: _____

Address: _____

Home Phone: (____)_____ Best time to call: _____

Work Phone: (____)_____ Best time to call: _____

Cell Phone: (____)_____ Best time to call: _____

E-mail: _____

Occupation: _____ Date of birth: _____

Employer/school: _____

Who should we call in case of an emergency?

Name _____

Number: (____)_____ Relationship _____

1. Availability

a) How many hours per week can you contribute to the program? _____

b) When are you available?

	Mon	Tues	Wed	Thurs	Fri	Sat	Sun
Morning							
Lunch hour							
Afternoon							
Evening							
Night shift							

c) Any dates not available (e.g., holidays):_____

d) Commitment for this year: _____

_____

_____

2. Relevant Experience

a) Please list any previous volunteer experience: _____

_____

_____

b) Please list any previous employment experience: _____

_____

_____

_____

c) Briefly describe hobbies, interests, clubs or activities that you enjoy:_____

_____

_____

_____

3. Goals

a) Briefly describe why you offered to volunteer in this organization (for example, community involvement, further work experience, concern for this cause, enjoy being with people like [name]): _____

_____

_____

_____

b) Do you have specific achievement goals that you plan to accomplish through this volunteer experience?_____

_____

_____

_____

6. Appropriate tasks

a) Which of these areas are you interest in? (Check all that apply.)

❑ Newsletter committee

❑ Fundraising

❑ Advertising

❑ Develop web site

❑ Other specific areas

_____

_____

_____

b) Are there any tasks you do not want to do?

_____

_____

_____

jobs. Depending on the nature of the work, you might also want to use group meetings with role-playing sessions to help the new people get used to their new jobs.

Now you can put the volunteers into their new positions and proceed with on-the-job training. But don't abandon them! This is a hard time for them; this is the test. They need a lot of support at this stage and want to feel needed and recognized. Hold regular meetings of new volunteers at which they can share their feelings and experiences in their new jobs. To ensure support and follow-up, you can have supervisors check up on the newcomers and encourage them.

Another approach is to pair new volunteers with more experienced ones. Asking volunteers who have been with you for a number of months to orient new volunteers is often effective. These old hands lend confidence to the newcomers with an attitude that says, "I was just as unfamiliar with this as you are, but soon you will feel as comfortable as I do now." The experienced volunteers can also translate any jargon your organization uses and introduce the new person to others. The fresh volunteer, in turn, may help re-energize the volunteer who has been around for a while.

When a volunteer has held a position for several weeks and is prepared to stay, review the job description with him or her. If the volunteer's description of the job still matches yours, you can now ask the volunteer to make a commitment to fill that position for a fixed period of time. If the whole process has gone smoothly, you can let the volunteer begin to work independently. He or she should now be able to ask for help when needed.

If a volunteer doesn't like the job after a few weeks but still cares for the organization, see if he or she will try another job. Don't try to keep volunteers in jobs with which they aren't happy. If the job doesn't work for the volunteer, the volunteer won't work in the job.

People often complain that it takes a lot of work to get to the point at which the volunteer is producing for the organization. It's true! The process of recruitment and orientation *is* labor intensive. To manage the load, many nonprofits have a "Coordinator of Volunteers." Often this job is done by a volunteer!

If your *only* reason for wanting volunteers is to free the staff for other "more important" work, we suggest that you forget volunteers and look into labor-saving devices. It is the combination of the work that volunteers do and their ability to enrich the organization that justifies the investment for both parties.

6. Training, Promotion, and Appreciation

Once new volunteers are working well, you must still provide periodic training and growth opportunities. Volunteers need renewal, stimulus, feedback, and change, or they become stale and lose interest.

The need for support is particularly important at the 90-day mark of a volunteer's involvement. Up to that time, there is a honeymoon period in which volunteers may forgive problems. After three months, neglect may lead to cynicism or early departure.

A combination of formal and informal training will fill the ongoing need for renewal for several years. Training can range from simply passing on an interesting magazine article to sending volunteers to seminars and conferences. Many continuing-education programs offer courses that are good training for volunteers. The costs of training should be borne by the organization.

Give your volunteers regular opportunities for reflection and self-evaluation. This way, both you and the volunteer can identify when he or she is ready for a change or a promotion. If you promote a volunteer within the organization, he or she will again need to go through orientation and training stages. Don't drop a volunteer, no matter how experienced, into a new job without support.

Sometimes, a volunteer's growth may require that he or she move to another agency. What is most important is that the voluntary community as a whole can continue to provide new and exciting opportunities for the volunteer and benefit from his or her efforts. Keep the volunteers' best interests in mind and be aware of their changing needs. That is the organization's side of the contract with the volunteer. Besides, if you fail to meet their needs, you will soon lose them anyway.

If several groups can cooperate and pool their efforts in identifying, recruiting, and training volunteers, everybody stands to gain. The chances of gaining new volunteers and promoting others will be far greater through interagency cooperation. Some areas have volunteer centers that match up volunteers and agencies.

Providing thanks and recognition to your volunteers should be a regular feature of the program, not something that is done only when the person leaves. It may be as informal as a birthday or Christmas card, or as formal as a presentation of a plaque at a banquet. Do it in a manner that is appropriate for the individual. The thanks will carry more meaning if it is personalized.

7. Retirement and Succession

Too many groups try to hang on to their volunteers, begging them to stay on, making them feel guilty for leaving. This is most unfortunate because the volunteer leaves the organization with a bad taste in the mouth, and that doesn't serve the individual or the group. Let your volunteers retire gracefully, with thanks and recognition. When they want to quit, accept it and thank them.

If the person's leaving creates a great gap, it may be appropriate to ask the retiring volunteer to recruit another person to fill the job. However, beware of downgrading. Ken saw one group at which the departing volunteer, a senior partner in a law firm, replaced herself with a junior partner. The junior partner served his term in office, then, in turn, recruited another lawyer who was not yet a partner, who, a year later, recruited a law student. In just a few short years the position moved from power to peanuts.

Of course, in the best of all worlds you would have a successor waiting to replace a key volunteer who retires. This is called succession planning. Sample 15 can be used to develop and evaluate possible successors for a key job and plan the recruitment. In many cases, you can get retiring volunteers to train their own replacements. It's efficient, effective, and everybody feels good.

In some groups, the volunteer jobs switch over at an annual meeting. Joyce's own alumni association works that way. Since members and volunteers

SAMPLE 15
SUCCESSION PLANNING SHEET

POSITION TO BE FILLED _____ BY WHEN_____				
Potential candidates	Candidate's interests	Rank candidates	Possible recruiters	Possible contacts

are spread across the country, succession planning is essential. Joyce has developed a simple form to help retiring volunteers explain their jobs to new volunteers. (See Sample 16.)

8. The Volunteer as Fundraiser

Why is fundraising different from any other volunteer job? Almost nobody wants to do it, and just about everybody is afraid to try. In fundraising, failure is visible and public. As a result, there are more ways to avoid fundraising than any other job, with the possible exception of defrosting the freezer!

The resistance to fundraising is incredibly high. Your fundraising volunteers will need a lot of help. They need support, encouragement, and training. If your volunteers are doing telemarketing, canvassing, or face-to-face fundraising, they need to be trained specifically for those techniques. The learning curve is all at the front end. Once they are trained and they succeed, they will keep producing for you.

There have been times when, after the training session and everything else, board members have said, "There's no way I can do this. I can't ask for money." You could say, "Sure you can!" and invalidate their concerns. Instead, say, "I understand. Is there another way you could help us with raising money?" Your volunteers have to be comfortable with their participation in fundraising or they won't succeed.

One of the most positive and exciting fundraising committees we have ever seen was headed by a vice president of sales from Xerox. He ran the fundraising like a sales campaign. The committee loved it. If your fundraising committee is dragging its heels, recruit a top salesperson.

9. Managing Staff/Volunteer Relationships

If surveyed, probably 40 percent of volunteers would report that they had been abused in their volunteer position, and another 40 percent would report themselves dissatisfied with how they are managed. Only 20 percent would say that they are pleased with the way they are treated by the organizations they serve.

What qualifies as volunteer abuse? Yes, volunteers face sexual harassment, verbal hostilities, and even physical threats when dealing with troubled people. So do staff. There are also forms of abuse unique to volunteers. Consider this short list of examples:

a) Placing Jane Novice, a first-time volunteer, on the board committee that faces the most controversial issues. After the unsuspecting Jane has accepted, you tell her that these issues exist, the chair has just resigned, she is currently a committee of one, and that she will have to recruit the rest of the committee members.

b) Plunging Jane into demanding action such as counselling or handling a crisis phone line alone with no orientation, training, or back-up support.

c) Keeping Joe Faithful, a longtime volunteer, stuck in the same job year after year, long past the time when he is bored and wants to progress to new challenges and responsibilities.

d) Allowing John Oldtimer, one of the original board members, to continue wasting his time and talents on an organization that doesn't want what he is offering.

e) Asking Kim Peaceful to take on more responsibility or give a speech as a "reward" for good work, when Kim just wants to be allowed to continue doing familiar, relaxing tasks within her competency.

That's a mere start to the list of abuses that staff members perpetrate against volunteers and volunteers sometimes perpetrate against each other. Now, let's take a look at the other list — the volunteers staff members hate.

SAMPLE 16
VOLUNTEER POSITION DESCRIPTION

Steering Committee Position Description

Position title:_____

Position previously filled by: _____

Telephone number:_____

Major activities:

_____

_____

_____

_____

_____

Major responsibilities:

_____

_____

_____

_____

_____

Reports to:

_____

_____

_____

Average time/month required:

_____

_____

Materials, resources, or access (e.g., printing, computer time, etc.):

_____

_____

_____

_____

a) Alice Professional, who demands that the underfinanced community group that she has deemed worthy of her time measure up to her professional standards.

b) Alex Runsitall, the committee member who wants to have a say on all important matters, even though his committee meets only once a year.

c) Annie Condescension, who treats volunteer work like a third-rate proposition. She is frequently heard to say, "It's only volunteer work. It doesn't have to be perfect. They won't mind if it's late." (This attitude does more to create staff disrespect of volunteers than anything else, except no delivery at all!)

d) Alan Overrule, who ignores professional staff judgments. Often found on boards or committees, he makes decisions on matters that he is not qualified to judge. We once heard about a Mr. Overrule who, as a newly recruited board member, ordered removal of a structure that was basic to the group's treatment methodology. His action resulted in mayhem within the facility.

Given the experience of both volunteers and staff with these kinds of abuse, it's no wonder that concern about volunteers continues to appear on the priority lists of conferences. But what are the solutions? "Maybe we need to put more effort into recruitment," said a client of ours who was worried about volunteer turnover. "You had better find out why they are leaving in the first place," we suggested, "otherwise you will just lose them as fast as you recruit them."

Volunteer turnover, poor attendance at meetings, low morale, low productivity — there are no simple equations that will diagnose the cause and prescribe the cure. The same symptom could have five different causes in five different organizations, and five different solutions as well. The first step in finding the solution in your organization is for senior staff and volunteers to admit that there is a problem. This is critical, because if they don't recognize the problem, they won't see the need for a solution. Then determine whether the people involved are truly willing to work to change the status quo. Don't assume that recognition of the problem means a commitment to change. Most people hate change.

If you can negotiate these two steps successfully, you are in a good position to analyze the situation. Start interviewing volunteers and staff to find out how they see each other, what they've experienced, and what they think the problems and solutions might be. Using this information, take a look at the big picture. What are the key issues? Is it leadership? Is it structure? Is it relationships between staff and volunteers or between different levels of volunteers?

When you have a comprehensive analysis in hand, you will know where changes need to be made to improve your organization. Enlist the help of those who were ready to recognize the problems and seem willing to change things to solve those problems.

10. Conclusion

This approach to volunteer management is a lot of work, but it's an approach that's based on the realities of running an organization. More important, it works. Whether you can develop your organization to its fullest potential depends on expanding your people resources when your dollar resources are fixed or shrinking. To meet the growing demands from your constituencies, you must be positive, forward-looking, and innovative.

CHAPTER 16
STRATEGIES FOR SURVIVAL

1. Be Self-Sufficient

The best survival strategy for nonprofit organizations is self-sufficiency. Public interest groups should make a deliberate attempt to function as self-sufficient, nonprofit businesses. Many nonprofit groups give away potentially marketable products. If there is a need for what you are doing — be it a book, newsletter, or film — in many cases you should be able to sell it and break even financially.

The voluntary sector needs an injection of marketing and entrepreneurial skills. It needs people who can interest a target public in a cause and convince them to invest their money in it.

2. Build Up Your Organization

Building an organization as the vehicle to carry forward your mission is a survival strategy. That may sound like a blinding glimpse of the obvious, but there are a lot of neglected organizations. The volunteers, staff, resources, structures, policies — all the things that together make up an organization — cannot be taken for granted. The

care and feeding of the organization is a necessity, not a luxury. If you don't take care of your organization, your organization will not be able to shoulder the burdens you want it to carry and your cause will be short-lived.

Within your organization, strive to build a strong, committed staff and board. When it comes to the crunch, when a group is on the brink of bankruptcy or oblivion, only a strong staff and board can pull it together and save it from falling apart.

3. Encourage Diversity

Developing diversity within the organization will help ensure its survival. Diversity means having a racial, gender, social, economic, and cultural mix within your board of directors. It means listening to your critics and lunching with your perceived enemies. Encouraging diversity means getting all the actors, all the people who have a stake in the issue, to sit down together. It means getting clients working as staff or board members to keep you honest and make sure you don't get pushed off your mission.

Diversity means listening to your funders and recruiting them as volunteers and consultants. Rosabeth Moss Kanter, a well-known management consultant, was asked, "What makes a good consultant?" She replied, "You have to be able to go into an organization you know nothing about, walk around in it for an hour, and say something intelligent about it." Consultants can do that because they are *outside* the organization. So listen to outsiders: they can tell you things about your group that you cannot see for yourself.

Diversity within your leadership gives you an early warning system for outside change that could affect you. If you are involved with social and political issues, your organization is very vulnerable to changes in legislation, in political agendas, and in funding priorities. If you have a diverse board, you have more radar stations to warn you so that you can adjust in time. Diversity gives you adaptive capacity. Without it, your group could go the way of the dinosaur.

4. Manage Conflict

Diversity *is* important and powerful for organizations, but many groups are afraid of it, knowing intuitively that the price of diversity is conflict. Most people think conflict is bad and should be avoided, but conflict in organizations is inevitable, necessary, and healthy if you learn to manage it properly. It's only bad if you avoid working it through or if you personalize it.

Entire books have been written on conflict, and this isn't one of them. When you sense conflict between individuals, groups, or departments, get on it fast. Fed by avoidance, conflict will grow and it can become debilitating. Don't hesitate to get outside help if you need it.

Some of the most exciting and high-performing teams we have worked with were those that could manage conflict. Team members would openly state and explain different points of view and the group would work on the differences. The goal of the discussion wasn't to be right or to win, it was to look at all the information, ideas,

and implications and work to a consensus. The energy that comes from this kind of conflict resolution and the efficacy of the decision making can carry a team a long way.

5. Ensure Quality

The most common mistake made by nonprofit groups is trying to do too much with too little, too fast. They have undisciplined passion and short-sighted strategies. Trying to change the world overnight achieves high staff and volunteer burnout, crisis fundraising, low credibility in the constituencies you are trying to influence, and an early demise. The quality of the group's work deteriorates.

Whether your group runs a program, provides a service, produces a booklet, or does research, focusing on quality instead of quantity will keep you on the right track. Use the quality of the work you do as a check against the seduction of undisciplined passion. A group that limits its mandate and ensures that what it does, it does well, has a good strategy for survival.

6. Continue Learning

Let your organization be about learning and having fun. Children learn through play and so do adults. People who are given the opportunity to learn and grow in their work are the most productive.

Be theory-based in your work. Determine which theories work or don't work for you, but don't assume you know better than all the research and all the theorists. That is simply arrogance. Kurt Lewin, one of the founders of organization development, said, "There is nothing so practical as a good theory." Make the theories work for you.

7. Conclusion

There is an incredible range of nonprofit groups in the world working to build a better society by helping abused children, former psychiatric patients, First Nations people, illiterate people,

people with illnesses, immigrants, or minority language groups; by saving historical buildings, the environment, animals, or dead elm trees; by making life more beautiful through arts and culture and religion, or by addressing any of the countless other causes that are part of our world.

We hope we've given you a few shortcuts to financing the changes needed to make a better world. And we thank you for all the hard work and sacrifices you make along the way. The path may not be easy, but the results are worthwhile. Good luck!

AFTERWORD

What follows was written by Joyce's dear friend and mentor, the late Dick Arima, a top management and organization development consultant of international repute. For those of us in helping organizations and helping roles, this goes to the heart of the challenges and dilemmas we face.

Fairness

For those who want to help the less privileged, whether they are disadvantaged by gender, race, social status, age, or another reason, the question of fairness becomes an issue at one time or another. How can the less privileged get a fair chance in institutions and organizations? Recent revisions in the Canadian Human Rights Act address this question.

All organizations have rules governing employment, membership, promotions, terminations, and hierarchies within the group. While some of these rules are explicit and formalized, others are implicit and subjective. Hence, extending fair-play privileges to the less privileged entails not only attention to the formal rules, which are relatively easy to monitor, but to the informal rules as well. These informal rules present difficulties because the perpetrators themselves are often not conscious of them.

If you want to help the less privileged, you should understand your personal stand on fair play. If you do so, your aid will be more consistent and focused. You will also avoid ambivalence on the issue, an ambivalence that is likely to be detected by those you are helping.

Use the list below to help you identify your attitude toward how society should deal with inequality:

a) *Patronization: Maintain the rules and systems of the privileged, reward the less privileged who work hard and "know their place in life."*

The helper who espouses this value teaches the less privileged how to be effectively compliant and how to stay out of trouble. The consequence for the less privileged is that it will help them to survive. However, they will remain subjugated.

b) *Competition: Every man for himself. Democracy is based on individual hard work and aspiration, and the cream will rise to the top regardless of the system.*

The helper who espouses this value enables individuals to become more competent and competitive. The consequence for the less privileged is that individuals may gain some of society's rewards such as better pay, jobs, or housing. However, these individuals will have to be over-achievers in order to compete with the privileged and could be disappointed if there are ceilings for such rewards for the less privileged.

c) *Assimilation: Don't fight the rules, adapt to them. Work harder and work smarter.*

The helper who espouses this value ensures that the less privileged under-stand the rules. Additionally, the helper can enable the less privileged to work effectively within the bounds of the rules. The consequence for the less privileged is that the rewards will be more bountiful than competition without awareness of the rules. However, through assimilation people can lose their sense of cultural identity, and in hard times, all the effort that went into assimilating does not guarantee continued privileges.

d) *Compensation: Extra assistance to the less privileged because they are starting off with a handicap. They are not the inventors of the rules nor the maintainers and, therefore, they start at a point behind the privileged.*

The helper who espouses this value advocates the cause of the less privileged, sponsoring and championing them and challenging the formal and informal rules on their behalf. It is expected that the less privileged will work to help themselves during this advocacy. The consequence for the less privileged is more equality of privileges because organizations become more aware of unfair rules. However, overdependence on sponsors may lead to feelings of inadequacy.

e) *Equality: Strive for pluralism, an integration of diverse cultural characteristics in organizations rather than one culture group dominant over other culture groups.*

The helper who espouses this value assists the less privileged to value their cultural heritage. The helper can do what is possible to assist institutions to value other culture contributions and to change those systems that deny those contributions. The consequence for the less privileged is equal opportunity, not only in employment, promotions, and other concrete rewards, but also in formulating the formal and informal rules by which these benefits are awarded.

— Dick Arima

APPENDIX

Here is a partial list of resources you may find useful. There are many others. A listing here is not an endorsement. Being left out is not condemnation. If your favorite is missing, please contact Ken Wyman (e-mail: kenwyman@compuserve.com).

Contact the organizations listed for current prices and information. They may charge extra if your payment does not accompany the order. All information is subject to change.

National Organizations
Canada

Canadian Centre for Philanthropy (CCP)
425 University Avenue, 7th Floor
Toronto, ON M5G 1T6
Tel: 416 597-2293
Fax: 416 597-2294
Web: www.ccp.ca
E-mail: general@ccp.ca

CCP covers all aspects of organizational management as well as fundraising. Special seminars on a variety of topics. Monthly newsletter. Offers computerised foundation searches. Membership fees and charges apply to services.

CCP publishes *The Canadian Directory to Foundations and Grants,* in both print and online editions, which gives details of available funding, cross-indexed by subject, geography, and individual names. The directory outlines the criteria and interests of every Canadian foundation and many American foundations that give to Canadian charities, including the name and address of the contact person. The directory also shows how much was given, to which charity, and for what purpose. There are also excellent articles on how to get foundation grants. Read these before submitting any applications.

The Centre also publishes a companion guide, *Building Foundation Partnerships: The Basics of Foundation Fundraising and Proposal Writing* by Ingrid van Rotterdam. The guide covers everything you need to know to locate and attract foundation funding, including critical first steps, the ABCs of research, and the essentials of a successful program plan and proposal.

CCP's list of publications also includes *Planning Successful Fund Raising Programs,* by Ken Wyman. How and when to plan, who to involve, how to find time. Includes homework exercises and checklists that you can use to improve your planning process now.

Community Partnership Program/Programme des partenariats communautaires, Department of Canadian Heritage/Patrimoine canadien
15 Eddy Street, 7th Floor, Room 5/15,
rue Eddy, 7ième étage, pièce 5
Ottawa, ON K1A 0M5
Fax: 819 994-1314
Web: www.pch.gc.ca/cp-pc
E-mail: Community_Partnerships@pch.gc.ca

This agency of the Canadian federal government produces a variety of free materials for nonprofit organizations. For budget reasons they are only available in electronic format. For information on these publications, or an up-to-date list of all publications available, contact the Community Partnership Program at the address above or download a copy from the Internet. They request that you not telephone.

The following publications are available for downloading at <www.pch.gc.ca> under the Community Partnership Program, They will continue to be available in printed form from Volunteer Canada, Volunteer Calgary, Volunteer Vancouver for a nominal price to allow the centres to recover their costs:

- *Face to Face: How to Get Bigger Donations from Very Generous People,* by Ken Wyman (1993). How-to manual with focus on major individual donations.

- *Fundraising for Grassroots Groups: Fundraising Ideas that Work,* by Ken Wyman (1993). Practical, ready-to-use ideas for small- to mid-size nonprofits.

- *How to Estimate the Economic Contribution of Volunteer Work*, by David Ross

- *Low-Cost Small-Scale Publishing,* by Doug McKercher

- *A Springboard to Tomorrow: Creating Youth Volunteer Programs that Encourage the Development of Skills*

- *Bridges to the Future: Programs for Volunteers with Special Needs*

- *Family Volunteering: The Ties that Bind.* Preparing your agency for family volunteering.

- *Promoting Volunteerism,* by Janet Lautenschlager. Strategies and approaches to promoting volunteerism. Includes list of reference tools on public relations, publicity, media relations, and public education, and how to buy or borrow them.

- *Publicity! How You Can Publicize Volunteerism and National Volunteer Week in Your Community*

- *Stronger Together: Recruiting and Working with Ethnocultural Volunteers*

- *Volunteering for Work Experience: Developing and Maintaining Employment Skills through Volunteer Work*

- *Volunteering in the Work Place*

- *Volunteering: A Traditional Canadian Value,* by Janet Lautenschlager. A short history of volunteerism in Canada that shows what can be accomplished through the active involvement of ordinary citizens.

- *Why People Volunteer*

Volunteer Canada
330 Gilmour Street
Ottawa, ON K2P 0P6
Tel: 800 670-0401
Tel: 613 231-4371
Fax: 613 231-6725
Web: www.volunteer.ca
E-mail: volunteer.canada@sympatico.ca

Promotes the establishment of volunteer centres and provides support to several hundred volunteer centres across Canada. Engages in research, training and other national initiatives designed to increase community participation across the country.

National Organizations
United States

Independent Sector
1200 18th St. NW, Suite 200
Washington, DC 20036
Tel: 202 467-6100
Tel: 888 860-8118 (to order publications)
Fax: 202 467-6101
Web: www.independentsector.org
E-mail: info@independentsector.org

A nonprofit coalition of corporate, foundation, and volunteer members created as an information exchange and spokesgroup. Publishes variety of books, pamphlets. Membership dues based on size of organization (0.25 percent of salaries paid), but no cost to be added to mailing list for publications catalogues and updates.

American Association of Fund Raising Counsel
(AAFRC)
10293 N. Meridian Street, Suite 175
Indianapolis, IN 46290
Tel: 317 816-1613
Tel: 800 46-AAFRC
Fax: 317 816-1633
Web: www.aafrc.org
E-mail: info@aafrc.org

Publishes *Giving U.S.A.: A Philanthropic Annual Report. Giving Updates* published quarterly. Mailing list of AAFRC members also available.

Association of Fundraising Professionals
1101 King Street, Suite 700
Alexandria, VA 22314
Tel: 703 684-0410
Tel: 800 666-FUND
Fax: 703 684-0540
Web: www.afpnet.org

Formerly known as the National Society of Fund Raising Executives. Membership organization for professional fundraisers. Several excellent conferences and publications. Local chapters across North America. Good Web site even for non-members.

Regional Or Local Associations And Interests (Canada)
Local chapters of AFP in Canada:

AFP **Calgary Chapter**
Kim Lenters
Chapter Administrator
424, 234-5149 Country Hills Blvd. NW
Calgary, AB T3A 5K8
Tel: 403 297-1033
Fax: 403 297-1035
Web: www.afpcalgary.com
E-mail: afpcalgary@shaw.ca

AFP **Edmonton Chapter**
Gerry Backs
c/o Alberta Cancer Foundation
10405 Jasper Avenue, #1220
Edmonton, AB T5J 3N4
Tel: 780 412-6335
Fax: 708 412-6337
E-mail: gerrybac@cancerboard.ab.ca

AFP **Quebec Chapter**
Danis Prud'homme
Coordinator Development Office
HEC Montreal,
3000 Côte-Ste-Catherine Road
Montreal, QC H3T 2A7
Tel: 514 340-6340
Fax: 514 340-5615
E-mail: danis.prudhomme@hec.ca

AFP **Ottawa Chapter**
Linda Eagen
c/o Ketchum Canada
86 Meadowcroft Cresent
Ottawa, ON K1J 1H2
Tel: 613 282-2690
E-mail: leagen@ketchumcanada.com

AFP Saskatoon Chapter
Dept. 586 106 – 3120 8th Street E
Saskatoon, SK S7H 0W2
Tel: 306 966-1929
Web: members.shaw.ca/afpsaskatoon
E-mail: afpsaskatoon@shaw.ca

AFP Toronto Chapter
Cynthia Quigley
Chapter Administrator
260 King St. East, Suite 412
Toronto, ON M5A 4L5
Tel: 416 941-9212
Tel: 800 796-7373
Fax: 416 941-9013
Web: www.afptoronto.org
E-mail: cquigley@afptoronto.org

AFP Vancouver Chapter
Krista Thompson
c/o Surrey Memorial Hospital Foundation
13750 96th Avenue
Surrey, BC V1M 3X7
Tel: 604 585-5542
Fax: 604 585-5550
E-mail: afp@mpsexecutive.com

AFP Vancouver Island Chapter
Jennifer Jasechko
c/o Suburbia Studios
590 Beaver Lake Road RR#3
Victoria, BC V9E 2J7
Tel: 250 744-1231
E-mail: Jennifer@SuburbiaStudios.com

AFP Winnipeg Chapter
LuAnne Lovlin
c/o The Winnipeg Foundation
1350 One Lombard Place
Winnipeg, MB R3B 0X3
Tel: 204 944-9474 Ext. 32
Fax: 204 942-2987
E-mail: llovlin@wpgfdn.org

Atlantic Canada

Society of Fund Raising Executives
PO Box 3064 South
Halifax NS B3J 3G6
Web: www.sfre.org
E-mail: membership@sfre.ns.ca

Membership Group. Chapters in several cities, especially in the Maritimes. Excellent newsletter. Seminars and monthly lunches.

Western Canada

Volunteer Calgary
Suite 900, 640 8th Avenue SW
Calgary, AB T2P 1G7
Tel: 403 265-5633
Fax: 403 265-8981
Web: www.volunteercalgary.ab.ca
E-mail: volunteer@volunteercalgary.ab.ca

Volunteer Vancouver
Suite 301, 3102 Main Street
Vancouver, BC V5T 3G7
Tel: 604 875-9144
Fax: 604 875-0710
Web: www.vancouver.volunteer.ca
E-mail: volvan@volunteer.ca

Central Canada

Ontario Prevention Clearinghouse (OPC)
180 Dundas Street, Suite 1900
Toronto, ON M5G 1Z8
Tel: 416 408-2249
Tel: 800 263-2846
Fax: 416 408-2122
Web: www.opc.on.ca
E-mail: info@opc.on.ca

Focus on non-traditional fundraising strategies such as resource networking, capacity building, asset mapping and collaboration. They also provide workshops and have publications on topics such as community development, some of which are available free online. Mostly for health organizations.

Corporate Donations

Organizations

Canadian Centre for Business in the Community
(CCBC)
The Conference Board of Canada
255 Smyth Road
Ottawa, ON K1H 8M7
Tel: 613 526-3280
Tel: 866 711-2262
Fax: 613 526-4857
Web: www.conferenceboard.ca/ccbc
E-mail: ccbc@conferenceboard.ca

CCBC is a nonprofit unit of The Conference Board of Canada. It provides objective information and analysis in the area of corporate giving (among other duties). It is set up to serve corporate donors, not charities. However, it does have a variety of interesting publications for sale.

CCBC recommends that any group launching a corporate donations request send information about itself to the CCBC office. While CCBC cannot match nonprofit groups with donors, it wants to have background data handy in case the companies ask for verification.

**The Council for Business and the Arts
in Canada**
165 University Avenue, Suite 705
Toronto, ON M5H 3B8
Tel: 416 869-3016
Fax: 416 869-0435
Web: www.businessforarts.org
E-mail: info@businessforarts.org.

The CBAC is an organization of businesses whose purpose is to encourage corporate support for the arts through research, seminars, publications, counselling, and information services. CBAC offers a long list of excellent publications. They do not give money, but can provide limited help to arts groups that need to connect with corporate supporters. Publishes *The Ten Lost Commandments of Fund Raising* among others.

Useful Publications

Corporate Ethics Monitor
Ethicscan Canada
Lawrence Plaza Postal Office
P.O. Box 54034
Toronto, ON M6A 3B7
Tel: 416 783-6776
Fax: 416 783-7386
Web: www.ethicscan.ca
E-mail: ethic@concentric.net

Profiles of companies including their charitable giving. Newsletter published six times yearly. Also features columns and issues on a range of corporate responsibility issues.

Canadian Key Business Directory
Dun and Bradstreet Canada
5770 Hurontario Street
Mississauga, ON L5R 3G5
Tel: 905 568-6000
Fax: 905 568-6197
Web: www.dnb.ca

Data on corporations. Rapid corporate mergers and personnel changes mean you must do final double-check on names and addresses by phone.

Scott's Directories
Southam Information and Technology Group
1450 Don Mills Road
Don Mills, ON M3B 2X7
Tel: 800 668-2374
Tel: 416 442-2010
Fax: 416 510-6870
Web: www.scottsinfo.com
E-mail: scottssales@corporate.southam.ca

Directories of businesses. Volumes on the manufacturing sector for Ontario, Quebec, Western Canada, and Atlantic Canada. The *Trade Directory* covers Toronto only and includes a wider range of businesses, totalling 22,000 listings, organized alphabetically, by street, and by type of product. Listings of the key executives, number of employees, etc.

Government Grants

KWIC Index to Your Ontario Government Services
Publications Ontario
50 Grosvenor Street
Toronto, ON M7A 1N8
Tel: 416 326-5300
Tel: 800 668-9938
Fax: 416 326-5317
Web: www.gov.on.ca/MBS/English/publications
/popular/107948.html

One route to Ontario grants. Frustrating — but nothing better available.

Special Events

Organizing Special Events and Conferences
by Darcy Devney
Pineapple Press
P.O. Box 3889
Sarasota, FL 34230
Tel: 800 746-3275
Fax: 941 351-9988
Web: www.pineapplepress.com
E-mail: info@pineapplepress.com

A practical guide for busy people.

Guide to Special Events Fundraising
by Ken Wyman
Available on-line at <www.pch.gc.ca>.

See Community Partnership Program for further information.

Toronto Events Calendar
99 Kimbark Blvd
Toronto, ON M5N 2Y3
Tel: 416 782-3322
Fax: 416 787-9299
E-mail: torontocalendar@rogers.com

Will list free up to five events per organization per issue in their calendar. Also contains event ideas and lists of venues and corporate sponsors. A good way to keep track of what everyone else is doing and avoid conflicts.

Directory of Sponsorship Marketing/IEG
Sponsorship Report
640 North LaSalle, Suite 600
Chicago, IL 60610-3777
Tel: 312 944-1727
Tel: 800 834-4850
Fax: 312 458-7111
E-mail: customerservice@sponsorship.com
Web: www.sponsorship.com

Directory of major events and who sponsors them. Newsletter. More than 30 publications. Annual conference. Excellent for research.

Direct Mail and Telephone Campaigns

The Canadian Marketing Association
1 Concorde Gate, Suite 607
Don Mills, ON M3C 3N6
Tel: 416 391-2362
Fax: 416 441-4062
Web: www.the-cma.org

(Formerly the Canadian Direct Marketing Association.) Members include business and government. Fundraisers and telemarketers have special groups. Chapters in Montreal, Calgary, Ottawa and Vancouver, and forming elsewhere. Various fees.

Useful information and books (some free) on direct marketing. Seminars and conventions across Canada. Awards for best mailings. "Do Not Contact" service helps people get their names off mailing lists, and helps direct marketers avoid sending them unwanted mail. Code of Ethics helps keep direct marketing honest. "Operation Integrity" is an intermediary in complaints about direct mail fundraising.

Fund Raising Letters
Finn Communications
1840 S. Elena Avenue, Suite 105
Reddondo Beach, CA 90277
Tel: 310 373-0743
Fax: 310 373-2889
Web: www.johnfinn.com
E-mail: john@johnfinn.com

A substantial binder full of materials from an experienced US direct mail copywriter.

Successful Direct Mail & Telephone Fundraising
Mal Warwick & Associates, Inc.
2550 Ninth Street, Suite 103
Berkeley CA 94710-2516
Tel: 510 843-8888
Fax: 510 843-1042
Web: www.malwarwick.com
E-mail: info@malwarwick.com

Several books and newsletters devoted exclusively to direct mail and telephone fundraisers. Created by Mal Warwick, progressive direct mail expert and author of *Revolution in the Mailbox.* Canadian content from contributing editor Stephen Thomas.

Teach Yourself To Write Irresistible
Fund-Raising Letters
Precept Press
Division of Bonus Books Inc.
160 E Illinois Street
Chicago, IL 60611
Tel: 312 467-0580
Tel: 800 225-3775
Fax: 312 467-9271
Web: www.bonus-books.com
E-mail: bb@bonus-books.com

A self-teaching textbook for fundraisers that goes right to the heart of the matter: involving you directly in planning, creating, evaluating and polishing fundraising letters.

Foundations

Organizations

Canadian Centre for Philanthropy (CCP)
425 University Avenue, 7th Floor
Toronto, ON M5G 1T6
Tel: 416 597-2293
Fax: 416 597-2294
Web: www.ccp.ca
E-mail: general@ccp.ca

Council on Foundations
1828 L Street NW
Washington, DC 20036
Tel: 202 466-6512
Fax: 202 785-3926
Web: www.cof.org

Foundation Center
79 Fifth Avenue/16th Street
New York, NY 10003-3076
Tel: 212 620-4230
Tel: 800 424-9836
Fax: 212 807-3677
Web: www.fdncenter.org
E-mail: orders@fdncenter.org

Publishes a wide variety of books on foundations and related fundraising. Guides to foundations for 30 different fields. Free catalogue.

Directories

Canadian Directory to Foundations and Grants
Canadian Centre for Philanthropy (CCP)
425 University Avenue, 7th Floor
Toronto, ON M5G 1T6
Tel: 416 597-2293
Fax: 416 597-2294
Web: www.ccp.ca
E-mail: general@ccp.ca

Thomson Gale
27500 Drake Road
Farmington Hills, MI 48331-3535
Tel: 248 699-4253
Tel: 800 877 4253
Fax: 800 414 5043
Web: www.gale.com
E-mail: galeord@gale.com

Corporate Giving Directory, Foundation Reporter, Prospector's Choice and other publications and CD's.

Fundraising Overview: Books and Periodicals

Advancing Philanthropy
Publications Department
Association of Fundraising Professionals
1101 King Street, Suite 700
Alexandria, VA 22314-2967
Tel: 703 684-0410
Tel: 800 666-FUND
Fax: 703 684-0540
Web: www.afpnet.org

Official journal of the AFP (formerly NSFRE). Information, issues and answers on philanthropic development. Included with AFP membership.

Fundraising for the Long Haul
Fundraising for Social Change
both by Kim Klein
Chardon Press
3781 Broadway
Oakland, CA 94611
Tel: 510 596-8160
Tel: 888 458-8588
Web: www.chardonpress.com
E-mail: info@grassrootsfundraising.org

Many excellent publications.

The Ten Lost Commandments of Fundraising
by Lyman Henderson
The Council for Business and the Arts in Canada
165 University Avenue, Suite 705
Toronto, ON M5H 3B8
Tel: 416 869-3016
Fax: 416 869-0435
Web: www.businessforarts.org
E-mail: info@businessforarts.org.

A slim volume that should be in every fundraising library. Lyman is a volunteer fundraiser par excellence and a generous major individual donor.

The Grass Roots Fund Raising Book
Successful Fundraising: a Complete Handbook for Volunteers and Professionals
both by Joan Flanagan
McGraw-Hill/Professional
Box 545
Blacklick, OH 43004
Tel: 800 621-1918
Web: www.books.mcgraw-hill.com

The Successful Volunteer Organization
by Joan Flanagan
ISBN 8092-58374
McGraw-Hill/Contemporary Publishing

Currently out of print. It's worth looking for in your local library or used book stores.

Canadian Glossary of Fundraising Terms
by John M. Bouza, Doris M. Smith
John Bouza & Associates
216 Crichton Street
Ottawa, ON K1M 1W4
Tel: 613 744-7711
Tel: 800 387-4020
Fax: 613 744-2115
Web: www.bouza.com
E-mail: bouza@bouza.com

More than 400 fundraising terms defined and cross-referenced. Clear and concise.

How to Start and Run a Nonprofit Organization
Achieving Excellence in Fund Raising
Henry A. Rosso and Associates
Jossey-Bass Inc.
10475 Crosspoint Boulevard
Indianapolis, IN 46256
Tel: 877 762-2974
Fax: 800 597-3299
Web: www.josseybass.com

A detailed guide written under the direction of one of America's most distinguished fundraising professionals. Winner of the NSFRE Research Prize.

Fighting for Hope: Organizing to
Realize Our Dreams
Joan Newman-Kuyek
Black Rose Books
C.P. 1258 Succ. Place du Parc
Montreal, QC H2W 2R3
Tel: 800 565-9523
Fax: 800 221-9985
Web: www.web.net/blackrosebooks/
E-mail: blakrose@web.net

Practical ideas on community organizing, forming groups, holding meetings, planning, funding, and community economic development.

Managing the Non-profit Organization
Peter F. Drucker
HarperCollins
55 Avenue Road, Suite 2900
Toronto, ON M5R 3L2
Tel: 416 975-9332
Fax: 416 975-5223
Web: www.harpercollins.ca

Money, Money, Money: How to Get It!
T. Ouellette
Alberta Council On Aging
#401, 10707 100 Avenue
Edmonton, AB T5J 3M1
Tel: 780 423-7781
Tel: 800 423-9666
Fax: 780 425-9246
Web: acaging.interbaun.com
E-mail: acaging@interbaun.com

How to incorporate and register as a charity, market your project, write proposals for government and foundations, plan special events, and more.

In-Kind Donations

In Kind Canada
6535 Millcreek Drive, Unit 78
Mississauga, ON L5N 2M2
Tel: 905 816-0900
Fax: 905 816-0870
Web: www.inkindcanada.ca
E-mail: contact@inkindcanada.ca

Gifts In Kind International
333 N Fairfax Street
Alexandria, VA 22314
Tel: 703 836-2121
Fax: 703 549-1481
Web: www.giftsinkind.org

Telefax library: 888 288-4043. Press 1 and enter your fax number to receive a listing of the available books.

National Association for the Exchange of Industrial Resources (NAEIR)
560 McClure Street
Gailburg, IL 61401
Tel: 800 562-0955
Fax: 309 343-0862
Web: www.naeir.org

Government Regulations

The Law and Volunteers
Mary T. Satterfield and Karla K. Gower
Johnstone Training & Consultation
1310 Upper Dwyer Hill Road
R.R. 2, Carp, ON K0A 1L0
Tel: 613 256-5516
Fax: 613 256-0902
Web: www.jtcinc.ca
E-mail: jtcinc@jtcinc.ca

This guide conveys the relationship between the engagement of volunteers in the delivery of service, the standard of services expected from them, and the consequences that flow from failure to meet the community standard.

Canadian Taxation of Charities and Donations
Arthur B.C. Drache, Q.C.
Carswell
One Corporate Plaza
2075 Kennedy Road
Toronto, ON M1T 3V4
Tel: 416 609-3800
Tel: 800 387-5164
Fax: 877 750-9041
Web: www.carswell.com

Expensive, but your lawyer and accountant should review it on any difficult matters. Updated as new regulations are released.

Canada Customs and Revenue Agency (formerly Revenue Canada)
Charity Law Hotline
Tel: 800 267-2384
Web: www.ccra-adrc.gc.ca

Official answers for charities, nonprofits, and donors on their regulations. You can call anonymously. Free.

Internal Revenue Service
Exempt Organizations Information
Tel: 800 TAX-1040

Securing Your Organization's Future
Michael Seltzer
The Foundation Center
79 Fifth Avenue
New York, NY 10003-3076
Tel: 212 620-4230
Tel: 800 424-9836
Fax: 212 807-3677
Web: www.fdncenter.org
E-mail: orders@fdncenter.org

Major Gifts and Planned Gifts

Canadian Association of Gift Planners
10665 109 Street
Edmonton, AB T5H 3B5
Tel: 780 430-9494
Tel: 888 490-9494
Fax: 780 438-4837
Web: www.cagp-acpdp.org
E-mail: cagp@tnc.ab.ca

Canada's first professional body dedicated solely to the development and growth of gift planning. Their work may be too complex for most grass roots groups, but the members can help you think through wills, bequests, life insurance, and other sorts of planned giving.

Planned Giving for Canadians
by Frank Minton & Lorna Somers
Somersmith
P.O. Box 1083
Waterdown, ON L0R 2H0
Tel: 905 689-2538
Fax: 905 689-9268
E-mail: dsomers14@cogeco.ca

Comprehensive guide to planned giving — the process, tools, policie, and regulations. Produced in co-operation with Canadian Association of Gift Planners.

Planned Giving: Making it Happen
by Dr. Edward Pearce and Sherry Rodney Kushner
Strategic Ink Communications Ltd.
109 Vanderhoof Avenue, Suite 200
Toronto ON M4G 2H7
Tel: 416 696-8816
Fax: 416 696-5075
Web: www.strategicplannedgifts.com
E-mail: info@strategicplannedgifts.com

Planned Giving for the One Person Development Office
by David G. Schmeling, CFRE
Deferred Giving Services
614 S Hale Street
Wheaton, IL 60187
Tel: 630 682-4301
Fax: 630 682-4301
Web: www.deferredgivingservices.com
E-mail: Schmeling@aol.com

Megabits: Who Gives Them, Who Gets Them
by Jerrold Pacas
Precept Press
Division of Bonus Books Inc.
160 E Illinois St.
Chicago, IL 60611
Tel: 312 467-0580
Tel: 800 225-3775
Fax: 312 467-9271
Web: www.bonus-books.com
E-mail: bb@bonus-books.com

Examines reasons why people give. Lists 65 Tenets for Success in seeking large donations.

Pinpointing Affluence: Increasing Your Share of Major Donor Dollars
by Judith E. Nicholls, PhD, CFRE
Precept Press
Division of Bonus Books Inc.
160 E Illinois Street
Chicago, IL 60611
Tel: 312 467-0580
Tel: 800 225-3775
Fax: 312 467-9271
Web: www.bonus-books.com
E-mail: bb@bonus-books.com

The Seven Faces of Philanthropy: A New Approach to Cultivating Major Donors
Russ Alan Prince and Karen Mary File
Jossey-Bass Inc.
10475 Crosspoint Boulevard
Indianapolis, IN 46256
Tel: 877 762-2974
Fax: 800 597-3299
Web: www.josseybass.com

Based on extensive research with extremely wealthy people, the authors describe seven personality profiles, and how to work with each type of donor.

Take the Fear Out of Asking for Major Gifts
James A. Donovan
Donovan Management Inc.
P.O. Box 195068
Winter Springs, FL 32719
Tel: 407 366-8340
Fax: 407 977-9668
Web: www.donovanmanagement.com
E-mail: dmimgt@aol.com

A guide for professional staff and trustees of nonprofit organizations with step by step instructions, self-study exercises, checklists, charts, and graphs. Quantity discounts available.

We Gave Away A Fortune
Christopher Mobil and Anne Slepian
New Society Publishers
P.O. Box 189
Gabriola Island, BC V0R 1X0
Tel: 250 247-9737
Fax: 250 247-7471
Web: www.newsociety.com
E-mail: info@newsociety.com

Out of print, but check libraries.

Where the Money Is: A Fund Raiser's Guide to the Rich
Helen Bergan
BioGuide Press
P.O. Box 42005-W
Arlington, VA 22204
Tel: 703 820-9045
Web: www.bioguidepress.com
E-mail: hbergan@cs.com

Emphasizes prospect and donor research in pursuit of donations from the rich.

Media and Publicity

Sources: The Directory of Contacts for Editors, Reporters and Researchers
489 College Street, Suite 305
Toronto, ON M6G 1A5
Tel: 416 964-7799
Fax: 416 964-8763
Web: www.sources.com
E-mail: sources@sources.com

Directory available online and sent free to journalists semi-annually. You pay to be listed. Vital if you want the media to contact you when they are working on news or feature stories.

Getting Publicity: A Do-It-Yourself Guide for Small Business and Nonprofit Groups
by Tana Fletcher
Self-Counsel Press
1481 Charlotte Road
North Vancouver, BC V7J 1H1

Tel: 604 986-3366
Tel: 800 663-3007
Fax: 604 986-3947
Web: www.self-counsel.com
E-mail: service@self-counsel.com

Health Promotion Calendar
Publications
Ontario Hospital Association
200 Front Street West, Suite 2800
Toronto, ON M5V 3L1
Tel: 416 205-1345 to add information to the calendar
Tel: 416 205-1350 to order the calendar
Fax: 416 205-1301
Web: www.oha.com
E-mail: publications@oha.com

Annual lists of events and health charity "days," "weeks," and "months" from September 1 to August 31. List health-related events free. Submissions should include contact person; brief details of cause, purpose, theme and/or event(s); timeframe: date, day, week, month, etc.

News Canada
111 Peter Street, suite 810
Toronto, ON M5V 2H1
Tel: 416 599-9900
Fax: 416 599-9700
Web: www.newscanada.com
E-mail: info@newscanada.com

Need help reaching the media? This commercial service rents up-to-date media lists for newspapers, radio, TV, magazines, and weeklies in 256 Canadian regions, or by 230 subject topics. They also distribute media information at relatively low costs.

Statistics
Canada

Canada's Charitable Economy: Its Role and Contribution
Larry W. Smith (Department of Economics, University of Waterloo)
The Canadian Foundation for Economic Education

110 Eglinton Avenue West, Suite 201
Toronto, Ontario M4R 1A3
Tel: 416 968-2236
Tel: 888 570-7610
Fax: 416 968-0488
Web: www.cfee.org

Comprehensive analysis of donors, donations, volunteers, charitable organizations, etc.

Statistics Canada
Statistical Reference Centre
R.H. Coats Building, Lobby
Holland Avenue
Ottawa, ON K1A 0T6
Tel: 800 263-1136
Fax: 877 287-4369
Web: www.statcan.ca
E-mail: infostats@statcan.ca

Statistics Canada is an agency of the Canadian Federal Government that collects and publishes statistics on numerous social and economic issues. Its most recent survey relating to fundraising is the *1997 National Survey of Giving, Volunteering and Participating.* The results of this survey have been published under the title *Caring Canadians, Involved Canadians,* August 1998, catalogue number 71-5420XIE.

Canada West Foundation
PO Box 6572, Station D
Calgary, AB T2P 2E4
Tel: 403 264-9535
Tel:1 888 TALK CWF
Fax: 403 269-4776
Web: www.cwf.ca
E-mail: cwf@cwf.ca

Conducts research on issues of importance to western Canadians, including nonprofit sector studies, urban policy, health care reform, gambling policy, taxation, and economic development. Publishes *Pocket Fact Finder* annually, which contains statistics on Canadian imports, exports, provincial population, demographics, immigration, interprovincial migration, etc.

United States

National Center for Charitable Statistics
2100 M Street, NW
Washington, DC 20037
Tel: 202 261-5801
E-mail: NCCS@ui.urban.org
Web: nccs.urban.org

NCCS is a project of the Center of Nonprofits and Philanthropy at the Urban Institute. NCCS was formerly part of the research division of Independent Sector

Volunteers

Development and Direction for Boards of Directors
John E. Tropman
Canadian Centre for Philanthropy
425 University Avenue, 7th Floor
Toronto, ON M5G 1T6
Tel: 416 597-2293
Fax: 416 597-2294
Web: www.ccp.ca
E-mail: general@ccp.ca

Learn a revolutionary and effective method for running board meetings that result in high quality decision-making. Exercises to evaluate your board and its operations.

Democracy in Small Groups: Participation, Decision-Making and Communication
John Gastil
New Society Publishers
P.O. Box 189
Gabriola Island, BC V0R 1X0
Tel: 250 247-9737
Fax: 250 247-7471
Web: www.newsociety.com
E-mail: info@newsociety.com

Offers a variety of solutions to the problems commonly faced by small, democratic groups, exploring the dynamics of practicing democracy.

Promoting Volunteerism
Janet Lautenschlager
15 Eddy Street, 7th Floor, Room 5/ 15, rue Eddy, 7ième étage, pièce 5
Ottawa, ON K1A 0M5
Fax: 819 994-1314
Web: www.pch.gc.ca

Leading Today's Volunteers
Flora MacLeod
Self-Counsel Press
1481 Charlotte Road
North Vancouver, BC V7J 1H1
Tel: 800 663-3007
Tel: 604 986-3366
Fax: 604 986-3947
Web: www.self-counsel.com
E-mail: service@self-counsel.com

Recruiting Volunteers for Difficult or Long-Term Assignments
Steve McCurley
Johnstone Training & Consultation
1310 Upper Dwyer Hill Road
R.R. 2, Carp, ON K0A 1L0
Tel: 613 256-5516
Fax: 613 256-0902
Web: www.jtcinc.ca
E-mail: jtcinc@jtcinc.ca

How do you recruit volunteers for jobs that require a long or deep commitment? McCurley discusses redesigning the job, expanding recruiting efforts, team volunteering, apprenticeships and volunteers' need for psychological growth.

Be a Local Hero: A Guide to Volunteering in Toronto
Darby McNab
Whitecap Books
170 Shields Court, Unit 2
Markham, ON L3R 9T5
Tel: 905 470-8484
Tel: 888 870-3442
Fax: 905 470-6787
Fax: 888 861-6630
Web: www.whitecap.ca
E-mail: ianw@whitecap.ca

List of organizations by area of interest, with variety of time requirements, and cross-referenced to skills and age group. If this first edition is successful, updates and other cities will be considered

Video

Ask Somebody for Money Today

The best of Joan Flanagan's workshops. Three one-hour fundraising-training videotapes: *Getting Started*; *Asking for Money*; and *Fundraising Forever*.

Partners in Caregiving Program

Department of Psychiatry and Behavioral Medicine
The Bowman Gray School of Medicine
Medical Center Boulevard
Winston-Salem, NC 27157
Tel: 336 716-2011
Web: www.bgsm.edu

The Fund Raising Game

A video education tool with 270-page handbook designed for volunteers, board, and staff in all kinds of charities and nonprofit groups. It was produced by The Trillium Foundation of Ontario and TVOntario and consists of eight half-hour shows:

- The fundraising pyramid system
- Making people want to give
- Designing direct mail — when and how to
- Special events that raise more money
- Upgrading gifts to major individual levels
- Recruiting volunteers for fundraising
- Grants from corporate and institutional donors for money, in-kind donations and sponsorships
- Creating workable action plans with realistic deadlines and do-able tasks

Host and creative consultant Ken Wyman offers his own expert advice, while tips and strategies from experienced fundraisers help reinforce important fundraising principles. The series is closed captioned. For details and order form, contact Ken Wyman & Associates Inc. in Toronto.

64 Lamb Avenue
Toronto, ON M4J 4M3
Tel: 416 362-2926
Fax: 416 352-5470
E-mail: Kenwyman@compuserve.com

Courses in Fundraising and Nonprofit Organization Management
Canada

Courses may be offered by distance education (marked *) and/or day or night in-class instruction. Compiled in part with information from <charityvillage.com/learn/index.asp>:

Algonquin College (Ottawa)*

Banff Centre for Management: Community and Not-For-Profit Leadership programs

British Columbia Institute of Technology: Fundraising Management Certificate Program

Cabot Institute of Applied Arts and Technology

Cambrian College

Canadian Society of Association Executives: Association Management Education (AME) program

Canadore College

Concordia University: Graduate Diploma in Administration

Conestoga College: W. E. Hobbs Fundraising Institute

Confederation College

Dalhousie University: Non-Profit Sector Leadership Program

Fanshawe College: Certificate in Fund Development

George Brown College

Georgian College

Grant MacEwan Community College
(Edmonton)*

Guelph University

Humber College

Laurentian University

Laurentian University (Sudbury)*

McGill-McConnell Program: Master of
Management for National Volunteer
Sector Leaders

McMaster University

Mohawk College

Mount Royal College

Mount Royal College (Calgary)

National Program in Fundraising Education

Nova Scotia Community College

Okanagan College

Queen's University: Public Policy and the
Third Sector

Ryerson Polytechnical University:
Certificate in Interdisciplinary Studies
in Nonprofit and Voluntary Sector
Management

Simon Fraser University: Nonprofit
Management and Leadership Program

St. Clair College

St. Lawrence College

The College of the North Atlantic
(St. John's)

Université du Québec à Montréal

University of Manitoba

University of New Brunswick

University of Ottawa

University of Victoria

University of Western Ontario

University of Winnipeg: Philanthropy and
Development Specialization

Vancouver Community College: Nonprofit
Sector Management Certificate Program

York University: Nonprofit Management
and Leadership Program

United States

For a list of more than 240 colleges and universities with courses in nonprofit management:

pirate.shu.edu/~mirabero/Kellogg.html

For a list of graduate schools offering nonprofit education:

www.nonprofit-info.org/misc /acad.html

Other courses

Check with colleges, universities, the United Way and other public groups.

Periodicals on Fundraising and Nonprofit Management

Canadian Fundraiser
The Hilborn Group Ltd.
Box 86 Station C
Toronto, ON M6J 3M7
Tel: 416 696-8146
Fax: 416 345-8010
Web: www.charityvillage.com
/charityvillage/cfr.html
E-mail: circulation@hilborn.com

Newsletter published 24 times a year.

Canadian Fundraiser e-News
circulation@hilborn.com

Charity Auction Newsletter
E-mail: mwinter@flite.net
Web: www.benefitauction.com

Free monthly e-mail offering tips, reviews, and resources to help you produce, grow, and manage your non-profit auction.

Chronicle of Philanthropy
1255 Twenty-Third Street, NW
Washington, DC 20037
Tel: 202 466-1234
Fax: 202 223-6292
Web: www.philanthropy.com
E-mail: editor@philanthropy.com

Tabloid 24 issues a year and online newsletter.

Community Action
Box 448
Don Mills, ON M3C 2T2
Tel: 416 449-6766
Fax: 416 444-5850
Web: www.communityaction.ca
E-mail: info@communityaction.ca

"A news journal for people in community service organizations," published 22 times per year. Among articles and job ads, it reports grants given by foundations and government (mainly Ontario). Lists interesting new publications.

Fundraising Free Press
Web: www.cdsfunds.com/cgi-bin/newsletter.pl
Free e-zine from a consulting firm.

The Sponsorship Report
P.O. Box 378
Station Main
Campbellford, ON K0L 1L0
Telephone: 705 653-1112
Fax: 705 653-1113
Web: www.sponsorship.ca
E-mail: dbp@redden.on.ca

Newsletter that documents who sponsors what in Canada. Directory of sponsorship consultants. Annual conferences. Good articles online.

Grassroots Fundraising Journal
Chardon Press
3781 Broadway
Oakland, CA 94611
Tel: 510 596-8160
Tel: 888 458-8588
Web: www.chardonpress.com
E-mail: info@grassrootsfundraising.org

Research on Donors and Prospects

The BIG Database
Metasoft Systems
1080 Howe Street Suite 203
Vancouver, BC V6Z 2T1
Tel: 604 683-6711
Tel: 888 638-2763
Fax: 604 683-6704
Web: www.bigdatabase.ca
E-mail: sales@bigdatabase.ca

Canadian and selected US foundations, corporations, major individual donors and government grants. Updated on Internet.

Prospect Research Online (PRO)
iWave
P.O. Box 143
Charlottetown, PE C1A 7K2
Tel: 800 655-7729
Fax: 902 894-2659
Web: www.iwave.com
E-mail: admin@iwave.com

Web Sites Every Fundraiser Should Visit

Our top picks, in alphabetical order. The list could easily be much longer. If your favorites are missing, please contact Ken Wyman (E-mail: kenwyman@compuserve.com).

www.afri.org
The website of the American Fund Raising Institute. With an American emphasis, this site specializes in information about capital, annual, and planned giving campaigns.

www.ccp.ca
Canadian Centre for Philanthropy. Lots of good research on line.

www.chardonpress.com
Fundraising for social change is the theme of this site from Kim Klein, author of the *Grassroots*

Fundraising Journal and other good written material. On-line stories, free newsletter, nonprofit links, and a book catalogue where you can browse selections or search by topic, author, title or organization.

www.charity.ca
One of many sites that will collect and process online donations for any charity, for a fee. Not a magic money tree, but a simple solution for those who are not ready to set up a web site offering secure transactions. Useful articles too.

www.charitychannel.com
Offers many nonprofit discussion forums on specific topics and Guestshare, a space to share documents among nonprofit professionals trying to solve similar problems.

www.charityvillage.com
One of Canada's — maybe the world's — most useful Web sites for nonprofits. News, jobs, professional associations, how-to articles, and special events

www.community-fdn.ca
This is the site of Community Foundations Canada (CFC). CFC is the national membership organization for community foundations across Canada. CFC does not give grants or other funding, but its member community foundations do give money to projects that strengthen the community. The site contains a list of all the community foundations across Canada and links to some of their websites.

www.fdncenter.org/pnd
Sign up for free e-mail weekly version of Philanthropy News Digest, a news service of the Foundation Center. Mostly American information about grants and grantors' requests for proposals. Updated weekly.

www.fundraising.co.uk
This British Web page has developed a strong following based on its library services and in-depth coverage of events, jobs, news, grants, and funding opportunities. Its "stay in touch" feature sends you e-mail about site updates.

www.fundsnetservices.com
Research and locate international funding. The information is very useful, but to receive full value from this site a monthly membership fee is needed.

www.gilbert.org
A site maintained by The Gilbert Center, which is fundraising consultant Michael Gilbert and a group of colleagues. There are pages on nonprofit news, online fundraising, and social ecology.

www.greenability.org
Online courses on fundraising, created by Ken Wyman.

www.guidestar.org
GuideStar is a searchable database of over 850,000 nonprofit organizations in the United States. The site also contains news items about charities.

www.idealist.org
One of the few sites that specifically offers training for nonprofit and community organizations on how to use the Internet.

www.nonprofitcareer.com
The Nonprofit Career Network, which maintains this site, uses the site to bring together job seekers looking for work in the nonprofit sector with nonprofit organizations seeking qualified candidates to fill job openings.

www.nonprofits.org
The Internet Nonprofit Center, which maintains this site, is a project of the Evergreen State Society. The site contains a "nonprofit locator," a list of questions and answers about issues ranging from accounting and audits to telemarketing and volunteer recruitment.

www.nutsbolts.com
Practical "how-to" management tips. You can browse some of the articles from current and back issues of their printed monthly newsletter Nuts and Bolts, geared towards the busy nonprofit professional.

www.pch.gc.ca/cp-pc/ComPartnE/pub_list.htm
The site of the Community Partners Program of Canadian Heritage not only has excellent books on fundraising available for downloading free of charge (including three by Ken Wyman), but it also has links to several other related Web sites including Volunteer Canada, Canadian Centre for Philanthropy, Charity Village, the Coalition of National Voluntary Organizations, Community Foundations of Canada, United Way of Canada, and VolNet, the Voluntary Sector Network Support Program.

www.philanthropy.com
On-line source for current and back issues of Chronicle of Philanthropy newspaper.

www.tgci.com
The site of The Grantsmanship Center Inc. (TGCI), based in Los Angeles. TGCI's purpose is to offer training in how to obtain grants and produce information about government funders, community foundations, and international funding sources, the TGCI Magazine, *Winning Grant Proposals,* and TGCI publications.

www.web.net
Nonprofit web service devoted to social change. News, alerts, events, links to other websites. Best with paid membership.

OTHER TITLES IN THE SELF-COUNSEL BUSINESS SERIES

BUSINESS WRITING BASICS
Jane Watson
$12.95CAN/$9.95US
ISBN: 1-55180-386-0

- *Write with your reader in mind*
- *Add personality to your writing*
- *Take the stress out of report writing*
- *Impress clients, colleagues, and even the boss with superior business-writing skills.*

Mastering the art of written communication is an important key to business success. A poorly written letter can embarrass an organization, but a professionally penned document will enhance the image of a company and the writer.

This information-rich book offers tried-and-true techniques to help business people become solid writers. It covers all the skills needed to write effectively.

Includes:

- Writing memos that get read
- E-mail and fax etiquette
- Recent changes to business-writing practices
- More than 200 tips and hints for improving writing skills

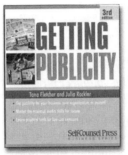

GETTING PUBLICITY
Tana Fletcher &
Julia Rockler
$20.95CAN/$15.95US
ISBN: 1-55180-312-7

If you'd like to know all the inside secrets for attracting publicity to your business, your association, or yourself, you need this book. Step-by-step instructions illustrate just what it takes for any enterprise to generate media attention.

Aimed specifically at individuals and organizations whose ambitions are bigger than their bankrolls, *Getting Publicity* emphasizes low-cost, do-it-yourself promotional strategies, and is filled with inexpensive and practical tips for capitalizing on the power of publicity.

Includes:

- Becoming your own publicist
- Putting together a publicity plan
- Creating publicity opportunities
- Understanding the media
- Preparing publicity materials
- Announcing a new product
- Mastering the media interview
- Writing and public speaking

LEADING TODAY'S VOLUNTEERS
Flora MacLeod &
Sarah Hogarth
$13.95
ISBN: 1-55180-247-3

- *Manage volunteers effectively*
- *Implement a successful volunteer program*

Motivation is the biggest challenge facing non-profit organizations. Today, only one in five adults donates time to a group, and with funding drying up and contributions slipping, organizations now, more than ever, need their unpaid angels.

Managing volunteers and making sure they feel they are full-fledged contributors to the organization is a full-time job. This book will help you set up a program that organizes, evaluates, and recognizes your volunteers. Includes:

- Attracting new volunteers
- Interviewing and selecting the right volunteers
- Orientation and training
- Maintaining volunteer commitment
- Evaluating volunteer performance

MARKET RESEARCH MADE EASY
Don Doman,
Dell Dennison &
Margaret Doman
$18.95CAN/$14.95 US
ISBN: 1-55180-409-3

- *How to analyze the market*
- *How to gauge the success of your advertising campaign*
- *How to plan strategically*

Whether you are starting a new business, launching a new product, setting a marketable price point, or trying to increase market share, good market research can tell you what you need to know. A successful business can't do without it.

The good news is that you can do it yourself. Market research is not the exclusive territory of high-priced professionals. It is simply a process of asking questions or finding existing information about the market, the competition, and potential customers.

This practical, easy-to-read book will lead you through the process of planning, implementing, and analyzing market research for your company, without spending a lot of time or money.

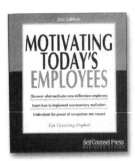

MOTIVATING TODAY'S EMPLOYEES
Lin Grensing-Pophal
$21.95CAN/$16.95 US
ISBN: 1-55180-355-0

- *Discover what motivates new-millennium employees*
- *Learn how to implement non-monetary motivators*
- *Understand the power of recognition and reward*

When you are watching the bottom line, it's easy to forget how your employees are feeling about their jobs. But unproductive staff can be one of the biggest threats to that bottom line, as many business owners have discovered to their cost.

A favorable working environment combined with good worker benefits has eclipsed salaries as the prime concern of the work force. Here is a book that tackles the job-satisfaction issue head-on. It offers creative options that will help companies increase worker effectiveness.

This book will answer the following questions:

- How do I identify effective motivators?
- Why should my company establish job standards?
- Is it important to involve employees in goal-setting and decision-making?
- How do I know whether I am hearing what employees are really saying?
- How do I handle problem employees?
- What non-monetary incentives will work for my employees?
- How can I give workers a sense of "ownership" of their jobs?

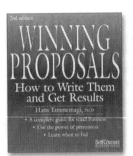

WINNING PROPOSALS
Hans Tammemagi
$15.95
ISBN: 1-55180-254-6

- *Unleash the power of persuasion*
- *Learn when to bid*
- *Discover the client-centered approach*

Proposals have become one of the most important tools of modern business. A proposal is both a sales presentation and a marketing tool. Without winning proposals, many companies would cease to grow or even exist.

This book teaches readers how to prepare proposal that will impress, persuade, and get results. It takes you beyond formulas and recipes, revealing the psychology needed to give your proposal that special edge for success. This is the essential guide for all those who seek to win support, from salespeople to business-people, from fundraisers to researchers pursuing grant money.

While, including the basic components of a winning proposal—from introduction to budget — this guide also covers:

- Accepting a request for a proposal
- Adding unique selling points
- Adapting to your client's needs
- Establishing credibility

THE HR BOOK: HUMAN RESOURCES MANAGEMENT FOR SMALL BUSINESS

Lin Grensing-Pophal
$22.95
ISBN 1-55180-241-4

Finding and keeping good employees is crucial to the efficient operation and success of every business. From hiring and orientation to developing company policies and negotiating employment contracts, today's employers have the opportunity to select and nurture the employees who most closely fit their company's culture and performance objectives.

The HR Book contains checklists and completed samples of all the forms necessary to maintain a streamlined, productive work force. This book covers all the essentials of human resource management:

- Preparing for hiring
- Knowing the law
- Developing interview ____tioning skills
- Selecting your cand____
- Starting employees ____ rack
- Conducting perform____ ____ions
- Maintaining a fully ____ ____ork force

Order Form

All prices are subject to change without notice. Books are available in book, department, and stationery stores. If you cannot buy the book through a store, please use this order form.

(Please print.)

Name _____

Address _____

Charge to: ❑ Visa ❑ MasterCard

Account number _____

Validation Date _____

Expiry date _____

Signature _____

YES, please send me:

____ *Business Writing Basics*

____ *Getting Publicity*

____ *Leading Today's Volunteers*

____ *Market Research Made Easy*

____ *Motivating Today's Employees*

____ *Winning Proposals*

____ *The HR Book*

Please add $5.95 for postage and handling.

Canad___ ____nts, please add 7% GST to your ____

WA____ ____ease add 7.8% sales tax.

❑ ____ ____or a free catalog.

IN ____
Ple___ ____ order to:
Sel____ ____ss Inc.
170___ ____eet
Bell___ ____ 98225

IN ____
Ple___ ____ order to the nearest location:

Sel____ ss   **Self-Counsel Press**
148____ ____oad   4 Bram Court
No____ ____, BC   Brampton, ON
V7.____   L6W 3R6

Visi____ ____ Web Site at:
www.____com